Complete Dictionary

of

Graphic Arts and Desktop Publishing Terminology

With an Overview on Industry Growth and Technology

by

Harvey R. Levenson, Ph. D.
Department Head
Graphic Communication Department
California Polytechnic State University
San Luis Obispo, California

Summa Books
560 N. Moorpark Rd., Suite 134
Thousand Oaks, CA 91360

Cover and Book Design: Thomas D. Kinsey
Illustrations and Graphics: Kerri Kramer

First Printing 1994
Second Printing 1995, revised

ISBN 0-932423-09-4

Printed and bound in the United States of America.

Acknowledgements:

Thomas D. Kinsey was responsible for writing and researching the terms in this book under the direction and active participation of the author.

Thomas D. Kinsey has over 30 years of computer, and graphic arts experience. Working for such companies as: Linotype-Hell, Astro Division of Canon USA, HB Prepress Systems, TeleData Scan & Type, Compucorp, and Delphi Information Sciences Corporation.

"The printer is the friend of intelligence, of thought; [the printer] is the friend of liberty, of freedom, of law; indeed the printer is the friend of every [person] who is the friend of order... Of all inventions, of all the great results in the wonderful progress of mechanical energy and skill, the printer is the only product of civilization necessary to the existence of free [people]."

Charles Dickens

Dedication

This book is dedicated to

Barbara, Mark, and Damien

and to your continued learning, growth, and benefit
through the power of the printed word.

Table of Contents

PART I: OVERVIEW

Introduction

Today, desktop publishing is everybody's business. From home user to classroom to business world, desktop publishing is rapidly becoming a necessary way of preparing and distributing printed information. This book was written for anyone presently doing desktop publishing for the preparation of print media and for those planning to learn desktop publishing.

The purpose of this book is to combine the terms and language of desktop publishing and graphic arts. Such an integration will help improve understanding and communication among users of desktop technology, printers, publishers, print buyers, and others involved in graphic arts. This book is for professionals and novices, for students and teachers, and for anyone who works closely with printers, or with materials to be printed, or who plans to do so in the future.

With the rapid changes in technology and the spread of the "Information Superhighway," comes the need for common languages to aid in the way people communicate. This is especially true in fields that are quickly changing from manufacturing to information dissemination and service. Graphic arts, with its focus on the preparation, production, and distribution of print media, is a field in the state of transition.

Having started as a craft in 1456 with Gutenberg's invention of the process for duplicating movable type, the graphic arts has evolved from a craft to a manufacturing industry. It is increasingly becoming a service profession that provides print media to the public through the most advanced computerized and electronic devices interfaced with technologies such as lasers, satellite transmission, CD-ROM's and multimedia.

The advent of desktop publishing has broadened the scope of graphic arts to include not only traditional printing establishments, but publishers, designers, advertising agencies, print buyers, and any individual who desires to produce something as simple as a one-color letterhead to a complex multicolor brochure, magazine, book, or other publication. Computerized technology and desktop publishing have allowed the author and originator of an idea for print, to become the producer of the print media.

Technological Transitions in the Graphic Arts

Contrary to the assumptions of some, print is not dead as a means of conveying information for advertising, entertainment, education, or any other purpose. Nor is it dying. In direct contradiction to popular McLuhanist predictions of the 1960's, (*The Gutenberg Galaxy, The Medium is the Message, Good-bye to Gutenberg,* and *Understanding Media*) the demand for graphic communication in all forms has never diminished. In fact, the printing profession has experienced more growth from 1960 to to the present than it did in all the years between 1456 and 1959. Access to desktop publishing at relatively low cost in all sectors of personal and professional life has contributed to this growth, particularly since 1985.

The enormous growth and vitality of the graphic communication profession indicates that ink-on-paper will be the primary way of producing graphic images well into the future. The vast majority of high quality commercial and specialty printing will continue to require traditional presses, however, the copy preparation and other prepress functions will use modern desktop and electronic publishing techniques.

Recent speculation concerning the growth of relatively new technologies such as impactless and ink-jet printing has been premature: while certainly feasible technologies, they have merely scratched the surface of becoming viable alternatives to the dominant processes of offset lithography and gravure printing. However, as new technologies become increasingly compatible with desktop publishing, industry must stay on the threshold of continuing education and research activities in these areas.

Educators and other professionals have studied the printing professions' vital statistics and realize the seemingly unrelenting trend of continued growth in nearly all of the industry's segments. For example, between 1974 and 1984, the number of traditional printing establishments has grown from 40,000 to well over 50,000. Approximately 1.3 million people were employed in these plants, with a 1983 gross sales revenue of over $91 billion. By 1994, the industry had grown to approximately 60,000 establishments employing nearly 1.6 million people with a 1993 gross sales revenue of about $177 billion. Estimated 1994 gross sales revenue will reach the $196 billion mark. The industry could reach gross annual sales well beyond $250 billion by the year 2000, when multimedia and other new communication technologies are considered. Much of the recent growth is represented by new companies that began with relatively low-cost desktop publishing systems. These new firms bypassed the need for the expensive, cumbersome prepress equipment purchased by the more established companies in the graphic arts.

While there is widespread optimism about the continued growth of graphic communication, managers and other professionals in the printing industry must realize that being part of this growth means adapting to certain changes. The printing profession is in a continuing dynamic state of change due to advances in technology, competition, and customer and societal demands. Customers demand information quickly and want and expect their products promptly with higher quality and lower prices. This induces the profession to research ways to improve its manufacturing capabilities and service efficiencies. Educational institutions and industry are now participating in research to learn how to best educate students to meet the changing and stringent demands of the profession and its customers.

Color Growth Typifies Change

Growth in the printing industry over the past 10 years was primarily in the color markets. Some graphic communication experts even claim the industry would have declined if it had not been able to satisfy customer demands for color printing.

The popularity of color television is largely responsible for the growth of color printing. Publishers and printers realized they would lose much of their business to the television medium if they were unable to provide the same color image appeal. Ironically, much of the technology the graphic communication profession adopted to produce fast, high quality, color printing came from technology first used for telecommunications. This particularly applies to front-end systems used to prepare, assemble, proof, and make ready copy for printing. However, such technology has now found applications to improve press and distribution capabilities through laser imaging, robotics, satellite transmission, and other electronics-related technology born out of the telecommunications industry.

What we see in the 1990's is the growth of a graphic communication profession that does typically what it has done since its inception - place an image on paper. The dynamic state of the profession applies primarily to changes in technology to improve the speed, efficiency and the quality of images placed on paper either with conventional printing inks or more recently with toners.

A Chronology of Change in the Graphic Arts

1456: Earth-Shaking Type

In the 1960's, media futurist Marshall McLuhan said that Gutenberg's invention of the process of duplicating movable type was ahead of the Industrial Revolution in Europe by about 400 years. This process made printing the most advanced technology of its time, and the most powerful because of its potential to influence fundamental institutions such as religion, education, politics, and law.

Although Gutenberg's invention was relatively simple by today's standards, for the first time in world history, documents could be produced in a relatively efficient manner for mass distribution. With only minor modifications in the process, Gutenberg's method of producing type and printing survived for 441 years.

1897: Enter the Linecasters

Invention of the Linotype machine by Ottmar Merganthaler was a revolution, not only in printing technology, but in the entire field of communications. Based on the concept of moving elevators, rotating matrices, and about 1000 simultaneously moving parts, the Linotype machine increased the efficiency of producing various publications beyond the highest expectations of those involved in the process of print production.

The Linotype machine and its counterparts, the Intertype and Monotype machines, were developed between 1897 and 1915. These devices used molten metal to mechanically produce lines of type or individual type characters in the case of the Monotype machine. These systems for typesetting became the mainstay of printing technology.

1954: Photo Threatens Metal

The technical viability of the Linotype and similar typesetting machines and the job security that they provided for operators, were jeopardized in 1954 when the commercial applications of photocomposition became a reality. Photocomposition represented the next significant revolution in the printing industry.

In 1954, Harris Intertype Corporation introduced the Harris Fotosetter, the first commercially viable application of phototypesetting. Based on the concept of projecting a type image onto photographic film or paper, it revolutionized the way typographic images were prepared for printing. No longer did the printer have to deal with cumbersome heavy type forms, nor did operators have to subject themselves to hazardous molten metal "squirts" from Linotype machines. Photocomposition produced type that was lightweight, easy to handle, and store. Additionally, it was generated on equipment that was relatively safe and easy to operate.

The technology of photocomposition virtually changed the environment of copy preparation. As technology developed to incorporate the application of photo-optics, revolving film fonts, and high intensity strobe lights that were synchronized to expose many characters per second, the speed of copy output was increased to many times that of the Linotype machine. Additionally, photocomposition grew in spite of union pressure to protect the unionized Linotype operators.

1968: The Electronic Age

Only 14 years after the introduction of commercially viable phototypesetting, the printing industry experienced the first application of microwave relay image generation. This became the forerunner of satellite transmission for the simultaneous distribution of black and white copy to multiple printing sites. This technology was introduced in 1968 by *The Wall Street Journal*. The application of microwave and satellite transmission of copy made *The Wall Street Journal* the world's first electronically produced national daily newspaper and revolutionized newspaper production technology.

The application of microwave transmission, satellites, telecommunication (and later, laser technology) to the printing industry was the result of U.S. developments in aerospace between 1957 and the late 1960's. Major cutbacks in aerospace programs at that time resulted in massive layoffs of highly skilled aerospace technicians, engineers, and other professionals. Many found their way into the equipment manufacturing sector of the printing industry. The influx of such a skilled labor force into a relatively provincial industry had a revolutionary influence. Technological developments resulted in the design of printing equipment and in the way images were generated, manipulated, and made ready for printing.

1974: Front-End Systems

In 1974, the printing industry (now more frequently called the graphic arts or graphic communication industry) had electronic front-end systems that could draft, alter, and produce architectural renderings, technical illustrations, and automobile designs - all on a cathode ray tube (CRT). These technologies represented the beginning of the computer graphics era. The ability to scan and digitize copy, produce it on a screen through keyboard commands, and produce "hard copy" output of the image on a printer was now available.

Such technology also contributed to development of Electronic Funds Transfer System (EFTS), which had a monumental impact on the products produced by bank stationers.

It also contributed to development and application of the Universal Product Code (UPC) which had a favorable impact on package printing quality because of the stringent quality controls required in printing bar code symbols on packages.

1977: Computer Graphics

In 1977, three years after digital processes and the use of CRT's became commercially acceptable ways of displaying and manipulating copy, computer graphics became an important technology for the printing industry.

Four major systems using computer graphics hardware and software for graphic communication were introduced:

● Hazeltine and Rudolph Hell Corporations were among several suppliers who introduced computerized color reproduction and color correction systems. They accepted scanned, digitized images from color reflection and transparent art and displayed these images on a CRT. This allowed the operator to make appropriate color corrections and to activate an electronic scanner to produce a fully corrected set of color separation positives or negatives ready for image assembly (stripping) and platemaking. What had once been the tedious, time-consuming and costly task of manually retouching color art, and manually producing color separations, continuous tone films, appropriate masks, and halftones on a conventional process camera was now fully automated in one system.

● Genigraphics Corporation, a subsidiary of General Electric, introduced a system that combined type, color, and line illustrations on a CRT to produce color transparencies. The system was the first to use computer and digital processes to electronically integrate type, color, and illustrations that could then be displayed, altered and output from a keyboard.

● Experiments in the application of teletext were widely advertised in 1977, and the "promise" was to revolutionize the manner in which the public sought and used information. However, people were far from ready to relinquish the look, feel, and personal convenience of print. Therefore, teletext became the forerunner of the seemingly more acceptable videotex. This process used telephone lines to combine the display of copy and hard-copy printouts of what appeared on the video screen. This technology was particularly suited to providing data usually found in directories and for other similar applications.

● While it never became a common household apparatus, in 1977, the Mitsushita Corporation in Japan announced development of a color television that printed out any screen image in color with a mere push of a button. The system combined the technology of CRT imaging and ink-jet printing in a single unit the size of a 19-inch television. Although this system is still not commercially available, it could someday have a revolutionizing impact on how customers review and receive advertising. This would place a printing press in every home.

These systems have spawned even more advancements which promised to revitalize the printing profession over the next 20 years and will enhance the growth of printing. One such system, introduced in 1979 by the Scitex Corporation, was an advanced integrated prepress system designed specifically for the printing profession. It produced complete page layouts in full color on a CRT with sizing, distorting, typesetting, and electronic airbrushing capabilities. Several other graphic arts equipment manufacturers developed integrated systems that used electronic laser beam scanners to digitize copy, produce color separations, and handle copy preparation, page layout, sizing, distorting, and electronic color correction.

While originally in the $1 million price category, these systems have experienced price reductions over the last 10 years. Today, the capabilities of fully integrated systems are available at prices well below $100,000. While such systems have been installed by the nation's largest printing and publishing companies, (R. R. Donnelley & Sons, Time-Warner, Inc., *Newsweek*) it is anticipated that in the next 10 years similar integrated systems will be acquired by smaller commercial color and specialty printing companies.

1980: Print Boundaries Change

By 1980, the graphic arts industry had seen further proliferation of new technologies that combined print with electronic and telecommunications. Additionally, the printing and telecommunication industries realized that a third, yet to be defined medium, was developing that employed the concepts of print and telecommunication technology. Both industries had come to realize that survival and marketability of profitable products depended on a merger of the media to expedite the quality and speed. This was evidenced by a number of events which occurred shortly after 1980.

● *USA Today*, using electronic laser scanning satellite transmission and conventional printing technology, had become a viable competitive daily newspaper at a time when many dailies were facing a survival crisis.

● R. R. Donnelley & Sons, the nation's largest commercial printing company, and a bastion for conventional printing processes, purchased a cable television company. Speculation was that this investment would diversify the company into a multimedia distributor of data services to satisfy future customer needs.

● The Montreal book and directory printing plant of Ronalds Federated, one of Canada's largest printing companies, and Case-Hoyt Printing Company of New York were purchased by Bell of Canada. These moves signified the viability of printing as viewed by the telecommunications industry.

Early to Mid 1980's

From the early to mid 1980's, the graphic arts industry benefitted from: government deregulation of telecommunications; an increase in the commercial and non-commercial satellites placed in geostationary orbit; and from the further proliferation of printing technology that combined print and electronic concepts. During this period, an International Communication Policy was developed which paved the way for an "Information Superhighway." This policy advocated five fundamental principles to guide technology advancements in the U.S.

1. Free Flow of Information - Business and individuals would benefit from the free flow of information. Steps should be taken to deregulate communication to ensure that everyone has access to as much information as possible to streamline the way business is conducted and to enhance education. This encompasses political, economic, social, cultural, personal, business, and other kinds of information typically disseminated by the printing and publishing industry.

2. Privacy - With the deregulation of communication, the need to protect privacy of corporations and individuals developed. With the vast amount of information changing hands through sophisticated electronic communication channels, matters deemed confidential would have to be protected. Hardware and software developers who wanted to protect confidential information and proprietary digital data were also concerned with security.

3. Free Market Forces - The government should move as quickly as possible to minimize or eliminate regulation in the domestic telecommunications area, and avoid the imposition of any regulation in the information and computer industries wherever possible. The general approach to information and telecommunications issues in the United States would be influenced by a broad government trend toward less regulation of communication related to business and economic activities.

4. Free Trade - With increasing amounts of internationally traded goods and services, free trade is important. Since internationally traded goods and services are

an important source of information, restraints on the expeditious delivery of such information could impede international marketing and business.

5. Availability of Telecommunication to the Public - Telecommunication and information dissemination are merging in a most profound manner. In fact, it is difficult to distinguish between them in many areas of application. The government strongly supports the introduction of new communication carriers, new services into the marketplace, and the maintenance of customer choice with respect to the kinds of facilities and services received.

Indeed, laws have been established to achieve many of the goals noted in these five fundamental principles.

With the International Communication Policy came a government "open skies" policy allowing any qualified commercial operator to place a communication satellite in orbit or access transponder time on existing government or private satellites. This stimulated investment in private aerospace ventures and has resulted in the rapid growth of satellite communication for business, entertainment, and educational purposes.

The new government attitude regarding technology and communication influenced the printing and publishing industries, particularly in the areas of newspaper and magazine production. For example, nearly all of the major national news magazines (*Time, Newsweek, Business Week*) moved to transmission as a means of expediting production. This allowed their publications to be printed simultaneously at various sites around the nation. *The Wall Street Journal, USA Today*, the national edition of *The New York Times*, and other national publications have enhanced their use of satellite transmission for sending and receiving data. Commercial printers such as R. R. Donnelley & Sons started using transmission to communicate with its newly established facility in the United Kingdom.

Mid to Late 1980's

From the mid to late 1980's, low cost desktop publishing systems appeared with the Apple Computer Company as the driving force. This period saw the increased use of electronics and computers, particularly personal computers, in print production and competitive information media. Production functions like typesetting, image assembly and pagination shifted from the printer to the customer. This began the restructuring of the prepress process during which the print buyer became involved in the print production. These changes opened new markets for equipment and supply manufacturers. The impetus for this was the appearance of a revolutionary electronic page description language, Adobe PostScript. This important standard was able to digitally describe a page of text and graphics. Its uniqueness was that it allowed a multiplicity of computer workstations to communicate with a wide variety of printers - laser, dot matrix, ink jet, and electrostatic.

By the mid 1980's, digital color proofing became firmly established as the future replacement for more conventional proofing methods. The more sophisticated digital proofing systems replaced intermediate films, thus streamlining and speeding the proofing process. Digital proofs were generated as "hard proofs" after viewing of the "soft proofs" on CRT monitors. The digital proofing sequence involved digitizing copy through an input scanner, interactive manipulation of the image (text and graphics), the creation of a direct digital color proof (without the need for film), a quality evaluation, and then electronic corrections (if necessary). Once the digital proof was approved, the color separation would be produced on an output scanner.

Late 1980's to Early 1990's

From the late 1980's to early 1990's, technological improvements escalated through mergers, joint ventures, and acquisitions thereby allowing two or more companies to combine their specialties to produce better technology.

Some important mergers included the Linotype Company joining forces with Hell Graphic Systems, and Heidelberg East merging with Heidelberg West to form Heidelberg USA.

Some significant joint ventures were: Kodak joined IBM in development of ATEX; Hoechst AG joined Gerber Scientific to develop a laser-exposure for computer-to-plate applications; Dupont and Philips joined in developing and marketing optical memory disks; Dupont and Fuji Photo joined to purchase Crosfield Electronics; Sun Chemical and the Cerruti Group joined to develop and apply water-based inks for publication gravure.

Some important acquisitions during this period include: Scitex acquired Iris Graphics; Misomex acquired Baldwin Technology; 3M acquired DiaprintSpA; International Paper acquired Cookson Graphic Arts; Sun Chemical acquired United States Printing Ink; World Color Press acquired George Rice & Sons; and Banta Corporation acquired Danbury Printing and Litho.

The budding technology of high definition television (HDTV) began to show promise in solving the long standing problem with soft proofs - low resolution provided by standard CRT monitors. A good side effect of these experiments in HDTV showed that some resolution drawbacks could be overcome by increasing the lines per inch on the current color monitors.

During this period, technologies emerged indicating that the configuration of the typical printing press may be changing. A clear signal was presented by Xerox with the introduction of its Docutech system. The speed constraints of former electrostatic and electrophotographic reproduction systems were overcome and systems were designed to provide the commercial quality and speed of traditional presses for black and white reproduction. These systems operate from digital data and require no film or plates.

One of the most exciting printing industry concepts of this period was that of demographic binding and finishing. Combining the technologies of digital imaging and ink-jet printing, these techniques demonstrated how mass print media could be personalized. The first direct-to-press digital printing press appeared in a combined venture between Heidelberg and PressTek, Inc. They introduced a printing press that accepted digital data from a remote site directly to plates already mounted on the press. The data was received at the printing site, captured on a monitor, electronically adjusted to remove potential problems, and transmitted to the four-color press requiring a make-ready time of approximately 15 minutes. This is another example of a cameraless and filmless operation that will become commonplace in the years ahead.

Early 1990's to Present

Between the early 1990's and the present, digital photography became a practical process; CD-ROM and multimedia applications became part of how images are prepared for printing; the variable imaging digital printing press was introduced (Indigo and Xeikon); and the "Information Superhighway" emerged as the likely means for sending and receiving information in the future.

Electronic digital photography passed the concept stage and became a viable industry tool. Major publications embraced this technique as a common production procedure for capturing analog images, converting them to digital form, and reproducing them as printed images. This process requires no film, the camera is the imaging tool, and the computer platform replaces the darkroom. Filmless electronic cameras are the logical alternative to film-based imaging.

The continued growth and development of the graphic arts industry is based on diversification into multimedia and other fields not traditionally associated with printing and publishing. New developments allowed the user to interact with multiple types of media, such as text, illustrations, photographs, sounds, voice, animation, and video. Presently, CD-ROM is at the core of multimedia developments in graphic arts. With electronic books being the fastest growing multimedia market, the near future will show growth in electronic magazines as they are used on such applications as interactive sales, marketing, catalogs, and electronic direct mail consumer advertising. The traditional printing industry is being redefined to include these areas as part of how print is produced, or supplemented by other media.

Introduction of electronic variable imaging printing presses by Indigo and Xeikon represents a major advance in demographic, regional, and personalized mass reproduction of printed material. An outgrowth of digital imaging, variable imaging is the ability to change the image from one sheet to the next as paper passes through this new type of printing press. Thus information can be personalized and regionalized. Variable imaging not only allows changes to entire images from sheet-to-sheet, but also allows subtle changes in color, tones, densities, and other variables to provide the print buyer with the desired quality. In a way, the technology of variable imaging places color proofing back on the printing press, where it started prior to the development of prepress proofing systems.

Even though exciting new technologies in the development stages may someday revolutionize how print media is prepared, produced, and disseminated, most industry experts agree that traditional print reproduction processes and methods will remain viable well beyond the year 2000.

Three technologies of the 1990's have developed to support the ongoing use of traditional printing and will impact the way printing is performed through this decade and into the next. They are: HiFiColor, Stochastic Screening, and Waterless Lithography.

HiFiColor is color reproduction that goes beyond using yellow, magenta, cyan, and black inks in full-color reproduction. It involves using a fifth, sixth, or even seventh color to more faithfully reproduce original color artwork such as color transparencies, color prints, paintings, or other full-color copy. Using the additional colors also simplifies the process of maintaining color consistency during a press run while maximizing the reproducible color gamut. One problem with this process is the increased tendency to develop moire patterns from the use of the additional colors when traditional color separation techniques are used. Therefore, HiFiColor lends itself well to Stochastic Screening.

Stochastic Screening, also called frequency modulated screening, produces a random-appearing pattern of extremely small halftone dots of the same size with varying distances between the dots. There are no set or predetermined screen angles or screen rulings as in conventional color separation screening. This configuration of small dot size and varying dot distances prevents objectionable moire patterns. The printed results of stochastic screening appear as screenless and continuous tone, due to typically high printing resolutions of 2400 to 3600 dots per inch.

Waterless Lithography eliminates the need for a fountain solution, one of the most troublesome variables in the lithographic process. In producing waterless lithographic printing plates, a solvent is used that penetrates the exposed photosensitive coating of the plate and thereby establishes the image areas. The solvent dissolves the coating and releases a silicone polymer from these areas. This process depends on changing the surface of the plate so that the image areas have high free surface energy and the non-image areas have low free surface energy. The silicone polymer represents the low free surface energy (non-image areas) which repels ink and keeps the non-image areas from printing. The image areas, having high free surface energy, accept the ink and allow printing to occur.

The collective result of all the technological advances in the printing and publishing industry since the early 1990's has been a series of major contributions to the development of the nation's "Information Superhighway." Through satellite transmission and other means of telecommunication, interactive CD-ROM, digital photography, multimedia, and direct imaging from remote sites, graphic arts has become a major force in furthering the "Information Superhighway." Indeed, the printing and publishing industry has established an information network through its present potential of digitally linking the printing plant to the publisher, to the advertising agency or other clients, and to prepress vendors, service bureaus, distance learning centers, universities, and even to the home.

In conclusion, the history of graphic communication shows that technological transitions accelerate with time. Recent transitions in the profession involve a converging of technologies, including those typically associated with the printing industry as well as those coming from the electronics and telecommunication industries. Printing, publishing, and related graphic arts companies of the future will likely include technologies such as electronic digital photography; earth stations for satellite transmission; digital direct imaging; variable imaging printing presses; on-line computer-to-document printing; multimedia in the form of print, video, and audio; computer integrated manufacturing; robotics and artificial intelligence systems; voice recognition, virtual reality systems; and interactive teleconferencing with seminars, workshops, training centers, manufacturers' sites, and universities. This will all take place in a production environment requiring fewer cost centers, fewer square feet for production operations, and fewer production personnel. However, substantially more personnel will be needed in service areas such as sales, marketing, customer service, estimating, training, and related areas.

Profile of the Printing and Publishing Industry Today: Industry Segments

The new technologies, and most particularly desktop publishing, that have evolved over the recent years are used in all graphic arts industry segments. The printing and publishing industry is comprised of these main industry segments. They are:

- Commercial Printing
- Newspaper Printing and Publishing
- Magazine/Periodical Publishing
- Book Printing and Publishing
- Business Forms and Bank Stationery Printing
- Financial and Legal Printing
- Greeting Card Printing
- Yearbook Printing

- Packaging
  - Folding Carton Printing
  - Flexible Packaging
  - Corrugated Box Printing
  - Metal Decorating
  - Label Printing
- In-Plant Printing
- On-Demand (Quick) Printing
- Prepress Vendors
- Service Bureaus

Commercial Printing - Commercial printing is comprised of over 60,000 establishments in the United States and is the largest segment with regard to number of establishments. It is typically composed of general printing and companies in this segment must be equipped to produce a wide variety of products from simple letterheads to complex four-color printing. Most jobs are relatively short run and approximately 80 percent of all commercial printers employ fewer than 20 employees. This segment is highly competitive and relies on high volume and low profit mark-up to sustain itself. Being able to provide a diversity of services in prepress, press, post press and having access to a broad range of supplies such as paper and ink is crucial for commercial printers to remain competitive. Typically, the most rapidly growing area of commercial printing is color reproduction.

Newspaper Printing and Publishing - This industry segment is growing but not in the number of daily newspapers. In fact, all facets of newspaper products are growing except daily newspapers. The growing portion of the segment includes advertising inserts and special publications, such as weekly, community, and special interest newspapers. Another trend in newspaper publishing is toward the greater use of color. This was spearheaded by *USA Today* in the early 1980's and since then nearly all major metropolitan and many community newspapers have introduced color editions. Commercial access to satellite transmission has resulted in a number of newspapers providing national and even international editions. However, such growth will continue slowly because most newspapers rely on local news and advertising as the main way to appeal to their readers. Local newspapers are beginning to diversify their range of services into electronic data bases that supplement classified advertising with telephone and facsimile services that will generate automobile, employment, real estate, and other similar listings.

Magazine/Periodical Printing and Publishing - The trend in periodical printing and publishing is toward specialty publication. The general interest magazine has given way to periodicals focusing on the special interests of society. There is a magazine for nearly all interests and nearly every occupation has its own periodicals. The wide acceptance of desktop publishing has resulted in more magazine/periodical titles with smaller circulation than ever before. However, the collective circulation of all periodicals continues to increase. This segment is one that focuses on good quality coated paper coupled with good looking color. Continued improvements in color reproduction and distribution methods and the ability to produce regional or demographic editions, keep periodicals competitive with television. Magazines are also taking advantage of technology that allows demographic printing and distribution. Some are offering split runs, delivery by zip codes, and selective binding is being used for personalized advertising. Magazine production has become electronic in the preparation of layouts, pagination, and image assembly. This industry will continue to grow as a result of the increased availability of low cost and sophisticated desktop publishing systems.

Book Printing and Publishing - This has been a slow growth area for a number of years. Aside from textbooks, it appears that people do not read general books for enjoyment as much today. Competition from other media such as television, movies, videotapes, and even video games has influenced the degree to which people read. However, a growth area of the book publishing segment is in the production of manuals, how-to books, and technical books required to keep people apprised of rapidly changing technologies and new ideas in all fields.

This segment services primarily a black and white market using uncoated paper printed on standardized sheet-fed perfecting presses and web or belt presses. Any modest growth in book printing and publishing generally should be accommodated by moderate cost increases as paper mills and book printers become more efficient in the manufacture and printability of recycled, acid-free, and alternative paper sources. Growing competition from computerized information systems and CD-ROM applications is forcing book printers and publishers to diversify into these areas. New technologies are influencing how book printers and publishers produce their products. The interface of sophisticated typesetting/pagination software to LED (light-emitting diodes) printers provides opportunities for customized textbooks and limited-edition textbooks geared toward regional preferences. Related to this trend are simplified front-end systems coupled with high-speed presses that provide opportunities for high volume overnight production and dissemination. The availability of low-cost typesetting and book design technology is easing the entry of new publishing firms into this increasingly competitive industry. This trend is expected to push new book title production from approximately 50,000 to 55,000 per year to between 60,000 and 70,000 in the next few years.

Business Forms and Bank Stationery Printing - With the proliferation of electronic funds transfer systems (EFTS), bank stationery as a separate segment will gradually be eliminated and the remaining bank stationery products will eventually be produced by business forms printers. They usually produce three main products: snap-out or unit set forms, computer or continuous forms, and specialty forms. Snap-outs which have become popular for utility invoicing such as water bills, electric bills, and so on include the entire package of mailing envelope, invoice, and return envelope as one unit. This product represents approximately 40 percent of business forms products. Computer forms are typical of those used for inventory control, invoicing, classroom rosters, purchase histories, and so on. They represent about 55 percent of all business forms produced. Specialty forms such as sales books and related products comprise approximately five percent of business forms products. With the inclusion of bank stationery products, the business forms printers will eventually produce checks, bank-books, passbooks, deposit and withdrawal forms, and related items.

For many years the business forms industry segment has been highly profitable, because its specialized products were manufactured on standardized equipment with a relatively small variety of supplies. Business forms products are typically produced on uncoated paper and, while the use of color is growing gradually, there is still little color used on business forms making the products less complex than other types of printing. About 450 firms operate nearly 600 plants in this industry segment with the 20 largest companies producing 70 percent of the volume. They have moved rapidly into electronic and desktop publishing as forms printing has moved on-line with computer systems.

Financial and Legal Printing - This segment produces materials used for borrowing money, money transfers, and for informing the public and stockholders about transactions. The products include securities, stock certificates, prospectuses, lottery tickets, registration statements, loan coupon books, legal briefs and documents, travelers checks, bonds, leases, SEC filings, proxy materials, foreign currency, and related certificates and documents. This industry segment is typically national, but there are some companies that serve local and regional needs. Currency is printed by governments or by contract to financial printers. Until recently, much of the world's currency was printed in the United States because all the Third World and developing nations were concerned with security and quality control. However, with advanced technology, financial printing is rapidly becoming global.

Financial and legal printing is highly specialized with only a few companies controlling approximately 90 percent of the volume. One reason for this unique situation is that financial and legal printers are highly controlled by the SEC and the federal government due to the security requirements of the information contained in many financial documents, especially stock and bond transactions.

The accuracy and security of the information contained on financial and legal documents is of upmost importance. Security of many financial documents necessitate complex technology and creative anti-counterfeiting techniques, i.e., heat sensitive inks, holograms, watermarks, and special papers. As the need for the security of financial information and its rapid dissemination grows, electronic distribution systems have become an important part of this segment. Financial printing will continue to be dominated by a few companies capable of maintaining security of highly confidential information.

Greeting Card Printing - This segment is highly specialized, innovative and creative. Three companies produce about 80 percent of all greeting cards in the United States, with Hallmark having a dominant share of the market. Hallmark's focus on quality has become the benchmark, not only in this segment, but in other industry segments where quality is critical. Hallmark's rigid standards have resulted in one of the most demanding quality control and quality monitoring programs in the industry. The Hallmark company requires that each card must look exactly alike, with no color shift from one card to the next.

Products of this segment are produced on coated and uncoated paper and on specialty substrates including plastics and foils. Unlike general commercial full-color printing, the color requirements of greeting cards often demand the use of six, eight, and sometimes ten-color presses. They also use special metallic pigments, laminations, and coatings and often require specialty processes such as embossing, die-cutting, and holographic applications. A trend in this industry is to manufacture regional or demographic cards that are identified with a particular community, city or state, and personalized cards on which the consumer can interject a personal message or picture on a home desktop computer.

Yearbook Printing - This industry segment focuses on the specialized product purchased annually by nearly every high school and college student in the United States - the yearbook. With their standard formats, yearbooks lend themselves to highly routine production procedures in the way copy is prepared, how it is handled once reaching the printing plant, and how it is distributed to the schools. It is a segment that has a relatively unsophisticated client base, i.e., high school students and young adults who are unaware of printing quality potential. They typically accept a product considered marginal in quality by more sophisticated printing buyers. The product's emotional appeal to its buyers far outweighs concerns for quality and maintaining tight production and delivery schedules.

Nearly all copy preparation is done by school students in accordance with instructions for layout, type, and picture use provided by the yearbook printer. This being the case, copy and particularly picture quality often lack the technical standards demanded in high quality printing. Production tolerances are relatively wide and the skill requirements of technicians and equipment operators are not as high as in other printing segments. The main delivery requirement is that the product be delivered anytime before graduation, usually in May or June. However, even in cases where this deadline is not met, the unsophisticated clients voice few complaints once the product in received.

This segment is traditionally one that produces its products in black and white, however, recent market forces have increased the degree to which full-color reproduction is required. This move has forced some yearbook printers to upgrade their equipment and improve their products. With its standard equipment and procedures, its low investment in quality assurance, its relatively low wage base, and the low number of competitors, the yearbook industry segment tends to be highly profitable.

Packaging - This area of printing is a large segment with gross annual sales revenue nearly equaling all general commercial printing in the United States. There are five packaging industry segments including folding carton printing, flexible packaging, corrugated box printing, metal decorating, and label printing. The component that runs through each of these segments, although to a lesser extent in corrugated box printing, is the importance of quality consistency. Packaging companies, particularly those that produce packages having pictures of food products, flesh tones, and other natural colors realize that the human eye is most sensitive to natural colors. People are reluctant to select packages from a shelf having a picture of food that does not look appetizing or a picture of a person whose flesh tones are unrealistic. Therefore, quality assurance and quality control are vitally important in nearly all phases of package printing. Typically what differentiates the five packaging industry segments is the substrate being printed and the printing process used.

Environmental concerns are increasingly plaguing the package printer in the area of disposal of expensive non-biodegradable packages. They are under pressure to develop effective methods of printing on package materials that are easily recycled. Package printing is growing rapidly throughout the world as more international brands are marketed. An increasing amount of package printing is done by product producers who found it more efficient and economical to develop their own package printing facilities.

Folding carton printing occurs on heavy substrates and boards that are easily folded into a permanent form. Cereal boxes, detergent boxes, and many cosmetic and general product boxes represent this category of package printing. Package engineers are usually involved in the design of folding cartons to ensure stability, durability, appropriate display characteristics, and storability of cartons. The substrates used sometimes have a liner and are typically highly coated. Folding carton printing is normally a sheet-fed process using standardized but relatively large four, five, and six-color printing presses. The fifth and sixth units are used to add additional colors beyond the four process colors and to add varnish or for other finishing applications to enhance the visual appeal of the printed carton. Paper mills sometimes see diversifying into the folding carton printing business as a lucrative opportunity to convert their main product, paper and board, into usable and marketable products. In essence, this industry is made up of a small number of large printing and converting companies which do the majority of folding carton printing in the United States.

Flexible packaging usually involves the use of substrates other than paper and board. The main substrates of this industry segment include foils, plastics, cellophane, and other pliable materials on which a printed image can be produced. Such materials have little or no ink absorptivity, extremely high ink holdout, and are typically printed using processes other than lithography. The main processes used in flexible package printing are gravure and flexography, and to a limited extent, screen printing. The high solvent content of conventional gravure and flexography ink enhance the bonding quality of the inks to the substrate and the overall image appearance. Flexible packages are usually produced in extremely high volumes for major product manufacturers and lend themselves to being printed on high-speed web presses typically used in gravure and flexography printing. Unlike lithography, the matter of ink drying is more complex in gravure and flexography printing, particularly when printing on high ink holdout substrates. Drying must occur after each color is printed and must be instantaneous to avoid smears and loss of image gloss. Therefore, highly complex and expensive drying methods must be used, such as infrared, ultraviolet, and electron beam dryers. These dryers are housed between each unit of the press so each color is dried immediately after its application to the substrate.

Corrugated box printing is often considered on the low end of the packaging industry from a quality standpoint. Corrugated boxes are typically made of low quality, highly absorptive craft paper and board with irregular and non-white surfaces that do not lend themselves to high quality printing. The typical packaging carton with its thick sides (top and bottom liner) is intentionally made highly compressible for protection of the items stored inside. The thickness of the substrate and its compressibility are other attributes that make corrugated boxes poor printing surfaces. Any printing found on such boxes is usually in one color, normally black. Flexography is the preferred process for such printing. In cases where product manufacturers and distributors desire attractive printed graphics on corrugated boxes, they usually prepare and print such graphics on large wrappers or labels which are applied to the outside of the corrugated box.

Metal decorating is printing on metal such as aluminum, steel, and other hard metal surfaces. While foil printing can be considered a form of metal decorating, it is usually not included in this industry segment and is classified as flexible packaging. Metal decorating is the most specialized of the packaging segments. Metal can be printed in sheets on sheet-fed presses, in rolls on web presses, or on specialty presses that print the metal after it has been formed into a container. This latter process is the way soda and beer cans are printed. Using sheet-fed and web printing, the container is formed after the image is printed. Lithography is the main metal decorating process although flexography and screen printing are sometimes used. Screen printing is popular for printing pre-formed containers. Metal decorating requires highly specialized inks that must dry instantly, adhere to metal, and resist scratching.

Label printing refers to printing that will be applied to an already formed container made of any substrate or material including board, foil, metal, plastic, and glass. Any major printing processes can be used to produce labels including lithography, gravure, flexography, and screen printing, but lithography and flexography are the most popular. When lithography is used, printing usually takes place on large sheet-fed presses where many labels can be assembled or stepped and repeated for printing on a single sheet. The sheet backs receive any necessary adhesive and are then die cut to size. Flexography label printing usually occurs on narrow-width flexographic web presses, many of which do on-line finishing such as die cutting, scoring, removal of paper surrounding the die cut labels, and slitting. The substrates used in this process are often pressure sensitive with a peel-away backing applied prior to printing. There are over 2000 label printers in the United States, some of whom use four, five, six and up to eight-color presses. An understanding of adhesion and gluing requirements is important as the most beautiful label has no value without proper adhesion. Various substrates require different adhesion properties and weather and storage environment conditions sometimes have a bearing on the effectiveness and longevity of labels. Typical label products include package labels, pre-glued labels, pressure sensitive labels, self-adhesive labels, flat labels, roll labels, bar code labels, flat wrappers, heat sealed wrappers, and glued wrappers.

Overall considerations that relate to most of the packaging printing industry segments are: the importance of consistent quality; working with standardized formats for sheet-fed and web presses; understanding and working with many and varied substrates; and using highly specialized inks that are rub resistant and dry quickly. Two other broad considerations relate to Federal Drug Administration (FDA) requirements and the use of the Universal Product Code (UPC).

The FDA has placed some regulations on the package printing industry, particularly in cases where food packaging is involved, i.e., any possible contamination of the food by the package itself must be prevented.

The UPC was devised with the immediate goal of speeding the supermarket checkout process and the long-term goal of realizing the not yet achieved "shelfless" supermarket. The UPC is composed of numbers, letters, and vertical lines of varying thicknesses and spacing. It represents millions of bits of information such as price, inventory, location in store, discounts and sales, age of product, shelf life, product sales, and so on. However, today the symbol is used primarily for price control and checkout scanning. Additionally, the UPC must be printed under very high quality standards in order to work, and this requirement has resulted in an overall improvement in package printing. As presses had to be recalibrated for the effective printing of the UPC, printers found that they significantly improved the resolution and quality consistency of the package itself.

In-Plant Printing - The in-plant printing industry is made up entirely of captive plants servicing one client - the company which owns the in-plant printing establishment. The purpose of this segment is to service the parent company with its specific printing needs. In-plant printing establishments could range in size from a one person operation to an operation employing thousands of workers. Most in-plant departments are small and employ several people, very few employ over 100. In-plant operations are found in the manufacturing companies that have an ongoing need for brochures, manuals, company reports, and newsletters; universities that have a continuous need for department publications, reports from administration to faculty and staff, and course materials; insurance companies and financial institutions that must regularly publish reports to customers, policy holders, and investors.

Products of the in-plant printing industry range from simple business cards and letterheads, business forms, sales brochures, newsletters, technical reports, and direct mail advertising pieces to fancy and complex four-color annual reports. The larger in-plant facilities could be equipped with the most sophisticated printing equipment available anywhere. The smaller ones are typically equipped with relatively simple and smaller format equipment for the production of uncomplicated and routine items needed by the parent company. Today, there has been rapid growth of the in-plant printing industry segment with the increased availability of desktop publishing opportunities, electrostatic printers, and turn-key operations. With the "miniaturization" and cost reduction of such equipment, many companies that previously relied on the services of a commercial printer now find it economical to acquire their own production equipment and produce their own printing.

On-Demand (Quick) Printing - On-demand printing, often called quick printing, represents one of the newer industry segments. Establishments in this business area offer walk-in storefront service much like the printers of old that had print shops side by side with grocery stores, hardware stores, and so on. Today's on-demand printer is equipped to provide printed products immediately through sophisticated desktop computers and electrostatic printers. Such printers specialize in small volume and simple formats. They can typically provide simple binding and finishing services. The latest trend in on-demand printing services allows the customer to participate in production through desktop publishing computers that are used for an hourly fee. In this manner the customer becomes the producer and controls all prepress operations. From the computer output, the copy is usually mass produced on a high-speed electrostatic copier.

In 1969 there were approximately 1,100 quick printers also known then as copy shops in the United States. Today there are about 30,000 establishments in the on-demand printing business. About 80 percent are individually owned businesses and approximately 20 percent have more than one location. A growing number of on-demand printing establishments are franchises. The franchise printers benefit from discounts provided by nationwide group purchasing and periodic training programs in marketing, sales, and production. While nearly all on-demand printing serves local communities, a few of the larger franchise printers operate internationally through sophisticated computers for transmission and receipt of copy.

Prepress Vendors - Prepress vendors have traditionally been referred to as trade shops and provide prepress services to printers that are not equipped to do their own prepress work. Services include: composition and imaging; line, halftone, and color separation negatives and positives; electronic prepress services; photoengraving; and platemaking. This area was recently revived in the 1980's due to the availability of sophisticated integrated Color Electronic Prepress Systems (CEPS) that provide efficiencies in productivity and quality that conventional prepress technology is unable to provide. Basically, one CEPS replaced the need for separate departments for typesetting, graphic arts photography, image assembly or stripping, and in some cases platemaking. Unfortunately, these systems were very expensive and were not affordable to most printers. Therefore, to enjoy the benefits that CEPS offered, many printers returned to purchasing services from prepress vendors who had invested in integrated systems. The vendor justified the investment by providing prepress services simultaneously to numerous printers locally or nationally.

Through the availability of low cost color desktop publishing systems and the increase in the number of prepress vendors providing such electronic services, color is becoming less expensive and more common. Prepress production has become simplified and there is less labor and fewer skills needed in the prepress functions. With modular software and the standards that have been developed, electronic prepress systems from different manufacturers can be used together. This industry segment is characterized by acquisitions and mergers among prepress vendors to make access to expensive CEPS equipment and service affordable.

Service Bureaus - The newest printing industry segment is the service bureau. It is the one industry segment that fully acknowledges the printing industry's place on the "Information Superhighway" and is committed to using desktop publishing in preparing and reproducing copy for printing. A service bureau typically works from computer disks or a modem. Often such companies have no typesetters or cameras on the premises. Most service bureaus will only accept electronic copy and do not accept traditional paste-ups or mechanicals. Some service bureaus will output computer files to Resin Coated (RC) paper, film, or four-color separations. Many provide electronic scanning services, slide imaging services, and ink-jet or other digital proof output. They also provide black and white line art, halftone negatives, color separations, electronic trapping and masking, and high resolution scans of color photography and illustrations. With today's direct imaging printing presses, service bureaus can send electronic files on disk or by modem to direct imaging presses where plates are electronically imaged within 15 minutes or less. The press may be at a remote site or be part of the service bureau equipment.

Traditional Printing Processes

Letterpress - Letterpress is printing from the surface of a raised image. It is the oldest of the present printing processes and has declined in use over the past 30 years as more efficient, economical, more rapid, and higher quality printing processes evolved. Less than five percent of all printing in the United States involves the letterpress process. Its primary application today is embossing, die-cutting, and foil stamping. The typical letterpress plate is made of zinc, copper, and a multi-metal formulation composed primarily of lead, or photopolymer. In letterpress printing, ink is placed in the press ink fountain, it is distributed onto ink rollers, the rollers place ink on the raised image of the plate, and then the plate transfers the image onto a substrate (usually paper). In this process, the image on the plate must be wrong-reading (or a mirror image) so the printed image on the substrate will be right-reading.

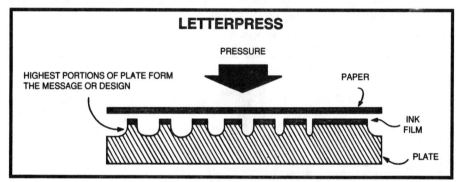

Reprinted with permission of the Mead Corporation

Lithography - Lithography is printing from a flat surface where the image areas and non-image areas are on the same plane. The process is based on the principle that grease and water do not mix. The image and non-image areas are separated chemically in such a way that the image on the plate will accept a greasy ink and the non-image areas will accept water and afterward reject ink. On a typical lithographic press there is an ink fountain and a water or dampening fountain. Ink is distributed from the ink fountain down a set of ink rollers. Simultaneously, the water fountain is distributing a dampening solution, primarily composed of water to dampening rollers. The rollers dampen the plate before ink is applied. The water sticks to the non-image areas which were chemically treated to accept the water. The ink rollers then apply ink to the image areas on the plate. The inked images are then transferred to a rubber-like blanket which is wrapped around a cylinder that comes in contact with the plate cylinder. The image is transferred from the imaged blanket to the substrate being printed.

The blanket performs two tasks:

1. It allows a right-reading image on the plate to become right-reading on the

substrate. If the blanket cylinder was not in place, the image would go from right-reading on the plate to wrong-reading on the substrate. With the blanket in place, the image goes from right-reading on the plate to wrong-reading on the blanket to right-reading on the substrate.

2. It reduces the amount of water which reaches the substrate. When printing on paper, moisture which absorbs into the paper causes problems such as paper distortion or dimensional instability.

The lithographic plate is typically made of aluminum although other metals and paper can be used. Lithography is presently the most popular and widely used printing process for most printed products ranging from simple one color printing to high quality full-color printing. Approximately 55 percent of all printing in the United States is produced with the lithographic process.

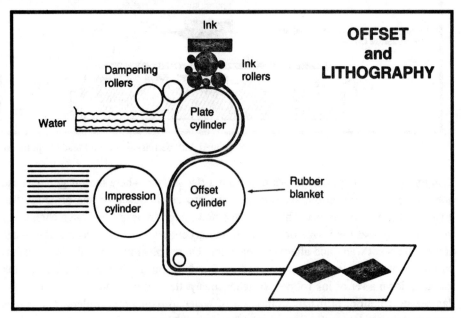

Reprinted with permission of Graphic Communications Today.
Source: National Association of Printing Ink Manufacturers

Gravure - In principle, gravure printing can be thought of as the opposite of letterpress printing. Whereas letterpress prints from a raised surface, gravure prints from a recessed surface. In other words, the image area is beneath the plate surface and the non-image area is the plate surface. The typical gravure plate is a large copper cylinder. Through a chemical, electro-mechanical, or laser engraving process, an image is etched or engraved onto the copper cylinder in the form of microscopic wells. Ink from the ink fountain is applied to the copper cylinder. The ink fills the wells and adheres to the surface of the cylinder. A doctor blade, made of hard rubber or plastic, passes over the cylinder and the ink is scraped off the cylinder surface or non-image area. After this occurs, the substrate being printed comes in contact with the cylinder at high speed and high pressure. As the paper is rapidly pulled over the plate cylinder, a capillary action sucks the ink from the microscopic wells and onto the substrate, producing the image. This all occurs at very high speed. Gravure printing involves

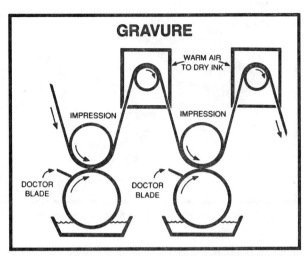

Reprinted with permission of the Mead Corporation

high costs and a lot of time in preparing the plate cylinder. It is, therefore, economical for very long press runs where the cylinder does not have to be changed often. Typically, printing which requires tens of millions of impressions lends itself to the gravure process. Another unique aspect of gravure is its image quality potential. The process allows for smooth tone transitions from highlight tones to middle tones to shadow tones. Because of this, the process is often used when extremely high quality printing is required. Gravure is a popular process for long run publication printing, package printing on non-paper or board substrates such as foils, plastics, cellophane, and other substrates that have little or no absorptivity. It is also a popular process for printing on specialty items such as wall coverings, linoleum, and for producing synthetic wood grains on pressure sensitive substrates.

Flexography - Like letterpress printing, flexography involves printing from a raised image on the plate. The difference is that the flexographic plate is typically made of synthetic rubber or of a photopolymer material. While some of the harder flexographic photopolymer plates print relatively sharp, high resolution images, synthetic rubber plates are not suitable for high quality printing. They are used for long-run imaging requiring one or two flat colors where sharpness is not a critical concern. Flexography is a popular process for label printing, packaging, corrugated board printing, printing on non-paper substrates such as cellophane, plastic, polyester, foils, and other substrates where there is little or no ink absorptivity. In recent years, flexography has

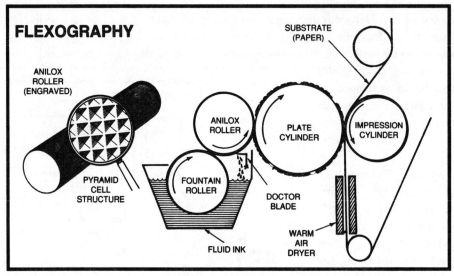

FLEXOGRAPHY

Reprinted with permission of the Mead Corporation

become popular for newspaper printing since the process lends itself to the use of water-based inks which do not rub off when handled.

Screen Printing - Screen printing is probably the simplest of the major printing processes. The image to be printed is formed on a screen made of synthetic fibers. A stencil is placed over the screen which represents the non-image areas. The screen area not covered by the stencil represents the image area. Here ink passes through the screen on the substrate being printed. Stencils can be formed in numerous ways. A negative or positive film can be exposed to a photographic emulsion on the screen.

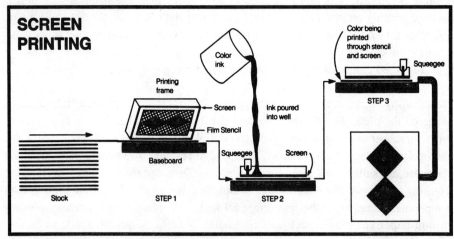

SCREEN PRINTING

Reprinted with permission of Graphic Communications Today.
Source: National Association of Printing Ink Manufacturers

When developed, the image and non-image areas are clearly defined. Stencils can be created by applying pressure sensitive stencil material or by painting a liquid stencil on the screen. Once the stencil is formed, the screen is brought in contact with the substrate being printed, ink is placed on the screen and a squeegee drags the ink over the stencil. The ink not blocked by the stencil will go through the screen and onto the substrate to form the printed image. Screen printing is normally a slow, manual process which lends itself to printing not requiring long runs. It is often used for printing on fabric such as on T-shirts, for short run posters, bumper stickers, and even billboards. It is also an excellent process for printing on leather, glass, wood, and ceramic surfaces. For greater speed, there are automatic single and multi-color screen presses and even web screen presses.

Non-Impact and Digital Printing Processes

These consist of ink-jet, electronic, electrophotographic, magnetographic, ion deposition, light emitting diode (LED), liquid crystal shutter (LCS), electron beam imaging (EBI), thermal printing, and electrostatic printing. These are all digital printing processes in which data representing the images is in digital form. These processes are used mainly for short runs and for printing variable or personalized information such as addresses, codes, computer letters, etc.

Ink-Jet Printing - Ink-jet printing is used mainly for variable printing like addressing, coding, computer letters, sweepstakes forms, and other personalized direct mail advertising. The process is based on the principle of squirting microscopic droplets of ink onto a substrate from a print head containing one or more nozzles. There are two main types of ink-jet printers: continuous drop and drop-on-demand. In the continuous drop process, a continuous stream of ink droplets is generated through a nozzle under constant pressure. In the drop-on-demand process, ink drops are expelled from the nozzle only when needed. There are three types of drop-on-demand methods: (1) piezoelectric where a piezoelectric crystal produces an electric charge that causes the ink drop to be expelled; (2) bubble jet/thermal liquid ink where an electric charge is applied to a small resister causing a minute quantity of ink to boil and form a bubble that expands and forces the ink droplet out of the nozzle; (3) solid ink which involves a solid wax-based ink that melts quickly and solidifies on contact with a substrate.

In continuous ink-jet and drop-on-demand processes, the ink droplets are deflected to the image area via electrostatic charges. Unneeded droplets are not charged and are deflected into a gutter for recycling. A disadvantage of ink-jet printing is that inks are water soluble and can easily smudge when subjected to moisture. New applications for ink-jet printing are short-run color printing and the production of color, digital, hardcopy proofs for color reproduction. Newer multiple-jet continuous drop ink-jet color

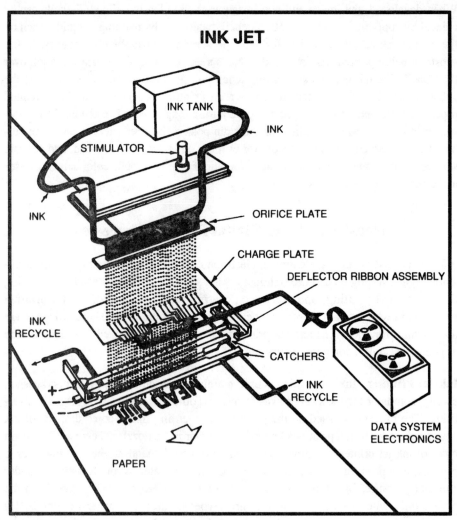

INK JET

INK TANK

INK

STIMULATOR

INK

ORIFICE PLATE

CHARGE PLATE

DEFLECTOR RIBBON ASSEMBLY

INK
RECYCLE

CATCHERS

INK
RECYCLE

DATA SYSTEM
ELECTRONICS

PAPER

Reprinted with permission of the Mead Corporation

proofing and printing systems produce images with improved color quality, saturated colors, and image smoothness without graininess.

Electronic Printing - The process has been popularly called desktop publishing. It uses intelligent copier technology for input and low cost, low resolution laser printers for output. It is used in offices, by in-plant and quick printing establishments for printing short-run products like on-demand printing, reports, college workbooks, technical manuals, parts catalogs, and other similar products.

Electrophotographic Printing - This is a method similar to a high-speed copier

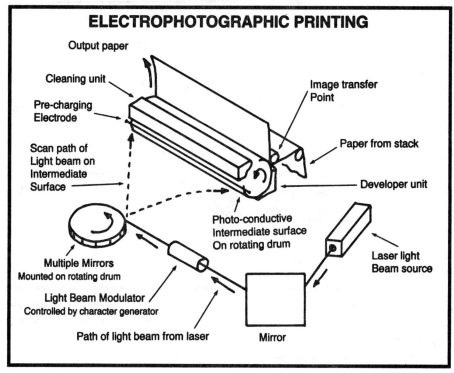

ELECTROPHOTOGRAPHIC PRINTING

Output paper

Cleaning unit

Pre-charging Electrode

Scan path of Light beam on Intermediate Surface

Multiple Mirrors
Mounted on rotating drum

Light Beam Modulator
Controlled by character generator

Path of light beam from laser

Image transfer Point

Paper from stack

Developer unit

Photo-conductive Intermediate surface On rotating drum

Laser light Beam source

Mirror

Reprinted with the permission of InterQuest
Source: Xerox Corporation

systems operating on the principles of xerography. It is the process used in many laser printers and copiers that operate from digital data. It uses an electrostatic photoconductor that is charged by a corona discharge, imaged by a moving laser beam that has been modulated by digital signals from a PostScript based digital imaging system. The process is developed by dry or liquid toners, and a system for transferring the toned image on the photoconductor to a substrate. In this process the laser beam is focused on a rotating mirror which deflects the beam through a focusing lens that forms a latent image on a photoconductor. Present systems work well for single color specialty printing but are very slow (up to 300 feet per minute).

Magnetographics - A plate or cylinder pressureless printing process which is similar in principle to electronic printing except the photoconductor and toners are magnetic and a device similar to a printing press is used. The process uses an array of thousands of heads to create a magnetic image on a drum. As the drum rotates, the magnetic image picks up toner. Excess toner is removed magnetically or by vacuum as the image is transferred to a substrate through a transfer roller. The image is fused to paper by heat that melts the toner after the magnetic image is removed from the drum by an erasing head. Through this sequence, the printing cylinder is charged, imaged, and

41

toned for the first impression and recharged and toned for succeeding impressions. Magnetography is a short-run process. Its main advantage is ease of imaging with digital data. Its limitations are slow speed and an absence of light-colored transparent toners. It is not yet suitable for process color printing, and toner costs are very high in comparison with ink costs.

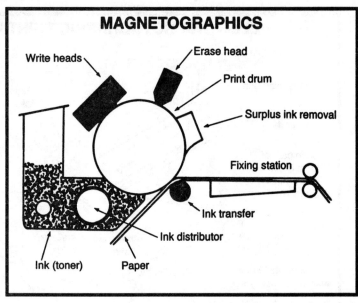

MAGNETOGRAPHICS

Write heads

Erase head

Print drum

Surplus ink removal

Fixing station

Ink transfer

Ink distributor

Ink (toner)   Paper

Reprinted with the permission of InterQuest
Source: Nipson Printing Systems

Ion Deposition Printing -
This is a process similar to other electronic printing systems. The process, having few moving parts, produces dots at high-speed using high-density ion currents. Images are produced directly from electrical pulses and involves a substrate passing, under pressure, between the imaged drum and a transfer roller. It consists of

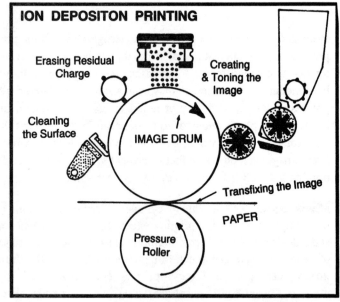

ION DEPOSITON PRINTING

Erasing Residual Charge

Creating & Toning the Image

Cleaning the Surface

IMAGE DRUM

Transfixing the Image

PAPER

Pressure Roller

Reprinted with the permission of InterQuest
Source: Delpha Systems

four simple steps: (1) an electrostatic image is generated by directing an array of charged particles (ions) from a patented ion cartridge toward a rotating drum that consists of very hard anodized aluminum maintained at a constant temperature; (2) a single component magnetic toner is attracted to the image on the drum as it rotates; (3) the toned image is transfixed to plain paper; and (4) after scraping the very small amount of toner (0.3 percent) left on the drum, it is ready for re-imaging. Ion deposition printing is used for printing of invoices, manuals, letters, and proposals, as well as specialty printing of tags, tickets, and checks. A disadvantage to this process is that images are easily rubbed. A system is being developed using new materials capable of producing high quality continuous tone four-color images.

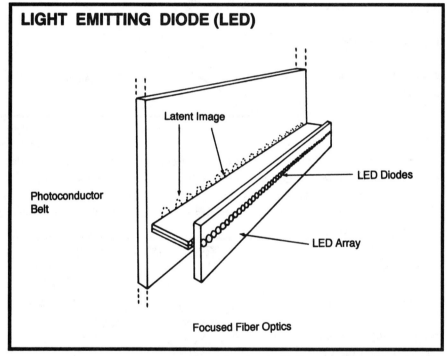

LIGHT EMITTING DIODE (LED)

Latent Image

LED Diodes

Photoconductor
Belt

LED Array

Focused Fiber Optics

Reprinted with the permission of InterQuest
Source: Kentek Information

Light Emitting Diode (LED) Printing - This is a process that uses a light source to create an image on a photoconductor. The system employs an array of several thousand light-emitting diodes that provide direct imaging with no moving light beam. Light-emitting diodes are switched on and off to create an image on a charged drum.

Liquid Crystal Shutter (LCS) Printing - A process that is similar to the LED process. The difference is that LCS writes an image onto a photoconductor through staggered liquid crystal shutters instead of diodes. The system uses a high intensity fluorescent bulb for light exposure. Electrical signals open and close shutters depending on the areas to be imaged.

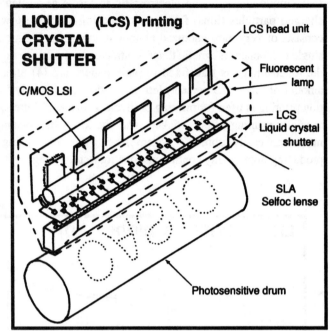

LIQUID CRYSTAL SHUTTER

LIQUID (LCS) Printing

C/MOS LSI

LCS head unit

Fluorescent lamp

LCS Liquid crystal shutter

SLA Selfoc lense

Photosensitive drum

Reprinted with the permission of InterQuest
Source: Casio

Electron Beam Imaging (EBI) Printing - A process similar to ion deposition printing, the difference being that the imaging is performed by controlling a beam of electrons instead of ions. The system uses high voltage and high frequency to excite free electrons onto a rotating drum. The electrons attract toner particles in the same way that laser printers do. High pressure rollers are used to fuse the toner to the paper.

Thermal Printing - This is widely used for non-impact printing. There are two thermal printing processes: direct thermal and wax thermal transfer. In direct thermal printing, a special coated thermographic paper is exposed to a head which reacts by turning the exposed areas into

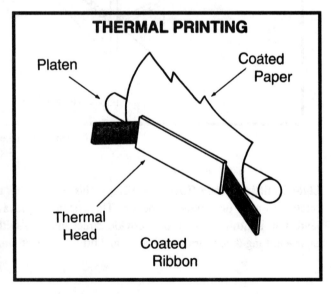

THERMAL PRINTING

Platen

Coated Paper

Thermal Head

Coated Ribbon

44

different colors, either black or blue. In the wax thermal transfer process the same chemical principle is used, however, a special coated ribbon is used which releases pigmented material. Characters are printed one at a time by a printhead that moves back and forth.

Electrostatic Printing - A process that is similar to xerographic or electrophotographic printing. It uses toner particles to form an image from an analog original. Unlike electrophotographic systems, there is no print drum. Toner particles are attracted directly to the paper through controlled conductivity. No optical system is used. The entire copier glass is exposed at once and an electrostatic charge is directly deposited onto the paper. Electrostatic printing systems use liquid or dry toners. In systems that require liquid toners, the toner is fused to the paper through hot air. When dry toners are used, the toner is fused to the paper via pressure.

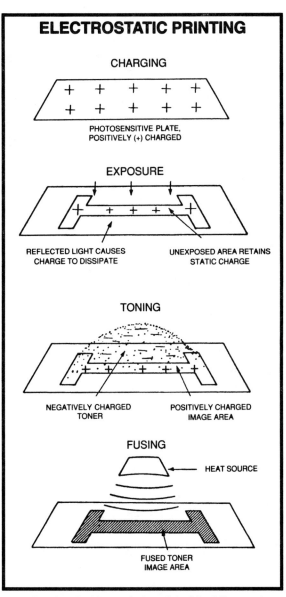

Reprinted with permission of the Mead Corporation

45

Electronic Digital Photography

Introduction

Electronic digital photography has surpassed the concept stage and will be a viable tool for the graphic arts industry in the years ahead. Major newspapers and news-magazines, typically among the first to adopt new technologies, have already embraced electronic digital photography as a common production procedure for capturing analog images, converting them to digital form, and reproducing them as printed images.

Electronic still digital photography transforms the analog values of an image into digital values and allows rapid image viewing, enhancement, modification, and overall improvement. The process requires no film and the camera is the imaging tool. As the printing and publishing industry continues to compete with electronic media and particularly television, and as the need increases for high quality imaging, rapid image transmission and meeting tight deadlines, filmless electronic cameras are the logical alternative to film-based imaging.

Advantages and Disadvantages

The advantage of using electronic cameras is that photographs are ready for instant viewing. This enables editing and image alterations quickly, thus expediting the preparation of images for transmission and printing. The present disadvantages are that the overall image quality from electronic cameras is not as good as from film-based images and electronic cameras are relatively expensive. These disadvantages are expected to be eliminated over the next few years as prices continue to drop and as the promise of high definition television (HDTV) and its higher screen resolution is realized.

Scanners

The nucleus of electronic still photography is the scanner. The scanner is the link between electronic images and computers. There are various types of scanners being used in electronic photography including: video scanners, hand-held scanners for flat art and text, flatbed scanners and overhead scanners for prints and transparencies, film scanners for negatives and transparencies, sheet-fed scanners for text, and drum scanners for prints, negatives, and transparencies. Rotary drum scanners still offer the highest quality for input and output images, but they are typically large and expensive. The less expensive charge-coupled device (CCD) scanners will show significant improvements as their dynamic range for recording color at high resolution improves. Users of electronic still video photography must learn to evaluate digital images on a screen with the same criteria that they typically evaluate prints and transparencies. Some of the criteria include: sharpness, copy range (highlight to shadow areas), gray balance, overall color correctness, and so on.

The "Electronic Darkroom"

With the expected rapid growth of electronic still digital photography will come a dramatic change in the photography work environment. Replacing the conventional darkroom is the electronic darkroom in which the computer platform replaces the process camera and the film processors as the key darkroom components. While the Apple Macintosh platform has dominated to date, other platforms such as MS-DOS, UNIX, and PC (IBM or compatibles) are being developed that are compatible with Macintosh or can be used independently. Therefore, setting up an electronic darkroom in the future will require careful evaluation of systems that best serve user needs. Decisions will also have to be made about the many versions of important peripherals needed for a complete electronic photographic system. These peripherals include: type and capacity of hard drive; type and size of monitor (monochromatic or color); scanner type, size, and capabilities; output devices such as printers and film recorders (thermal dye transfer, thermal wax, ink-jet, laser, electrostatic or photographic printers); type; and capacity of storage. With the emergence of universal page description languages like PostScript, images can be sent directly to many differently types of imagesetters or output devices.

Memory and Storage

Color digital image takes up a large amount of memory. Magnetic storage, still the major method of storage, is considered slow. Optical media is faster and has certain advantages for storing digital photographs. New developments such as Kodak's Photo CD allow high quality photo images to be stored in non-erasable memory for storage and retrieval. One disk can store up to 100 color digital images that are scanned from 35mm film at approximately the same resolution of 35mm negatives. The fastest image memory today is solid state memory, however the cost is presently prohibitive, but has the advantage of displaying images immediately.

Image Enhancement Software

Digital photographs can be created by direct electronic capture of the image with a digital camera, or by converting an analog image from a camcorder or still-video camera. The growing availability of image-enhancement software has done more to stimulate interest in digital photography than anything else. These new software packages not only modify and enhance photographs, but also assist in the control of input and output devices. They typically allow photo retouching, image manipulation, color correction of contrast and brightness, the production of color separations, and the creation of original electronic art. Some of the companies which produce image enhancement systems are: Agfa, Barco, Dupont, Hell, Scitex, Graphix, Dicomed, Kodak, ImageMaz, Imapro, Integraph, Management Graphics, Networked Picture Systems, and SupreSet.

48

The key to the future of digital electronic photography will be in the ability to compress image files. Compressed files will be easier to store and transmit. Breakthroughs will come with the elimination of image deterioration when compression is increased. Systems are presently being developed that will allow compression up to 220 to 1 with the user in control of acceptable quality loss.

There are a growing number of desktop software packages that allow users to integrate type and digital photographs. Common to most of the page layout programs is their text editing, layout capabilities, and their typographic controls. PageMaker from Aldus Corp. was an early package for use on the Macintosh. Ventura Publisher was one of the first packages for the IBM PC. QuarkXPress has become a program that is important for newspapers, magazines, and advertising.

Aldus PrePrint allows linkage, image enhancement, and printing options. It is compatible with files from PageMaker, Freehand and Adobe Illustrator, and it accommodates TIFF (Tag Image Format File), DCS (Desktop Color Separation), and Paint files. Aldus PageMaker serves the needs of the Macintosh and the IBM PC user with Windows 3.

Ventura software, one of the earliest of the page make-up software programs for the IBM PC and compatible computers has moved to a Microsoft Windows-base. In its latest version, Ventura has added four-color prepress products - Ventura Scan, Ventura Separator, Ventura PhotoTouch and Ventura ColorPro - that allow seamless integration of color scanning, separation, and photo editing.

Ventura Scan allows scanning of black and white, gray scale, or color images directly from within Ventura Publisher.

Ventura Separator produces CYMK separations of complete pages with all text, graphics, and continuous tone color images in place. It corrects for such things as printing press dot gain and provides for halftone screen angles.

PhotoTouch provides a range of creative tools to outline, airbrush, sharpen, blur, blend, smear, lighten or darken, shift hue, shift saturation, add or subtract color, and gradation.

Ventura ColorPro provides professional control of the high-end drum scanner in a Windows environment. It provides for undercolor removal (UCR), undercolor addition (UCA), and gray component replacement (GCR).

QuarkXPress manipulates color photographs, graphics, and text in a way that is suitable for high-quality reproduction. It has the ability to put together complete pages with type and pictures all in register. With QuarkXPress, trapping is done automatically. The system checks trapping values for the object color relative to background color and uses the minimum of these values. QuarkXPress emphasizes good typography which has given it a lead in the marketplace.

Digital Displays

The most practical means of viewing digital photo images directly from the computer is through the CRT. Liquid crystal display (LCD) screens, typically used in laptop computers, are beginning to appear, but presently have limited resolution capabilities. Projection LCD systems show greater promise since it is possible to create filters that more closely match color photographic printing and the inks used on printing presses, more so than the phosphors of CRT systems.

Developments for the Future

The trend in computers and workstations used in digital photography is towards multi-tasking which allows more than one operation to be performed at the same time. In other words, while the computer is making a time consuming global change, the operator can be working on another task.

ImageSpan Division of GTE Corporation has a system that allows text and pictures to flow over copper telephone lines and satellite at rates as high as 1.5 million bits per second. This is much faster than the current transmission speed of 2400 to 9600 bits per second.

Object-oriented programming allows the reuse of objects created in different programs. This means a program that involves enhancement can have an object move to a program that is word processing.

The Open Software Foundation (OSF), a consortium of leading hardware manufacturers, including IBM, Digital Equipment, Hewlett-Packard, and others, will exchange elements of their proprietary systems in an effort to create an open version of UNIX that will run across their own and other hardware platforms.

Polaroid has been working for sometime on new technologies for all aspects of digital photography.

Japanese companies are working on the means of capturing digital images with CCD sensors. Matsushita, Sanyo, Toshiba, Mitsubishi, Sharp, Hatachi, and Konica are all playing important roles in electronic imaging. Sharp developed a system for sending color faxes called ColorFax. It can send a high quality 8" x 10" color image in three minutes. A thermal-dye transfer printer outputs the page.

Interest in three-dimensional images has led to a new technology called virtual reality, which combines vision, sound, and hand movements to create the feeling of being able to see and touch objects that exist only in the computer.

The Kodak digital camera system has a CCD that can produce about 10 million bits of color information. On drawback of current digital cameras is the lack of CCD sensors with a sufficiently high resolution to create "film-look" images. Most of the mass-produced CCD sensors have only about 380,000 pixels and the ability to record 2 to 2.5 million bits of color data.

By the year 2000, memory chip capabilities could reach as high as 1000 megabits using X-ray technology. The next generation of microprocessor from Intel will be the 586 microprocessor with more than 3 million transistors.

Neural network technology, which mimics the neural system of the brain, has developed to the point where it is being used for applications such as text recognition and image processing. Intel Corporation has developed a neural network chip that can learn and remember what it has been taught. Neural networks of tomorrow in digital photographic systems will handle judgmental aspects such as exposure, contrast, and focus. In digital photography, neural networks in image processing systems could be used for tasks such as color correction and adjusting colors in a digitized image for better appearance on the screen and when printed. The system could also enhance portions of a photograph that have muddy tones or other weaknesses.

Fuzzy logic mimics the reasoning of the human mind. Combining fuzzy logic with neural networks could create a powerful means for creating "decision-making" components for all aspects of digital photography, from the camera to the processing and enhancement station, and to the final output.

Multimedia

Introduction

Multimedia is a continuum of applications and technologies allowing for a wide range of experiences and applications that bring together multiple types of media such as text, illustrations, photographs, sounds, voice, animations, and video. It typically combines three or more technologies that improve communication and allows for potential interaction between the user and the media.

The continued growth and development of the graphic arts industry relies on the diversification into multimedia and other fields not typically associated with printing and publishing. Such fields include electronics, telecommunication, and overall communications. The traditional graphic arts industry is presently being redefined to include these areas as part of how print is produced and how print is supplemented by or supplements other media. This redefinition is occurring to some extent within the printing industry but to a larger extent from outside of the traditional graphic arts. For example, in September 1993, 400 representatives of the computer, electronics, telecommunication, and CD-ROM industries gathered in San Francisco at a conference entitled "The Electronic Book Fair." They discussed ways in which multimedia will reshape and replace traditional books, magazines, catalogs, and other forms of print media. This is a clear signal to the printing industry to learn about and diversify into multimedia or be overtaken by an aggressive industry that is receiving growing appeal from businesses and the general public.

With its roots in the technological revolution of the 1990's, by 1993 multimedia has received such a high degree of acceptibility that many of its software manufacturers, vendors, and title developers have begun to enjoy a profit. Compare this to the over a decade it took for *USA Today*, with its highly technologically advanced methods of producing a traditional print medium, to begin approaching profitability.

Digitization

The commonalities or standards that will run through each facet of multimedia are digitization and the use of the same digital information across different types of media. This could begin with a digitized photographic image stemming from video transmitted to a CD-ROM and end with multiple similar or variable images produced on a direct digital imaging printing press. This information could have come from a remote location such as a client, advertising agency, design studio, photography studio, publisher, or any other printing buyer. Implications for the graphic arts industry include print buyer interaction to make editorial and correction decisions by viewing the image from a remote site as it is being printed. Basically, the customer would be in control at all times.

Electronic Books

The fastest growing multimedia market today is book publishing. While a fully developed multimedia market does not yet exist, this industry segment is growing rapidly as the public seeks and is enticed by new ways of acquiring information. The potential for electronic books include the ability to quickly search and retrieve text and other elements, the elimination of constraints imposed by the linearity of a printed book, and the expansion of a printed book's content into a more detailed electronic book. For example, a typical 200 page printed book can be expanded into a 700 page electronic book.

It appears that multimedia is appealing to people's interest in communication with and receiving communication through multiple senses, i.e., sight, sound, and touch. Multimedia is not presently looked at as a replacement for traditional print, but it is certainly viewed as a supplement. It provides flexibilities that print on paper does not have. Paper is tactile, has very high resolution, is variable in format, and is a familiar medium. However, multimedia is user-modifiable, rapidly searched, indexed, cross-referenced, non-linear, and extensible.

The more progressive traditional book publishers are preparing to make multimedia part of their business, with the realization that book stores will soon have CD-ROM sections in the same way that they now have books on tape. Typical multimedia products could be dictionaries, atlases, encyclopedias, magazines, catalogs, special interest books, advertising, greeting cards, yearbooks, and more. Apple Computer's Winter 1992-1993 edition of "The Apple Guide to CD-ROM Titles" lists approximately 300 titles which is merely a small sample of what is available.

Today, the proliferation of electronic books is hindered in part because of non-standard CD-ROM delivery platforms or engines. However, the next few years will likely show the emergence of a few dominent platforms making it easier for publishers to decide what platform to support.

Electronic Magazines

Another potentially large market for multimedia is the electronic distribution of magazines. Extending the magazine into digital form allows the inclusion of sound, animation, video clips, an information database, and other elements of an interactive interface that permits the user to access specific information about a subject. The electronic magazine borrows from conventions of broadcast media such as TV, and radio, and print media. It can be distributed through CD-ROM's, diskettes, computer networks, and through emerging technologies such as interactive television.

It is not anticipated that multimedia will replace traditional magazines but will supplement present titles. For example, Times Mirror presently publishes *Field and Stream, Golf, Home Mechanix, Outdoor Life, Popular Science, Salt Water Sportsman, Ski, Skiing, Skiing Trade News, Sporting Goods Dealer, The Sporting News, and Yachting.* Each of these magazines lend themselves to multimedia counterparts and are likely to appear in electronic versions in the future.

Electronic Interactive Sales, Marketing, and Catalogs

A multimedia advertisement takes advantage of the power of combined media and interactivity to encourage customers to learn about and ultimately purchase a product or service. It can be distributed over networks, cable transmission, and on-line facilities such as Compuserve or America Online. An electronic catalog can use interaction and multimedia to provide a more convincing product than print-based catalogs or cable shopping networks. Most contain the actual products on CD-ROM and the potential of this medium includes ordering the product with a credit card in an interactive manner.

Multimedia Databases

Multimedia databases provide a variety of options for retrieving information. One database called Aldus Fetch is a multi-user, mixed-media cataloging, browsing, and retrieval tool that can index clip art, photo images, presentations, QuickTime movies, sounds, and other elements. Uses of multimedia databases include advertising, product planning, electronic catalogs, business directories, and so on. Some databaes are industry specific and are being developed for fields such as travel, real estate, insurance, criminal justice, and medial industries - all typical printing industry customers. A current problem in selecting a database is the lack of standards among many multimedia types. Whereas text and numbers are commonly represented in ASC II format (a format recognized by almost all systems or applications), movies, sounds, animations, and to some extent graphic formats are only recently moving towards standards recognizable by many systems.

Designing multimedia databases and programs require working with business professionals having skills that cross the various types of media. They include content experts, writers, editors, researchers, graphic designers, photographers, and scanner and image processing specialists. With words no longer the only way of describing content, specialists with experience and strengths in using CD-ROM's to effectively describe content and deliver a message are needed. These strengths include working with words, sound, video, 2-D and 3-D animation, still graphics, interactivity, and so on. The cost of designing and producing a database can vary greatly. For example, a CD-ROM can cost between $25,000 and $500,000 to produce.

Market Projections

By the end of 1992 there were approximately 1,080,000 installed CD-ROM capable machines including 180,000 DOS, 600,000 MPC, and 300,000 Mac platforms. By the end of the first quarter of 1993 the number grew to approximately 1,300,000 with 800,000 MPC and 500,000 Mac platforms. A conservative projection for the end of 1994 is that there will be approximately 2,000,000 multimedia ready machines with 1.2 million MPC and 800,000 Mac platforms. An optimistic projection is for approximately 3,000,000 multimedia ready machines by the end of 1994 with 1.7 million MPC and 1.3 million Mac platforms.

Projections to 1996 indicate that digital content will be available on all computer platforms, on television, and on satellite downlinks—all of which will be part of a home or business multimedia system. It is also projected that by 1996 CD-ROM hardware prices will drop. This will result in significant market growth. Additionally, CD-ROM ready machines will be common in businesses and in homes. CD-ROM's will be readily available in software and computer hardware stores, audio and video stores, bookstores, and through mail order distributors. It is anticipated that the cost of replicating CD-ROM's will drop as will the cost of related items and operations.

The projection for multimedia's future is highly positive. It is anticipated that by the year 2000 multimedia will represent a $1 trillion industry combining the cooperative efforts of sub-industries including personal computers, consumer electronics, printing and publishing, entertainment, and communications. Segments of the graphic arts industry not presently planning to be part of this super industry may be unable to compete and consequently be out of business by the year 2000.

Cross Reference Descriptions

Cross-referencing has been included as an important part of this useful reference book. Each definition, software or hardware product, or company noted is cross-referenced to one or more of the following categories. In addition, all terminology that is included in the main dictionary has been listed by name under its respective category at the end of the main body of definitions. This complete listing begins in the "Cross-Reference" Section.

It is the author's and the publisher's hope that these cross-references make this dictionary more useful to you.

Art and Copy Preparation - All facets of conventional and electronic design, layout, paste-up, and mechanical art preparation including overlay color separation.

Color Reproduction - Color theory, conventional and electronic color processes related to color separations and four-color printing.

Computer Hardware - All physical computer equipment including peripherals such as monitors, keyboards, and tangible interfaces for integrating and expanding computers.

Desktop/Electronic Publishing - Electronic systems and their electronically produced output such as books, magazines, and other print media. Includes related issues such as copyrights, author's alterations, format, style, and publishing.

Digital Photography - Photographic procedures, components, and processes to record images and output them digitally. Requires no film or other photosensitive material.

Environment - Items related to environmental issues and controls such as health, safety, ecology, pollution, recycling, and waste disposal.

Finishing - All operations and procedures that a substrate goes through after it has been printed, including collating, slitting, trimming, binding, stitching, die cutting, embossing, foil stamping, etc. Plus the corresponding finishing equipment and materials.

General Computer - Any items related to computers and electronic applications that are generic and not classified as hardware or software. This includes general terms applicable to any computer and computer functions.

Graphic Arts Photography - All photographic reproduction equipment and processes for printing including line, halftone, duotone, four-color photography, graphic arts cameras, scanning, and photographic manipulation of images for the final print reproduction.

Image Assembly - All conventional stripping of negative and positive line and halftone film in accordance with the layout and imposition of pages on press sheets or signatures. Includes electronic assembly of images and pages on a desktop or electronic publishing system.

Image Carriers - All printing plates and procedures for producing printing plates for all processes including lithography, gravure, flexography, letterpress, etc.

Ink - All aspects of printing ink characteristics, formulations, manufacturing, testing, and use of ink on printing presses.

Laser Applications - The general application and characteristics of lasers in the graphic arts as applied to prepress, press, finishing, and other related operations.

Marketing - All terminology that relates to selling and promoting desktop and graphic arts products and services.

Multimedia - Use of two or more media, simultaneously used or available to convey information or a message through print, sound, motion, and interactivity.

Printing Processes - All devices, components, and operations related to imaging a substrate. Includes all the conventional printing processes, the newer techniques such as laser, electrostatics, ink jet, and other nonimpact and electronic printing.

Proofing - All methods, processes, procedures, supplies, and technologies used to create a simulation of what a finished printed product should look like.

Quality/Process Control - All references to procedures, tests, equipment, and other devices designed to monitor, control, and improve quality.

Scanning - All devices and procedures for digitizing input copy, film, or other images. This includes desktop scanning, plate scanning, and high-end monochromatic and color separation film output scanning.

Software - All non-tangible components of computers related to programs and programming, general computer languages, interpretation, and page description language.

Standards - Areas of desktop publishing and graphic arts where standard operating procedures, languages, measurements, and interpretations have been developed.

Substrates - Any surface on which an image is placed but typically refers to the substrate representing the final printed product such as paper, board, foil, etc.

Telecommunications - Devices, procedures, and concepts for transmitting information long distances through telephone lines, microwaves, satellites, cable, and optical fiber.

Typesetting and Imagesetting - The inputting and outputting of words and/or pictures on photosensitive film, photosensitive paper, or on plain paper, and all related technologies, procedures, processes, and products.

Typography - All considerations related to the aesthetics of type design, selection of type styles, and determination of appropriate type size, letter spacing, word spacing, line spacing, and other aspects of how type is used in the design of desktop publishing and printing products.

Editorial Comment:

The names and titles of all proprietory software have been underlined to provide uniformity. Each software product noted is the property of the company listed at the end of each description of the software.

A0 through A5 - Metric paper sizes. A0 = 894mm x 1189mm (33.1 x 46.8 inches). A1 = 594mm x 841mm (23.4 x 33.1 inches). A2 = 420mm x 594mm (16.5 x 23.4 inches). A3 = 297mm x 420mm (11.7 x 16.5 inches). A4 = 210mm x 297mm (8.3 x 11.7 inches). A5 = 148mm x 210mm (5.8 x 8.3 inches). *Standards - Substrates*

AA's - See Author's Alterations.

Absolute Address - An exact area or location in computer memory with a specific address. *Computer Hardware*

Absolute Value - A number which is positive or a zero, and no sign (+ or -). *General Computer*

Absorbency - See Absorption.

Absorption - The degree to which a substrate can soak up vapors and/or liquids. A consideration in the determination of the right quantity of ink that is needed to create an acceptable impression. See Impression. *Printing Processes - Substrates*

Absorptance - The amount of light that is absorbed by a surface, as compared to the actual amount of light striking that surface. A major consideration in subtractive color. *Color Reproduction*

Abrasion - The scratching of printed matter during shipping and processing. *Quality/Process Control*

Abrasion Resistance - The ability of all printed materials (especially covers and the packaging itself) to resist abrasion. *Quality/Process Control*

Accelerator Card - A replacement board for the main processor or a board that handles tasks performed by the main processor more efficiently. *Computer Hardware*

Accents - Distinguishing marks that are positioned over a character. Most commonly used in foreign languages. See Fig. 1. *Typography*

Acute	Á á
Cedilla	Ç ç
Circumflex	Â â
Dieresis	Ä ä
Grave	À à
Tilde	Ã ã

Fig. 1 - Accents

Access Time - The exact time needed for the computer to request and receive information for processing. *General Computer*

Accordion Fold - A type of paper fold that requires multiple parallel folds and when extended it gives the appearance of an accordion. *Finishing*

Accordion Insert - An advertising piece which was accordion folded and inserted into a direct mail package. See Accordion Fold. *Marketing*

Accumulator - A location in main memory where the results of arithmetic calculations are stored. *Computer Hardware*

Accurate Screening - Adobe Systems' version of Supercell Screening. See Supercell Screening. *Color Reproduction*

Acetate - A thin, flexible sheet of plastic

that is clear (sometimes translucent), and has the ability to accept the inks that are used in the printing process. *Substrates*

Acetate Proof - A proof that has been created on clear acetate. *Proofing*

Achromatic - Any color without hue, i.e., gray, black, and white. *Color Reproduction*

Achromatic Reproduction - A method that is used when producing color separations which creates only the minimum amount of magenta, cyan, and yellow color needed for the separation. Black is added to create the needed depth of color, especially in the shadow areas. This process uses less ink overall and gives more control at the press. See Gray Component Replacement. *Color Reproduction*

Acquisition - The transfer of video analog data to a digital form. *Digital Photography - Telecommunications*

Acrobat - Software that allows sending any document electronically to any other Adobe Acrobat user, regardless of the computer system, the application software, or the fonts. The receiving user can add comments to the document after viewing the material and then send it to any other user. See Adobe Systems, Inc. *Software*

Acronym - A word that has been created from the first letters (sometimes the critical letters) in a multiword series, i.e., ANSI stands for American National Standards Institute, and DMA stands for Direct Marketing Association. *General Computer*

Across Web - A page that moves perpen-dicular to the movement of the web or roll. *Printing Processes*

Activate - Increasing the state of chemical activity. *Graphic Arts Photography*

Ad - See Advertisement.

Ad Director - Automates the publication ad layout process by automatically placing ads on pages. Allows user to control zoning, gravity, advertising ratios, color press configurations and coupon placement. Produces reports on issue costs, color usage and advertising ratios. See Managing Editor Software, Inc. *Software*

Ad Director with Forms Manager - Combines Ad Director with range of publication functions. Allows for the quick placement of inserts, new forms or forms templates, and allows for customized folios, deadline alerting, and the quick calculation of press set-up and running costs. See Managing Editor Software, Inc. *Software*

Additive Color Primaries - There are three additive primary colors: red, green, and blue. See Additive Color. *Color Reproduction*

Additive Color - A process of creating color that is comprised of the three primary colors - blue, green, and red. Then by adjusting or adding amounts of each color all the other colors can be created. When equal amounts of the three colors are mixed with the appropriate brightness (or light), white is created. Cathode-ray tubes use the additive color process. *Color Reproduction*

Address - A value that indicates the specific address or location of the desired

60

information in memory so the computer can easily find the needed data. *Computer Hardware*

Addressograph - A machine that prints by a process of controlled pressure that forces contact between the inked ribbon and the embossed plates. Primarily used for addressing the envelopes of mailing lists. *Printing Processes*

Adhesive Binding - See Perfect Binding.

Adhesive Bleed - The seepage from the pressure-sensitive material, i.e., label stock, that bleeds through the stock before and after printing. *Finishing*

Adobe Font Folio - The world's broadest collection of Type 1 typefaces on CD-ROM. Contains packages 1 through 325 of the Adobe Type Library. Includes: ATM, Type Reunion, TypeAlign, and Suitcase. For Mac & PC. See Adobe Systems, Inc. *Typography*

Adobe Systems, Inc - Develops, markets and supports computer software products, type, and technologies that enable users to create, display, and print electronic documents. Contact numbers: 1585 Charleston Rd., Mountain View, CA 94039-7900; (415)961-4400. *Software*

Adobe Type Library - More than 1,700 Type 1 typefaces that include the collections of: Miles/Agfa, Berthold, ITC, Linotype-Hell, Monotype, Morisawa, and Adobe. Most packages contain typefaces from one family or a group of typefaces with similar characteristics. Symbol typefaces comprise character sets for special purposes such as music notation or map making. Expert sets include special characters such as old style figures and small capitals. Non-Latin typeface choic-es include Japanese and Cyrillic. Some of the Adobe Type Library packages come from the Adobe Originals collection of new designs and classic revivals created by Adobe's type designers. For Mac, Windows, OS/2, and DOS. See Adobe Systems, Inc. *Typography*

ADPCM (Adaptive Differential Pulse Code Modulation) - A standard in audio encoding and data compression. *Multimedia - Telecommunications*

Advertisement (Ad) - A paid message in the form of text combined with graphics to tell about a company and/or its products. They are included in newspapers, magazines, and other publications and are created by a graphic artist. *Marketing*

Advertising Agency - A service firm that assists another company in the development of advertising and marketing programs. Most agencies are full service and provide a wide range of graphics, printing, advertising, and marketing services. Some are highly specialized agencies that focus on one or more specific services, i.e., direct mail, radio ads, media placement, etc. Agencies receive most of their revenue from commissions earned on ads placed in the various forms of media, i.e., TV, radio, newspaper, etc. *Marketing*

Advertising Contract - A binding contract between an advertising agency or a client and the provider of advertising space that includes the cost and placement (times and locations) of advertising messages. *Marketing*

Against The Grain - The process of folding or of printing on paper in a direction that is at a right angle to the grain. *Substrates*

Agate - A term that is used to define 5 1/2 point type. Most common use in newspaper classified advertising. *Typesetting and Imagesetting*

Agate Line - The unit that is used to compute advertising space column depth. Fourteen agate lines to the column inch is used as the newspaper industry standard. *Typesetting and Imagesetting*

Agency Commission - This typically refers to the 15 percent discount given to advertising agencies by the provider of advertising space, i.e., TV station, radio station, magazine, etc. *Marketing*

Aim Point - The starting point for ink density, during make-ready before any color adjustments. *Ink - Printing Processes*

Airbrush - A small pencil-like pressure gun that is used for the application of a fine spray of watercolor by compressed air. It is used for the creation of artwork and to create or correct graduated tones. *Art and Copy Preparation*

Air-Bubble Packing - Plastic packing material having a surface covered with many air pockets. Has excellent shock absorbing qualities, thus protecting delicate shipments from damage. *Finishing*

Aldus Corporation - Offers electronic production software that will automate the prepress workflow using off-the-shelf software tools. Contact numbers: 411 First Avenue South, Seattle, WA 98104-2871; (206)622-5500. *Software*

Algorithm - The specific sequence or set of instructions and/or procedures that must be followed to complete or solve a mathematical or logical problem. *General Computer*

Aliasing - The jagged appearance in graphic images of all diagonal lines, i.e., a stair-stepping effect. *Desktop/Electronic Publishing* The under sampling of the spatial frequency of a signal from its original frequency. *Digital Photography*

All Caps - See Uppercase.

Alphanumeric Characters - Characters that are a combination of all alphabetical characters and numeric characters plus other specific special characters (i.e., question mark, etc.) and control characters (i.e., spacing). *General Computer*

Alpha Test - The first phase of testing for a new software or hardware product. *General Computer*

Alt Key - A keytop function on PC's that when combined with other keys can produce special results, usually software related. *Computer Hardware*

Aluminum Foil - Aluminum that has been rolled to less than .006 of an inch thick. *Substrates*

Amberlith - Orange masking film by Ulano. *Art and Copy Preparation*

Ampere - An electrical current measurement unit, which indicates the volume of electrical current flowing through a given point or area, i.e., a conductor. *General Computer*

Amplifier - A mechanism for increasing signal power. *Telecommunications*

Analog - Everything we see, feel, and hear is analog in its natural form. Analog refers to the representation of data by a changing physical state, i.e., intensity, frequency, voltage, etc. *Digital Photography - General Computer*

Analog Computer - A special type of computer that processes information that is continuous versus information that is generated in discrete digital units. *Computer Hardware*

Analog Proofs - Proofs that are created from the film negatives and are used to give the customer a view of how the final printed job will look prior to printing, i.e., 3M Matchprints and Dupont Cromalins. See Matchprint and Cromalin. *Proofing*

Analog Recording - A method of representing an audio or video signal by direct transfer of the changing elements (amplitude and frequency). Analog recording involves the recording of the fluctuating voltages as changing flux densities on a magnetic medium, i.e., audio or video is converted into electrical impulses which form patterns in the oxide particles of tape representing wave-forms. *Digital Photography - Multimedia*

Analog-To-Digital Converter - A unit or mechanism that converts analog information to discrete digital information. See Analog Computer and Digital Computer. *Computer Hardware - Software*

Analog Transmission - A method of transmitting signals and information which are continuous and non-discrete. *General Computer - Telecommunications*

Angle Indicator - A clear polyester gauge that will indicate the exact screen angle on a halftone when laid over the image. *Quality/Process Control*

Angle Of Wipe - The angle that is formed between a gravure cylinder and its doctor blade. *Printing Processes*

Anhydrous - A process that is water free. *Printing Processes*

Animation - A software technique that adds movement to objects or drawings, making them lifelike. *Software*

Animator - The person who creates animation. *Multimedia*

ANSI (American National Standard Institute) - The organization that establishes the standards that govern many areas, i.e., computers, data transmission, communications protocols, etc. *Standards*

Anti-Aliasing - A software process that will smooth out the jagged appearance on lines that are not perfectly straight up or down, or even on circles and curves. This technique will also allow the operator to soften the hardness of jagged lines by modifying the pixels next to the line to show a smooth transition between all areas of lightness or darkness. *Software*

Anti-Foaming Agent - An ink additive for foam prevention. *Ink*

Anti-Offset Spray - A printing press spray that is used to prevent the unwanted transfer of wet ink from one sheet to the next sheet of paper. *Printing Processes*

Antique Finish - A rough surfaced substrate that is used primarily for book and booklet cover stock. *Substrates*

Anti-Skid Varnish - A special coating to help prevent any possible carton slippage. *Quality/Process Control*

Anti-Slip - A characteristic of film that minimizes film surfaces from sliding over each other. *Graphic Arts Photography*

Aperture - An opening in the camera that controls the diameter (size) of the beam of light entering the lens. *Digital Photography - Graphic Arts Photography*

Apple Computer, Inc. - Develops and markets a full family of Mac personal computer systems. Plus a broad range of printers, monitors, scanners and system software for Mac systems, as well as a range of software extensions and development tools. Also creates a variety of inter-operability, networking, and communication products that integrate Mac systems into different computer environments. Contact numbers: 1 Infinite Loop, Cupertino, CA 95014; (408)996-1010. *Computer Hardware - Software*

AppleScript Workflow Application ToolKit (AWAT) - A program that makes integrating AppleScript-aware applications easy. Provides a complete 4-D application shell, AppleScript 4-D external and instructions on how to execute AppleScripts containing 4-D parameters. See Productivity Enhancement, Inc. *Software*

AppleTalk - The LAN developed for the Mac. See LAN. *Software*

Application Program - A computer software program that was designed and developed to perform a specific job, i.e., invoicing, label preparation, etc. *Software*

APR Print - Extends Scitex APR (Automatic Picture Replacement) to several image formats in addition to Scitex PSImage. Files in TIFF, EPS, PICT, Sci-tex CT, or Scitex LW format can be placed, cropped, and scaled as "FPO" images in a QuarkXPress document. See Scitex Corporation Ltd. *Software*

Architecture - The internal structure of the microcomputer, i.e., how all the parts are connected. *General Computer*

Archival Paper - A non-acidic type of paper that has a long life. It is used for important books, records, and documents. *Substrates*

Archival Storage - Long-term record storage, usually on the slowest and least expensive type of media, i.e., floppy disks, tape drives, optical disks, etc. This type of information or data is usually compressed to hold a greater capacity. *Software*

Archive - The process of storing long-term data on low cost media, usually backup copies or seldom used information. See Archival Storage. *Software*

Argument - The values or numbers that are used by the program to complete the necessary calculations required by the formula. *General Computer*

Ares Software Corporation - Develops and markets leading-edge PostScript, True Type font portability, type library technology, font utilities, and graphics software products for Mac and Windows. Contact numbers: 565 Pilgrim Drive, # A, Foster City, CA 94404; (415)578-9090. *Software - Typography*

Artificial Intelligence - The ability of the computer to perform human-like intelligence activities, i.e., speech recognition, learning from experience, making logical inferences from limited data, and general creativity. *Software*

Array - An entire list or collection of character strings and/or numbers that are of a similar type or have the same name. Each element in an array can be directly addressed or located as needed. *General Computer*

Arrow Keys - Keyboard keys with functions that control cursor movement in all directions: down, up, left, and right. *Computer Hardware*

Art - Illustrations, graphics, and drawings that are created by an artist to be used for reproduction. See Graphic Designer. *Art and Copy Preparation*

Art Board - See Camera-Ready Copy.

Artist - See Graphic Designer.

Arts & Letters Apprentice 1.2 - A graphics and drawing program: Includes 4,000 artforms and clip-art symbols; 90 typefaces; charting; predefined color; line and fill styles; type controls; warp/perspective; text along a path; and interactive size/slant/rotate features. See Computer Support Corporation. *Software*

Arts & Letters Easy Draw - A series of software products that combine the informational and entertainment value of multimedia with the power of a complete drawing program. See Computer Support Corporation. *Software*

Arts & Letters EXPO Series - A complete drawing program with advanced features. Offers nine typefaces, bezier-curve drawing & editing tools; 350 clip-art images; complete typographic controls; support for ATM typefaces; and more. See Computer Support Corporation. *Software*

Arts & Letters Graphics Editor 3.12 Offers over 8,000 clip-art images; Activity Manager and Clip-Art Manager; 90 typefaces; type controls; warp/perspective; clipping masks and hole-cutting; shape and color interpolation; bezier-curve drawing and editing; and spot and four-color separation. See Computer Support Corporation. *Software*

Arts & Letters Picture Wizard 1.1 Drawing and graphics program for newcomers. Features concise and easy to understand instructions: 1,000 clip-art images; 15 typefaces; bezier line and curve editing; and more. See Computer Support Corporation. *Software*

Artwork - See Art.

ASA Rating - A rating on the sensitivity of film. It is established by the American Standards Association. *Graphic Arts Photography - Standards*

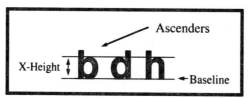

Fig. 2 - Ascenders

Ascenders - The portion of the lower case characters that are above the X-Height. See Fig. 2. *Typography*

ASCII (American Standard Code for Information Interchange) - The seven bit binary code that represents and is assigned to each character, number, and punctuation mark. *General Computer - Standards*

Aspect Ratio - The ratio between length (horizontal) and width (vertical) of an object, i.e., 1:1; 2:1; 3:1, etc. 4" X 5" film has a 5:4 aspect ratio. This can indicate the degree of distortion of the object. *General Computer*

Assembling - See Gathering.

Assembly Language - A low-level computer language that is unique to each type of computer. Each assembly language statement directs a single computer action, i.e., store, add, etc. The primary purpose of this language is speed of operation and greater control over movement of data. *Software*

Asynchronous - A method of communication between two different devices where the receiving data is not synchronized with the internal operations of the receiving computer. *General Computer*

Audio - The sound itself, i.e., music, sound effects, etc. *Multimedia*

Audiotex - A telephone-based service where specific audio information is received by dialing a phone number or by accessing the information over phone lines via computers. *Telecommunications*

Authoring Tool - A tool that is used in creating electronic books. *Multimedia*

Author's Alterations (AA) - Copy that is changed or altered from the original manuscript after it is typeset, at the request of the author or client. Will also indicate to the customer (author or client) those corrections that are chargeable to them by the printer, typesetter or color separator. *Desktop/Electronic Publishing*

Automatic White Balance - Automatically adjusts the still video camera's color rendition without requiring the user to take a reading of a scene and select filtration. The purpose is to produce pure whites in scenes regardless of the lighting, i.e., tungsten, sunlight, etc. *Digital Photography*

Automation - Machines that are now doing the jobs that were formally performed by people. *General Computer*

Autopositive Film - A special film that creates a positive rather than a negative image. *Graphic Arts Photography - Image Carriers*

Auto Trace - A software feature that converts bit-mapped or raster images to object-oriented graphics. *Software*

Back Flap - That portion of a hardcover jacket that folds around the back cover that is usually the location of the author's biography. *Finishing*

Backbone - See Spine.

Background - This is the function on a multi-processing, multi-tasking computer where a program is running in the background while another program or function is visible on the screen. *General Computer*

Background Color - The color that is displayed behind the main characters or objects in an illustration or photograph. *Color Reproduction*

Backing-Up - After a sheet has been printed, it is reversed and then printed on the other side. *Printing Processes*

Backlighting - The light that comes into the photo itself from the back. Typically, the sunlight that fills a room from a window in the background in the photograph. *Graphic Arts Photography*

Back Lining - The process whereby a fabric or durable paper is glued to the spine (a part of hardcover book) for added strength. *Finishing*

Back Margin - See Gutter Margin and Gutter.

Back Matter - Reference material, i.e., glossary, index, etc., that is located at the end of a publication. *Desktop/Electronic Publishing*

Back Printing - Printing the image on the backside of clear film. This allows the printing to show through to the front. *Printing Processes*

Back Spinner - Part of a perfect binder that removes excess glue. *Finishing*

Back-To-Back Register - When the images on either side of a page must align with each other. *Image Carriers - Printing Processes*

Backup - A copy or duplicate of a program or file that is created for protection against loss in the event of a lost original and for archiving purposes. *Computer Hardware*

Backup Blade - The supporting blade to the cylinder's doctor blade in gravure printing. *Printing Processes*

Backups - See Backing-Up.

Bad Break - When a new page is started or a paragraph is ended with a single word standing by itself (called a widow). This is considered bad design and poor typography. See Widow. *Desktop/Electronic Publishing - Typography*

Balance - All page elements are placed symmetrically so there is good balance between the elements. See Design Principles. *Art and Copy Preparation*

Balanced Screening Technology - Miles/Agfa's version of Supercell Screening. See Supercell Screening. *Color Reproduction*

Ballard-Shell - A copper layer that holds the gravure image. *Printing Processes*

Balloon Copy - Copy that is enclosed in a balloon-like graphic and appears like the words in the balloon are emanating from a person's mouth. *Art and Copy Preparation*

Bandwidth - The range of frequencies, from the lowest to the highest, that a system is capable of reproducing. Measured in frequency (Hz) within a specified amplitude tolerance (db). Also expressed as frequency response. *Digital Photography - Telecommunications*

Banner - A large sign (usually much longer than it is wide) which projects a message. *Marketing*

Bar Code - The pattern of vertical bands of varying widths that are printed on items sold in retail stores, i.e., books, food, etc. This allows the store selling the product to scan the price into the cash register in order to simplify the buying process. Also called Universal Product Code (UPC). *General Computer - Marketing*

Baronial Envelope - A large official looking envelope that is characterized by a large flap. Its formal look makes this an ideal direct mail piece, because the envelope creates the image of importance. *Substrates*

Base Art - See Camera-Ready Copy.

Base - The number of actual digits that comprise a numbering system, i.e., binary has two numbers, 0 & 1; decimal has 10. *General Computer* The ink toner at full strength. *Ink* The film or paper that supports the emulsion. *Image Carriers*

Base Alignment - The characteristic of type that allows differing sizes and designs of type to actually rest on an invisible line, that is called the baseline. *Typography*

Base Cylinder - The gravure cylinder (usually steel) that holds the copper surface. *Printing Processes*

Baseline - The invisible line that all characters of type will rest upon. See Fig. 3. *Typography*

Fig. 3 - Baseline

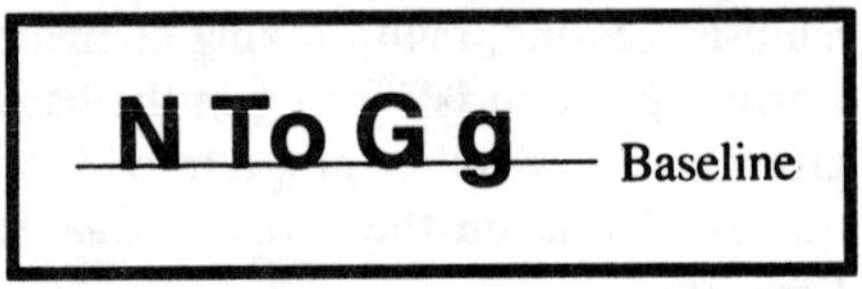

BASIC (**B**eginner's **A**ll-purpose **S**ymbolic **I**nstruction **C**ode) - A widely used and easy-to-learn computer language. It is most often taught to beginning programmers because it contains many of the basic concepts of the more complex languages. *Software*

Basic Size - The exact size that has been established for each type and grade of paper, i.e., bond, cover, etc. *Standards - Substrates*

Basis Weight - The weight of 500 sheets (ream) of paper expressed in pounds. Each grade of paper is weighted at a predetermined size, i.e., cover paper is weighted at the 20" X 26" size. *Substrates*

Batch - The process whereby data is collected and stored in the computer memory prior to processing. *General Computer*

Baud - The standard measure for the speed of data-transmission, i.e., bits a second. *General Computer - Telecommunications*

Baud Rate - The number of signal changes that actually occur per second, however, it usually refers to the speed a modem is able to send data. *General Computer - Telecommunications*

Bearers - Press mechanisms that function as a means of reducing printing surface pressures while printing is taking place. *Printing Processes*

Bed - The metal surface or working area of a paper cutter. *Finishing*

Belt Press - A large book printing press that prints multiple page books in a single pass, using two continuous synthetic rubber or photopolymer belts. The press starts with the paper roll and finishes with a ready-to-be-bound book at press end. *Printing Processes*

Benchmark - A test that is used for the measurement of computer software and hardware performance and the actual throughput. *General Computer*

Bernoulli - Removable magnetic hard disk. *Computer Hardware*

Beta Test - The final testing phase of computer hardware and software before it is released to market. It will often occur at a customer site. *General Computer*

Bevel - A printing plate where the edge was trimmed to an angle to provide a better gripping surface. This allows the plate to be clamped to the press for printing. *Printing Processes*

Bezier Curves - Lines and curves that are described mathematically as distinct objects. They can be rotated, moved, stretched, combined with other objects, and manipulated in enumerable ways. *Desktop/Electronic Publishing*

Bible Paper - A thin, strong, and light weight paper with good opacity. It is used for high-quality books with a large number of pages (like bibles and dictionaries) to keep the bulk down. *Substrates*

Bibliography - A recommended list of books on a certain subject that is usually included in the back of a book. This usually represents the author's suggested readings that either enhance or embellish the material covered in the book. *Desktop/Electronic Publishing*

Big Thesaurus, The - An easy to use, interactive thesaurus that works with all popular Mac applications. See Deneba Software. *Software*

Billboard - A large structure (usually about 12 ' x 25 ') located in a high traffic area, that holds a large advertisement on its surface. *Marketing*

Bimetal Plate - A durable printing plate that is used for high quality, long runs. It derives its unique characteristics from the metals used: copper and brass in the printing image section; aluminum, chromium, or stainless steel in the non-image sections. *Image Carriers*

Binary - Means two. Any system or condition that contains two parts. *General Computer*

Binary Numbers - A number system that has two digits - 0, 1. *General Computer*

Binaural Sound - 3-D sound. *Multimedia*

Bind - See Binding.

Binder's Board - The stiff, high-grade pulp board that is covered with cloth (or other similar material) and used to manu-

69

facture book hardcovers. *Finishing*

Binder's Waste - The amount of allowance given a bindery for waste, so the desired amount of finished product is delivered. *Finishing*

Bindery Service - A firm that performs collating and binding services for other companies, usually printers. See Binding. *Finishing*

Binding - The process whereby books, booklets, and catalogs are folded and/or collated into their proper page sequence. They are then stapled, glued, sewn or bound together with wire or rings, and cut to the desired size of the final printed product. *Finishing*

Binding Dummy - The assembly of blank signatures to show final thickness of the finished product and to show the amount of creep or thrust that is produced. *Finishing*

Binding Edge - That side of a book where each signature is glued, stitched or sewn together. *Finishing*

Binding (Mechanical or Manual) - A process whereby pages are joined together by circular shaped metal and/or plastic rings. See Spiral Binding. *Finishing*

Bind Margin - See Gutter Margin.

Bit - An abbreviation for binary bit. In the binary numbering system a bit is either a 0 or 1. *General Computer*

Bit Depth - The amount of bits that are used (i.e., 4, 8, 24 or 32) to represent color and grayscale. *Color Reproduction - General Computer*

Bit-Map - The collection of pixels in a file located in memory that can display or create a specific image or picture. *Color Reproduction*

Bit-Mapped Display - Monitors that can display graphics via bit-mapped images using pixel-level controls. *Desktop/Electronic Publishing*

Bit-Mapped Fonts - Non-scalable fonts. They create a jagged look if increased or decreased in size. *Typography*

Bit-Mapped Graphics - Objects that exist as a pattern of bits or dots. *Desktop/Electronic Publishing*

Bits Per Pixel - A reference to the brightness level that is assigned to each pixel. *Color Reproduction*

Bitstream - A stream or flow of binary information (bits) from one device to another. *General Computer*

Black - One of the four-color process inks. It exhibits a complete absence of reflected light. Black absorbs all light. *Color Reproduction - Ink*

Black And White - Originals and artwork that are comprised of only black on a white background. *Art and Copy Preparation*

Black Printer - A black ink plate which is used to increase the contrast and enhance the details. *Image Carriers*

Blanket - The synthetic rubber surfaced material that is responsible for the transfer of the print image from the plate on the cylinder to the substrate in offset printing. *Printing Processes*

Blanket Thickness Gauge - A device that indicates blanket thickness over its entire surface. *Printing Processes*

Blanking - The period of time between when the beam from the electron gun in a television is turned off and it resets. Blanking is used to prevent the scanning beam from being visible on the TV screen. *Digital Photography - Multimedia - Telecommunications*

Bleed - A special printing effect that extends a graphic element or printed image beyond the edge of a page or the crop marks. This overlap is trimmed off by the printer to produce a final printed piece. *Printing Processes*

Bleed In The Gutter - When a printed image completely covers the facing pages of a magazine across the margin in the center. *Marketing*

Bleed Through - The image on the back of a printed sheet that is visible on the front side. *Printing Processes*

Blind Embossing - The process of creating a raised image on a substrate by using heat and pressure on a special letterpress machine. *Finishing*

Blind Folio - The unprinted page numbers in a book or signature. *Desktop/Electronic Publishing*

Blind Image - An image with problems holding ink and will often not print at all. It is usually the result of excess moisture. *Printing Processes*

Blind Perf - A type of perforation that is not visible on the back or opposite side. It would be used to avoid disturbing the appearance of pictures or information on the back side. *Finishing*

Blister - A bubble or a raised area that is caused by moisture that is trapped on the surface of the paper. *Printing Processes - Substrates*

Blistering - See Blister.

Blister Pack - A type of packaging where the items to be sold are placed on a printed card and sealed in place under a plastic cover. *Finishing*

Block - Elements of text and/or graphics that are modified or controlled as a unit. *Desktop/Electronic Publishing*

Blocking - The situation where punched, trimmed, or drilled sheets will stick together. *Finishing - Printing Processes*

Blooming - Occurs when a certain light quantity is exceeded. When an intense beam of light is photographed, excessive photoelectric charges are produced by the CCD, it produces an overflow to adjacent picture elements. See CCD. *Digital Photography*

Blow-Up - The enlargement of any graphic or copy elements by photographic methods. *Art and Copy Preparation - Graphic Arts Photography*

Blueline - A proof that is created by exposing negatives placed over photosensitive paper to light. See Blueprint. *Proofing*

Blueprint - Proof that is created from photosensitive blueprint paper to check the position of all the image elements. After exposure to light, a proof is produced that is blue or black on a white background. When a negative is created the colors are reversed. See Blueline. *Proofing*

Blushing - A blur on the impression caused by trapped moisture between the ink and the surface. *Printing Processes*

BNC Connector - A bayonet-type video connector, with a twist lock for secure connection. *Digital Photography*

Board - A short term for printed circuit board. *Computer Hardware*

Boards - See Camera-Ready Copy.

Body - This refers to ink consistency, i.e., ink with too little body is runny. *Ink*

Body Height - The X-Height of type. See X-Height. *Typography*

Body Type - The specific typeface that is used in the main text. *Typography*

Bold-Face Font - Alphanumeric characters that have been designed to be bold - darker or heavier. *Typography*

Bold Italic Typestyle - A combination of the bold and italic styles. *Typography*

Bond Paper - The various grades of high-quality, professional looking, and durable paper that is used for certain business applications, i.e., business cards, letterheads, etc. *Substrates*

Book - Any 49 plus page publication that has a cover that is heavier than the text paper. *Finishing*

Book Block - A fully stitched (or glued

or sewn) book, just before the hardcover is attached. *Finishing*

Book Cloth - The cloth that is used on hardcover books. It is usually heavily starched and impregnated or covered with plastic. *Finishing*

Booklet - Any book of any height or width with 48 or less pages (except magazines) that has a cover that is heavier than the text paper. *Finishing*

Book Paper - The different grades of durable paper (coated or uncoated) that are used in book, magazine, and catalog production. *Substrates*

Book Printer - A printer specializing in book production. *Printing Processes*

Boot - A short program that is responsible for starting the computer and initiating the computer operating system and some utility programs. *General Computer*

Border - A design that can be as simple as a line or as complex as a very ornate drawing. It completely encircles a piece of artwork, an advertisement, or a flyer. *Art and Copy Preparation*

Boxboard - Stiff paperboard used to manufacture boxes. *Substrates*

Boxes - Containers made of cardboard. See Cardboard. *Substrates*

BPS (Bits Per Second) - See Baud.

Break For Color - The process of separating the CRC or film into the colors required for a multi-color printing job. See CRC. *Art and Copy Preparation - Color Reproduction*

72

Brightness - The ability of paper to reflect light, i.e., the highest quality coated stock has the greatest degree of brightness. *Substrates* The amount of the brightness level of each pixel on a scale from 0 (pure white) to 256 (100 percent black). See Brightness Level. *Color Reproduction*

Brightness Level - The amount of brightness of each pixel on a scale from 0 (pure white) - 256 (100 percent black). *Color Reproduction*

Brightness Resolution - The accuracy of the measurement of the brightness level of each pixel. *Color Reproduction*

Brilliance - A color's intensity. See Chroma. *Color Reproduction*

Bristol - A paper of intermediate thickness, usually between .006 and .01 of an inch. This is somewhere between what is commonly called paper and cardboard. *Substrates*

Broadband - A greater range of transmission frequencies than standard voice lines, i.e., fiber optics. *Telecommunications*

Broadcasting - The transmission of frequencies for use by consumer, i.e., television, radio. *Telecommunications*

Broadband Communication Network - The communication of information over high-capacity, special digital lines. *Telecommunications*

Broadside - An extra large advertising piece that is used when a hard-hitting impact is needed. It can also be used as an in-store poster for special events or when appropriate. *Marketing*

Broadside Page - A page that is printed sideways and the page must be rotated to read. *Desktop/Electronic Publishing*

Brochure - A piece of advertising literature (usually folded) that is used to narrate a story or describe a product or service. *Art and Copy Preparation*

Broken Type - A defect in a typeset character or symbol. *Typography*

Bronzing - A technique that applies wet bronze powder to a sheet of paper while the sizing ink is still wet in order to create a metallic look. *Finishing*

Brown-Print Paper - A photographic paper that is used for one color proofs. Silver nitrate is used for sensitizing. *Graphic Arts Photography - Proofing*

Brush Strokes - A Mac color painting application. See Claris Clear Choice and Claris Corporation. *Software*

Bubble Jet - A printing process that has compact and minute heating elements allowing ink droplets to be ejected by rapidly-forming solvent vapor bubbles. Popular for color ink-jet printing and also known as thermal liquid ink-jet. *Printing Processe*

Bubble Wrap - See Blister Pack.

Buffer - A temporary storage place in memory that is used to hold data. *Computer Hardware*

Bug - An error in either the software or the hardware. *General Computer*

Bulk - Paper thickness is often referred to as pages per inch (PPI) when selecting a particular paper for a book or when a specific thickness is desired. *Substrates*

Bulking - The process of making low-cost paper thicker in order to make it as thick as the more expensive higher-bulk papers. *Substrates*

Bulking Dummy - See Binding Dummy.

Bullets - Varying sized dots that are used to highlight listed items. The size of bullets are controlled by the indication of the desired point size, just as type size is selected. *Typography*

Examples:

Bundled Software - A marketing technique whereby a computer is sold with the programs as a package. It can also refer to a series of programs sold as a package. *Software*

Bump Exposure - A technique used in traditional halftone creation with a graphic arts camera. The halftone screen is removed briefly during a segment of extra light exposure in order to reduce the number or size of the highlight halftone dots. This increases the white or highlight areas because of the extra exposure of the film to the camera's lights. *Graphic Arts Photography*

Burn - The process whereby the image to be printed is imprinted or "burned" onto the plate material. Often referred to as plate exposure. *Image Carriers*

Burnish - A technique that is used for darkening an area that would normally be noticeably light. A steel burnishing tool is used to rub the area, thus allowing the selected area to absorb additional ink. *Image Carriers*

Burst Binding - A process that is designed to slit a book spine prior to perfect binding so the glue will penetrate the paper and properly adhere to the cover of the book. *Finishing*

Bursting Strength - The ability of any substrate to resist the pressure that is applied by a burst tester. See Burst Tester. *Substrates*

Burst Tester - A special device that tests (or measures) the resistance or strength of any substrate. *Quality/Process Control - Substrates*

Bus - A main highway within the computer that allows all the various components (i.e., Memory, CPU, Input-Output ports) of the computer to communicate with each other. The type of bus is a strong influence on computer throughput. *Computer Hardware*

Busy - A poorly designed ad that usually contains too much information and is not properly balanced. See Balance and Proportion. *Art and Copy Preparation*

Butt Register - The printing of multiple colors adjacent to each other where there is no need for chokes or spreads. *Printing Processes*

Bypass - A communication system that is able to avoid portions of the standard communication networks, i.e., telephone. *Telecommunications*

Byte - A single character or unit of information that consists of eight bits. All computer storage is expressed as a specific amount of bytes, i. e., megabytes, gigabytes, and terabytes. *General Computer*

C1S (**C**oated **1** **S**ide) - Paper that is coated on one side. The coated side is smoother and often glossy. This type of paper is often used for book or booklet covers and flyers that are printed on one side. *Substrates*

C2S (**C**oated **2** **S**ides) - Paper that is coated or even glossy on both sides and is commonly used on brochures. *Substrates*

C - A machine-independent assembly programming language that is often used on microcomputers which have a close connection to UNIX. *Software*

Cable Communication - A method of transmission that uses coaxial cable or fiber optics to send audio and/or video signals for communication as opposed to broadcasting through the air waves. Cable communication provides clearer signals and simplifies two-way, interactive communication. *Telecommunications*

Cable Television - A typical broadband communication system that transmits video signals to a television set. *Telecommunications*

Cache - A unique memory subdivision of central or main memory which is faster than RAM memory. Commonly used data and instructions are stored in cache for faster access. *General Computer*

CAD/CAM (**C**omputer **A**ided **D**esign/**C**omputer **A**ided **M**anufacturing) - Complex computer systems' software for design and manufacturing applications that use sophisticated GUI's. See GUI. *Software*

Caere Corporation - Information management products: OmniPage OCR software; PageKeeper for document management; OmniScan for hand held scanning, image-editing, and fax; Image Assistant for image-editing; and FaxMaster. Contact numbers: 100 Cooper Court, Los Gatos, CA 95030; (408)395-7000. *Software*

Calender - A special machine with rollers that compress and/or smooth a substrate. *Substrates*

Calendering - The pressing of paper between calender rolls to enhance the smoothness and the gloss of the paper. See Calender Rolls and Supercalendering. *Substrates*

Calender Rolls - The metal rollers (usually made of cast-iron) that are used in the process of making paper smoother. See Calendering and Supercalendering. *Substrates*

Calera Recognition Systems - Optical character recognition (OCR) software and hardware systems for converting scanned or faxed images into computer usable text. For Windows, Mac, OS/2, and UNIX. Contact numbers: 475 Potrero Ave., Sunnyvale, CA 94086; (408)720-8300. *Computer Hardware - Software*

Calibration - Adjustments that are made to a device that allow it to produce results that meet a specific standard. *Software - Standards*

California Job Case - A drawer or case that has specific compartments for storing the different characters, numerals, and symbols of metal foundry type. *Typesetting and Imagesetting*

Caliper - A unit of measurement for paper thickness that is expressed in mils (1,000ths of an inch). A micrometer is used to measure the caliper of any substrate. See Micrometer. *Quality/Process Control - Substrates*

Camera-Back Masking - A masking and color correction technique that is produced with a process camera. *Graphic Arts Photography*

Camera-Ready Copy (CRC) - The actual artwork that is prepared on a flexible, yet durable board. It will typically include the FPO low-resolution pictures of the photographs to be used, any graphics or illustrations, and all typeset text. This CRC will become the material that is to be used by the printer for creation of the final film and plates. Therefore, it must be clean and include all instructions to the printer, i.e., correct sizing of photographs, indications of the exact location of color separations, the correct PMS colors to be used in each area of the artwork, and other pertinent information. Also referred to as the mechanical. See FPO and For Position Only *Art and Copy Preparation*

Canvas For Windows - A virtual carbon copy of Canvas 3. A drawing environment for Windows. Gives users a much needed solution for technical drawing, integration of tasks that previously required dedicated programs, and professional quality output. See Deneba Software. *Software*

Canvas 3 For Mac - Mac drawing software. Its unique open architecture allows Deneba and third parties to add power by creating new tools. Deneba's Canvas ToolPAKS adds over 40 powerful utilities, and design and imaging features. See Deneba Software. *Software*

Canvas 3 ToolPAKS - A three-part upgrade to Canvas 3. Design adds enveloping, extrusion, "hot-linked" objects, and a pressure sensitive pen. Imaging adds tools for masking, adding textures, and changing scanned and computer art. Utility adds performance, new translators, and third party filters. See Deneba Software. *Software*

Capital Letter - See Upper Case.

Caps - See Upper Case.

Caps And Small Caps - The two different sizes of uppercase characters for each point size. See Fig. 32 on page 196. *Typography*

Caption - The legend or written description under any photograph, graphic, or illustration. For an example, see all the illustrations and graphics on pages 35 through 45. Each illustration or graphic has its own corresponding caption or legend. *Desktop/Electronic Publishing*

Carbon Dioxide Laser - An infrared laser beam that is used for cutting soft materials such as paper and rubber and has applications in laser die cutting and the laser engraving of flexographic plates. *Laser Applications*

Carbon Tissue - The pigmented, light-sensitive material that is sensitized and exposed for the purpose of etching metal cylinders or gravure plates. *Image Carriers - Printing Processes*

Cardboard - A thin, semi-stiff paperboard. *Substrates*

Carrier (Carrier Wave) - Radio wave that is modulated by a signal in order to efficiently transmit information. The carrier frequency is normally much higher than the signal frequency and can be modulated by varying its amplitude, frequency, or phase at the signal frequency rate. *Digital Photography - Telecommunications*

Carrier Sheet - Flexographic plates are adhered to this carrier sheet before mounting to a cylinder. *Printing Processes*

Carrier Wave - See Modulation.

Carton - A folded box that has been manufactured from bleached sulfate. *Substrates*

Cartouche - An ornate oval (sometimes oblong) border that is used to project elegance and importance. *Art and Copy Preparation*

Cartridge - A removable and transportable magnetic storage medium. *Computer Hardware*

Case - The hard covers on a casebound or hardcover book. *Finishing*

Case Binding - The process of creating a casebound book. *Finishing*

Casebound - A hardbound book, which is comprised of the cover boards, the covering and lining materials, and the book itself. *Finishing*

Casemaker - A machine that is used to manufacture hardcovers. *Finishing*

Casing-In - The process of combining a hardcover and a trimmed book to create a finished casebound book. *Finishing*

Cast-Coated - Coated paper that has been especially treated to produce a smooth, glossy enamel surface. It is an expensive, heavy sheet with excellent opacity. *Substrates*

Catalog - A booklet that contains details (including photos) on items that are for sale, with ordering information included. *Marketing*

Catching-Up (Scumming) - The condition where non-image portions of the plate are beginning to attract ink. This collection of ink is often referred to as a scum and it causes dot gain and ink spreading. *Printing Processes*

Cathode-Ray Tube (CRT) - The tube that projects electrons onto a screen for producing images in a monitor. If the tube has one gun, it will create a single color screen (usually green, amber, or white), and if there are three (red, green, and blue) guns the screen will produce color images. *Computer Hardware - Telecommunications*

CAV (Constant Angular Velocity) - Videodisc standard for storage and playback. Fixed disk rate speed. Also known as "Red Book." *Multimedia - Standards*

CCD - See Charged Coupled Devices.

CCD Camera - A small and lightweight camera containing a charged-coupled device (CCD), which is a transistorized light sensor on a circuit chip. It is extremely rugged and tiny compared to a camera tube. *Digital Photography*

CD-Audio - See CD.

CD (Compact Disc) - A standard format that stores audio data in a digital format on compact discs. Also known as Red Book. *Multimedia - Standards*

CD-I - See Compact Disk-Interactive.

CD-ROM (Compact Disk-Read Only Memory) - Optical storage media. *Computer Hardware - Multimedia*

CD-ROM/XA (Compact Disc-Read Only Memory/Extended Architecture) An advanced version of the CD-ROM for real-time playback. Similar to CD-I. See CD-I. *Computer Hardware - Multimedia*

Center Spread - Two facing pages that are located in the exact middle of a magazine. This section lays flat when the magazine is opened *Art and Copy Preparation - Marketing*

Centipoise - An expression for units of viscosity. *Standards*

Central Processing Unit - See CPU.

Centronics (Parallel) Interface - The standard interface for all parallel exchange of data between devices, i.e., computers, peripherals, printers, etc. *Computer Hardware*

CGA (Color Graphics Adapter) - A color video board for PC clones. *Computer Hardware*

CGM (Computer Graphics Metafile) - A standardized format for storing graphic elements. *Desktop/Electronic Publishing*

Chalking - The process whereby incorrectly dried ink is converted to dust and will no longer adhere to the paper or to other substrate. *Printing Processes*

Chambered Blade System - An enclosed inking system that holds and meters ink. *Printing Processes*

Change Font - The process of actually changing from the use of one particular typeface or font to another. The process can be different in each method of typesetting. *Typesetting and Imagesetting*

Channel - The foundation for the creation of an image, i.e., Grayscale (one channel); RGB (three channels); and CMYK (four channels). *Color Reproduction*

Character - One byte of information, i.e., letter or character, punctuation, number, and other control codes, like a space. *General Computer*

Character-Based Display - A simplistic computer display that is not capable of producing complex graphics, only text and some elementary graphics. *Comput. Hardware*

Character String - A set of bytes (characters) that are treated as a unit by the computer, i.e., "12-31-94," "Thomas A Moran," etc. *General Computer*

Characters - All the alphanumeric information (plus punctuation) that is called text or copy. *Art and Copy Preparation - Typesetting and Imagesetting*

Charged Coupled Device (CCD) - The solid state pick-up device that responds to light and records an image. Each CCD contains tens of thousands of light-sensitive photocells, each of which responds to the light that enters the CCD by building up an electrical charge. The amount of charge at each photocell element determines how bright the subsequent image will be at that point on the screen. *Digital Photography - General Computer*

Chemical Pulp - Chemically treated groundwood chips that are used in the manufacture of paper pulp. *Substrates*

Cheshire Label - A special computer generated label that is used heavily in direct mail and mail list management in place of the more expensive pressure-sensitive type of labels. *Marketing*

Chinese White - This is a semi-white (bluish cast), opaque paint that is used for various printing and graphic arts applications. *Art and Copy Preparation*

Chokes - This printing technique allows dark color areas to overlap very slightly into lighter color areas to eliminate any possible white gaps. *Image Assembly - Printing Processes*

Chopper Fold - The final fold on a web offset press that forms the finished signature. *Finishing - Printing Processes*

Chroma - The lack of dilution or the intensity of a color as determined by its freedom from the colors of black, white or gray. *Color Reproduction*

Chromacheck - An off-press Dupont color proofing technology that uses peel-apart overlays. *Proofing*

Chrome (Chromium) - A material that is applied to a printing plate that extends the life of the plate. This allows the printer to print more images than would otherwise be possible. *Image Carriers*

Chrominance - The part of the video signal containing the color information. *Digital Photography*

Cibachrome - Photographic paper, based on dye-bleach color, that is used to make color proofs, usually from positives. *Graphic Arts Photography*

Circular Screen - A round halftone screen that traditionally was used to indicate the screen angle of a color or black and white halftone, as it is rotated in various positions. *Graphic Arts Photography*

CITT (Convergent Image Thermal Transfer) - A technology that can control dot size on thermal transfer computer printers. *Computer Hardware*

Claris Clear Choice - A new software brand developed by Claris Corporation. It currently includes: Brush Strokes; Retrieve It!; and Power To Go. See Claris Corporation. *Software*

Claris Corporation - A leader in graphic user interface (GUI) applications and other desktop publishing solutions. Contact numbers: 5201 Patrick Henry Dr., Santa Clara, CA 95052; (408)987-7000. *Software*

Claris Draw - Powerful, intelligent drawing, and automatic business graphics solution for Mac and Windows users. See Claris Corporation. *Software*

Claris Impact - See Claris Draw.

Claris Works 2.0 - An integrated database, word processor, and spreadsheet with outlining, charting, presentation features, graphics, and paint capabilities all in a single program. *Software*

Clear Key - This keytop function clears the currently selected item. *Computer Hardware*

Click - The brief depression of a button on a mouse, while holding the mouse still. *General Computer*

Click Art Series - Full-color and black and white clip art and cartoons geared to all levels of interest: business, personal, holiday, professional, and children. See T/Maker. *Software*

Cling - A material's inclination to adhere to other material, often caused by static electricity. *Substrates*

Client - See Customer.

Clip Art - Illustrations, pictures, and unique designs that are already finished artwork. They are ready to be sized and pasted onto boards or CRC. Large libraries of finished clip art on innumerable subjects are readily available in electronic form or in preprinted formats. See CRC. *Art and Copy Preparation*

Clipboard - A memory feature that allows one to store information from one document or program to another provided both are compatible. *Software*

Clock - More properly called the system clock. The steady pulses of the system clock synchronize the internal operations of the computer and affect processing speed. The speed is expressed in hertz (Hz). *Computer Hardware*

Clock/Calendar - An electronic circuit within the computer that calculates correct date and time. Some circuits are battery powered and continue to work at all times, while others stop operating when the computer is turned off. *Computer Hardware*

Clone - In its strictest interpretation, it means an exact duplicate of something. In the computer world, it refers to a product (hardware or software) that represents a very close copy. Clones can present problems because of minor internal variations. *Computer Hardware - Software*

Closed Head - The uncut signature top. *Finishing*

Closed-Loop System - An automated and usually electronic system in which all operations and functions are interrelated for self-diagnosis, correction, and evaluation. *General Computer - Quality/Process Control*

CLV (Constant Linear Velocity) - Videodisc standard for storage and for playback. Variable disk rate speed. *Multimedia - Standards*

CMYK - A color model that is based on the four colors: (C) Cyan, (M) Magenta, (Y) Yellow, and (K) Black. It is the basis for all four-color printing. *Color Reproduction*

CMYK > RGB - Conversion from a CMYK format to a RGB format or an indication of the ability to perform this conversion. See CMYK and RGB. *Color Reproduction*

Coarse Screen - A screen with 100 or less ruled lines per inch that is used in the halftone creation process. Screens of 65 and 85 lines per inch are the most common. These screens are called coarse because they are used when printing onto the coarser newspaper type of groundwood paper. Higher or finer halftone screens (over 120 lines per inch) would print poorly due to the inability of the small dots to print smoothly on the coarser paper. See Fig. 4 and Fig. 5. - Halftone Screens. *Graphic Arts Photography*

Coated Paper (Stock) - Paper that has a smooth surface, with the finish varying from a matte to a high-gloss. *Substrates*

Fig. 4 - 65 Line Screen Halftone

Coating - An application of varnish that is applied to a substrate after it has been printed for extra protection. *Printing Processes* A light-sensitve material that has been applied to a plate. *Image Carriers*

Coaxial Cable - A cable that is often referred to as a coax cable. It has two conductors - an inside wire and an outside conductive shield, each separated by insulation. *Computer Hardware - Telecommunications*

Fig. 5 - 85 Line Screen Halftone

Codec - A chip or an algorithm for data compression and decompression. *Computer Hardware - Software*

Cold Boot/Cold Start - See Boot.

Cold Color - The range of bluish colors that project the feelings of calmness. *Color Reproduction*

Cold Composition - All the modern methods of typesetting and imagesetting, as opposed to hot metal composition. See Cold Type and Imagesetter. *Typesetting and Imagesetting*

Cold Type - All type that is produced by non-metallic methods, i.e., photocomposition and current imagesetter processes. *Typesetting and Imagesetting*

Collate - The process whereby single sheets of paper or signatures are merged together to create a fully paginated manual, book or booklet. *Finishing*

Collating - The function of putting a series of pages or signatures in the proper or correct page sequence. *Finishing*

Collating Marks - The numbered symbols of each folded signature that indicates the proper assembly sequence. *Finishing*

Collotype - An ink-water, screenless printing technique that prints on presses with uniquely designed dampening processes. *Printing Processes*

ColorAge, Inc. - A developer of networked color imaging and output technologies for corporate publishing and digital imaging. Freedom of Press and its ColorQSeries are the main corporate focus. Contact numbers: 900 Technology Park Dr., Billerica, MA 01821; (508)667-8585. *Computer Hardware - Software*

Color Analysis - The record of the exact amount of each of the colors used in an original color separation. *Color Reproduction*

Color Balance - The process of reducing or increasing the amounts of yellow, cyan, magenta, and black dots in a color separation to achieve the desired look. *Color Reproduction*

Color Bar - A bar that appears on the edge of the proof and on the final printed job. The purpose of the color bar often includes: ink density analysis, assessment of ink trap efficiency, measurement of dot gain, gray balance analysis, and assessment of overall print resolution. The segments of a color bar often include: solid ink patches, screens, overprint screens, overprints of solid inks, star targets, or other resolution targets. The printer checks the color bar on the proof with the color bar on the press copy to produce the desired result. *Color Reproduction - Quality/Process Control*

Color Break - The indications of the different colors used in the CRC through the use of overlays or instructions that have been indicated on the tissue overlay. See CRC. *Art and Copy Preparation*

Color Cast - An imbalance (no matter how slight) of any one color over the others. This imbalance can be corrected by the color separator by making adjustments in the amounts of magenta, cyan, yellow, or black. *Color Reproduction*

Color Central - An Open Prepress Interface (OPI) print and image server running on Mac, Windows, Windows NT, DEC Alpha, and Power Mac. See Aldus Corporation. *Software*

Color Chart - Printed color combinations of process colors for comparison to a sample. Color charts often show all possible color combinations. *Color Reproduction*

Color Circle - A diagram developed by GATF to evaluate hue error and gray content. See GATF. *Color Reproduction - Quality/Process Control*

Color Control Patch (Strip) - See Color Bar

Color Correction - The use of various traditional methods such as dot-etching or masking and/or the expert use of electronic scanners for the improvement of a color photograph. *Color Reproduction - Scanning*

Color Filters - The red, green, and blue colored screens or filters that absorb specific colors and modify others. *Color Reproduction*

Colorfit - A Mac program giving the user complete control of color on the Solitaire line of film recorders. See Solitaire and Management Graphics, Inc. *Software*

Color Gamut - All the possible hues of a color that can be printed from a specific set of colors. *Color Reproduction*

Color Guide - See Color Chart.

Color Hexagon - A graph developed by GATF for the purpose of comparing various ink sets and for comparing prepress results with reproduction results. See GATF. *Color Reproduction - Quality/Process Control*

Colorimeter - A device similar to a densitometer, but is specifically designed to measure color as it will be perceived by the human eye. *Color Reproduction - Quality/Process Control*

Colorimetry - Color measurement. *Color Reproduction*

Color Key - A 3M color proofing system. This system uses four individual pieces of color film (cyan, magenta, yellow, and black). They are combined after processing and are then placed on a white sheet of heavier paper. The result is a close representation of the finished color job. *Proofing*

Color Management System - A combination of software and hardware that will allow a color system to produce matching color across the many different components of the system, i.e., monitors, proofers, imagesetters, and the final printed piece. *Color Reproduction*

Color Monitors - Large 13" (and larger) color television-like devices that allow operators to check their work before final output and during job creation and editing. *Computer Hardware - Proofing*

Color Overlay - The colored transparent sheets that are used to indicate where each color will be printed on the proof or CRC. See Proof and CRC. *Art and Copy Preparation*

Color Photographs - Color photos in the form of transparencies, reflective prints or 35 mm slides. *Art and Copy Preparation - Color Reproduction*

Color Plate - The magenta, cyan, yellow, and black printing plates that are used in full-color printing. *Color Reproduction - Image Carriers*

Color Proofs - See Press Proofs, Prepress Proofs, and Progressive proofs.

Color Purity - See Saturation.

ColorQ Series - Software-based turnkey systems for connecting digital color copiers to networks for continuous tone color printing. Users can print high quality color files, quickly and easily with superior network performance and increased productivity. See ColorAge, Inc. *Computer Hardware*

Color Reference - Printed color combinations of process colors that have standard color densities and have been printed on standard papers. They are useful for color matching. *Color Reproduction - Quality/Process Control*

Color Scanner - See Scanners.

Color Separations - In order to print color originals, they must be separated into the three colors of magenta, cyan, and yellow. Black is then added for greater detail and enhanced dot density. *Color Reproduction - Graphic Arts Photography - Scanning*

Color Separator - See Separation Vendor.

Color Sequence - The order of the printing of each ink, i.e., cyan, black, magenta, yellow, PMS colors, varnish. *Color Reproduction - Printing Processes*

Color Space - A model that is used for the description of color in each particular color system. *Color Reproduction*

Color Strength - See Chroma.

Color Swatch - An actual color representation of a particular color. The Pantone color reference is an example of a color swatch. *Color Reproduction*

Color Temperature - Technical term used to indicate the temperature of a light source. In practice it is a measure of the warmness (redness) or coolness (blueness) of the light. The lower the number, the warmer the light. Tungsten lamps are about 3000k and daylight about 5000k. *Color Reproduction - Digital Photography*

Color Transparency - See Transparency.

Color Triangle - A graph developed by GATF to analyze hue error and gray content. See GATF. *Color Reproduction - Quality/Process Control*

Color Wheel - A wheel-like chart that is based on the three secondary printing colors - red, green, and blue. It is used to help understand color basics and how the many different colors are created in the printing process. *Color Reproduction*

Combination Plate - A photoengraving term that refers to a plate that combines halftone and line copy. *Image Carriers*

Comb Binding (Plastic) - See Binding (Mechanical or Manual).

Combination Folder - A series of different folds on a web offset that fold and cut a web into a finished signature. *Printing Processes - Finishing*

Combination Press - A special press arrangement with a series of different presses, i.e., offset, gravure, etc., in a line to create special printed products. *Printing Processes*

Combo Cache IIsi (Mac IIsi) - Cache card that speeds the IIsi up to 45 percent with a 32K cache. Adds a PDS slot, an optional 20 MHz math chip, and an additional PDS connector for future expansion. See DayStar Digital. *Computer Hardware*

Comdex - An acronym for Computer

84

Dealers' Exposition. Key computer show held annually at different locations. *General Computer*

Commercial Printer - A company that provides a full-line of printing services such as paste-up, typesetting and image-setting, graphic arts photography, image assembly, platemaking, press operation, binding, and finishing, etc. *Printing Processes*

Commercial Register - This refers to the correct alignment of dots in color printing. To meet specifications set by the printing industry, all four pieces of color film (magenta, cyan, yellow and black) must be aligned to ± a single row of dots. *Color Reproduction - Image Assembly*

Communication Satellite - A geosynchronous satellite that is functioning as a microwave relay station. See Fig. 6. *Telecommunications*

Comp - See Comprehensive Layout.

Compact Color Test Strip - A control strip developed by GATF to detect dot gain and incorrect process ink loading. *Printing Processes - Quality/Process Control*

Compatibility - This refers to the degree two devices or programs can work together, by accepting each other's data or instructions. *General Computer*

Fig. 6 - Communication Satellite

Compatible - See Compatibility.

Compile - The process of converting a high-level computer language, i. e., BASIC, into machine code or the native-language of the computer. *General Computer*

Complementary Colors - Colors that face each other on a color wheel, i.e., magenta and green, yellow and blue, etc. *Color Reproduction*

Complementary Color Removal - The process of removing the unwanted color from a complementary color through the use of light manipulation. *Color Reproduction*

Complementary Flats - This is when two flats are stripped for the creation of one offset plate. It is needed when a job requires that text be superimposed over a tint, a halftone, or over other image areas. *Image Assembly - Image Carriers*

Composing Service - A firm that produces typeset copy for other companies. *Typesetting and Imagesetting*

Composite Art - A finished page of artwork where the various colors are represented in black and white only. *Art and Copy Preparation*

Composite Color Images - The creation of a new color image through the process of combining other images that are from different areas. This new image is blended together to form an entirely new image. *Color Reproduction*

Composite Film - One positive or negative film that is created from multiple films via a process of double exposing. *Image Assembly*

Composite Signal - A video signal in which the luminance and chrominance information have been combined using a coding standard such as NTSC. This composite video format is used for all consumer video recording systems. See NTSC. *Digital Photography*

Composite Video - The video signal that is used in conventional television. *Multimedia - Telecommunications*

Composition - Text that has been typeset and ready to be included with the CRC. *Art and Copy Preparation* The combination of separately created video, animations, sounds, and graphics into one final product. *Multimedia*

Comprehensive Layout - A detailed layout that shows all elements included in the final CRC. This could even become the CRC once all finished elements are added. *Art and Copy Preparation*

Compressed Filed - In order not to waste pixels of the same color, this compression technique stores pixels of each shade to reduce memory storage space. *Digital Photography - General Computer*

Compression - See Data Compression

Compression Ratio - The size of the original file (or data) vs. the compressed version. *General Computer*

Computers - Devices that accept data, process that data with an internally stored program, and output the results on various output devices (printers, monitors, etc.). *Computer Hardware*

Computer Integrated Manufacturing (CIM) - The use of computers, special software, and data bases to automate all the manufacturing functions, i.e., accounting, assembly, etc. *General Computere - Software*

Computer Literacy - The ability to effectively understand and use computers and their software. *General Computer*

Computer Networks - A series of large and/or personal computer systems and their peripherals that communicate and share information. *Computer Hardware - Software*

Computer Security - All measures that are taken to protect the computer system and its information. Making backup copies of data and files is the most common type of security. *General Computer*

Computer Support Corporation - Arts & Letters multimedia and graphic arts software products for Windows. Available in 11 languages in 47 countries. Computer Support Corporation publishes a range of graphic arts programs. Contact numbers: 15926 Midway Rd., Dallas, TX 75244; (214)661-8960. *Software*

Computerized Composition - Typesetting functions, i.e., different typefaces and sizes, hyphenation, and justification, that are performed automatically on a computer. *Typesetting and Imagesetting*

Condensed Type - A type face that was designed to be thin and narrow so more information can fit into a given space. *Typography*

Conductivity - The ability to conduct an electrical charge. Typically used in graphic arts to assess fountain solution for lithographic printing, i.e., the degree of a solution's conductivity is based on the concentration of ions originating from minerals or other components in the water. *Printing Processes - Quality/Process Control*

Configuration - The sum total of a system's components, i.e., CPU, memory, keyboard, printers, external storage, etc. *General Computer*

Configure - The unique way each particular computer system has been set-up or installed. All the units in the system are hooked together to meet the user's needs and applications. *General Computer*

Consistency - Ink and varnish viscosity. *Ink*

Contact - See Contact Print.

Contact Exposure - The process of transferring an image from one format to another, i.e., positive to negative, film to plate, etc. This occurs by contacting one to the other in a contact vacuum frame. See Contact Frame. *Graphic Arts Photography - Image Carriers*

Contact Frame - A vacuum frame that is used to duplicate film, expose plates, or expose proofs by exposure to light. *Graphic Arts Photography - Image Carriers*

Contact Print - A photographic process that will create a print by exposing a positive or negative to sensitized paper or other image carriers. *Graphic Arts Photography*

Contact Printing - The creation of prints, from a negative, which are the identical size of the negative. *Graphic Arts Photography*

Contact Screen - A screen that is used in the process of creating a halftone from a photograph (continuous tone). *Graphic Arts Photography*

Container Board - See Corrugated Board.

Content - The actual story or information presented in the final graphic product. *Multimedia*

Content Editing - The checking of subject matter (word content) in an ad or publication rather than checking the spelling, grammar, etc. *Desktop/Electronic Publishing*

Continuous Forms - Computer business forms that are printed in long sheets, and perforations are used to separate each individual form. *Substrates*

Continuous Ink-Jet - Ink-jet printing in which a constant stream of ink is generated through a nozzle under pressure at high speed. The liquid jet breaks into a stream of droplets, which are uniformly sized and spaced when hitting the substrate. *Printing Processes*

Continuous Tape - The punched paper tape or magnetic tape that is used to control the older style phototypesetting machines. *Typesetting and Imagesetting*

Continuous Tone - Any photographic image with all the tonal values of color and shade. *Art and Copy Preparation - Graphic Arts Photography*

Contouring - The detail loss in an image.

That is, less gray levels are created than is necessary to accurately portray the image. Also referred to as "banding." *Desktop/Electronic Publishing*

Contrast - The variations in tone between the shadow, highlight, and midtone areas in a photograph or picture. *Graphic Arts Photography - Scanning* The placement of various sized elements in a design to create interest and appeal, provide variety, and to relieve monotony, i.e., the combining of different line weights. See Design Principles. *Art and Copy Preparation*

Control Key - A keytop function that when combined with other keys can produce special results, usually software related. *Computer Hardware*

Control Panel - That portion of the computer where system operations are controlled. *Computer Hardware*

Control Strip - See Color Bar.

Cool Colors - The range of colors in the blues, greens, and violets. *Color Reproduction*

Co-Operative Advertising - The mutual sharing of the advertising costs by a manufacturer and an agent or dealer. It is a major source of revenue for advertising agencies and graphic artists who create the ads. *Marketing*

Copper Plating - A gravure printing process whereby the copper coated plate is applied to a cylinder. *Printing Processes*

Coprocessor - A separate processor, different from the main processor or CPU, that performs special functions or pro-

vides assistance to the CPU. *Computer Hardware*

Copy - Handwritten or typewritten data or information that tells the operator what is required to enter into a typesetting system to create final output. Also, this term can refer to all typeset words and/or text that are incorporated into the final CRC. See CRC. *Art and Copy Preparation* The duplication or reproduction of information or files from one magnetic medium to another magnetic medium without affecting the original. *General Computer*

Copyboard - That portion of a graphic arts camera that temporarily holds material that has to be photographed for the purpose of being reproduced. *Graphic Arts Photography*

CopyBridge 3.1 - Links XyWrite or Microsoft Word editorial terminals to QuarkXPress for the Mac or PC page layout and design stations. The import and export of files is completely automatic. See North Atlantic Publishing Systems. *Software*

Copy Brushing - An electronic technique that allows damaged areas of a scanned photo to be corrected. Areas next to the damaged area are electronically duplicated and copied to the area to be corrected. *Desktop/Electronic Publishing*

Copy Editing - The checking of grammar, correct spelling, punctuation, and writing style in an ad or publication. See Editing. *Desktop/Electronic Publishing*

Copyfitting - The determination of the amount of type or copy that will fit into the copy space available in an ad, catalog, or other advertising piece. This usually includes changes in the size and boldness of the type. *Art and Copy Preparation - Typography*

CopyFlow 3.2 - Offers: batch import and export tools to QuarkXPress; speed page assembly; assigns names to Quark document boxes, associates them with the story and art files on disk, and carries out the batch operations of import, export, and flush. See North Atlantic Publishing Systems. *Software*

CopyFlow Geometry 2.0 - Creates QuarkXPress layouts, with text and art boxes in position, from ASCII files describing their geometry. Can also append pages to existing layouts and text and art files can then be imported into new pages automatically. See North Atlantic Publishing Systems. *Software*

CopyFlow Reports - Produces an ASCII file of document status information. The CopyFlow Report dialog box provides selections for configuring the information to be reported. See North Atlantic Publishing Systems. *Software*

Copy Preparation - The process of making sure all elements (illustrations, photographs, typesetting, etc.) of an ad, artwork, or other material to be printed are available for the preparation of the final CRC. *Art and Copy Preparation*

Copy Protection - Software diskettes or files that have been locked so they cannot be copied. *General Computer*

Copy Range - The density difference between the lightest neutral highlights where detail appears and the darkest neutral shadow where detail appears in original artwork for reproduction, i.e., the black and white photographs, and color prints and transparencies. *Art and Copy Preparation*

Copyright - This gives the author or creator of illustrations, photos, and written information the exclusive right to these creations for the length of their life plus 50 years. To acquire this right, the author or creator must include a copyright notice, i.e., Copyright © 1994 Thomas D. Kinsey, on the material to be copyrighted. On a book the copyright notice should be located behind the title page. Then, once the item to be copyrighted is finished and ready for distribution, an application for copyright is submitted to the Copyright Office, Library of Congress, Washington, D.C. 20559. *Desktop/Electronic Publishing*

Copy Viewer - See Light Box.

Corel Corporation - Developer and marketer of PC graphics and SCSI software. Corel DRAW is their main product and a leading graphics software. It is available in 16 languages. Contact numbers: 1600 Carling Ave., Ottawa, Ontario, Canada, K1Z 8R7; (613)728-8200. *Software*

CorelDRAW 4 - Creates illustrations and charts, edits photos, produces on-screen presentations, and animation functions. CorelDRAW 4 also includes over 750 fonts and more than 18,000 clip-art images and symbols, multi-page layouts, and fractal textures. See Corel Corporation. *Software*

Corel Professional Photos - 100 royalty free Kodak CD-format photographs on a variety of themes. See Corel Corporation. *Multimedia - Software*

Corel Ventura 4.2 - Fast font loading and support for Adobe Acrobat. Provided with Ventura DataBase Publisher 4.2, Ventura Separator and Ventura Scan, plus templates that allow the creation of a wide range of communication materials, over 600 fonts, and over 10,000 clip-art images. See Corel Corporation. *Software*

Corner Mark - See Crop Marks.

Corrugated Board - A heavy-duty composite paper that is used for boxes and other applications that require a stiff paper. *Substrates*

Cosmetics - The physical look of the printed piece. *Quality/Process Control*

Cover Paper - A heavier grade of paper that is used on larger catalog and book covers, or on any other printed piece where a more durable cover is needed. *Substrates*

CP/M (Control Program for Micro-computers) - The original operating system that was developed for the first microcomputers. *Software*

C-Print - A print that is created from photographic paper sensitive to the full spectrum of colors. *Graphic Arts Photography*

CPU (Central Processing Unit) - The computer's central "brain." The main control and computational section of the computer which executes all instructions and sends or receives all information to and from I/O (Input/Output Devices). *Computer Hardware*

Crash - A failure of either the computer, the software or one of the other computer peripherals (printers, external storage, etc.) within the computer system. *General Computer*

Crawl - The formation of droplets on the substrate, because the ink failed to adhere to the printed surface. *Printing Processes*

Crazing - Cracks that have developed where heavy coatings have been applied. *Substrates*

CRC - See Camera-Ready Copy.

Crease - See Score.

Creasing - The process of scoring. See Score. *Finishing*

Creasing Rule - The metal rule that is used for scoring or creasing. See Score. *Finishing*

Creep - The movement or the forward creep, while printing, of an offset press' blanket. *Printing Processes* The condition that occurs as press sheets are folded into signatures, continually larger trim sizes are needed, especially on the inner pages. This is especially true for saddle-stitched books. See Saddle-Stitched. *Finishing*

CristalRaster - Miles/Agfa's version of stochastic screening. See Stochastic Screening. *Color Reproduction - Graphic Arts Photography*

Cromalin - A color proofing method by Du Pont. In this system, film is exposed onto a white sheet of paper with ultra-violet, light-sensitive material. This film is colored with each of the four toners (cyan, magenta, yellow, and black), and is exposed in the proper order or sequence. This produces a very close representation of the final printed image. Color bars are usually included. *Proofing*

Crop - The removal of certain portions of an illustration, a photograph, or other similar types of graphic elements in order to fit that object into a desired area, or for the purpose of removing any unwanted or unneeded graphic elements. *Art and Copy Preparation*

Crop Marks - The pairs of narrow lines that define the boundaries of a page, or any other type of CRC. *Art and Copy Preparation*

Cross Direction - The direction of a substrate that is across or against the grain. This is often a serious problem in printing because when paper is printed across the grain it becomes weaker and can be susceptable to the type of problems that are created by moisture and humidity. *Substrates*

Cross-Fold - See Chopper Fold.

Crossline (Glass) Screen - A special screen housed between two glass sheets that was traditionally used to photograph images and convert them to halftone images. *Graphic Arts Photography*

Crossmarks - See Crop Marks, Register Marks.

Cross-Perf - A perforation in the web that prevents bursting of the signature while folding. *Printing Processes*

Cross-Platform - The ability of a software package to execute or run on various computer systems. *General Computer*

Cross-Web - See Across Web.

CRT - See Cathode-Ray Tube.

Crown - When the diameter of a roll of paper increases in the center. *Substrates*

Crow's Feet - A binding defect, i.e., a wrinkle or folding defect. *Finishing*

CTRL-ALT-DEL - By holding down the CTRL and ALT keys while pressing the DEL key a DOS-based PC will reboot. *Computer Hardware*

Curl - The distortion or rippling of paper. It is caused by moisture problems on one side of the paper, or by a coating on one side of the paper that is incompatible with the surface of the other side. *Substrates*

Cursor - An indicator on the terminal or monitor screen (which can be blinking) that will indicate where the next entered data will appear. *Computer Hardware - Software*

Curved Plate - A pre-curved plate that was designed to fit a press cylinder. *Image Carriers - Printing Processes*

Customer - The business or person who negotiates and purchases needed graphic arts and desktop publishing services for themselves or their company. *Marketing*

Custom Color - Ink colors in addition to the four process colors (CMYK), including PMS colors. *Ink*

Custom Publications - Specific books, newsletters, and magazines that are created by a single organization to promote its company or operation. *Marketing*

Cut - The process of diluting an ink or

varnish. *Ink*   To remove information or data from a document or file and paste (or place it) at another location. Also a Halo DPE file format for a paint program. *Desktop/Electronic Publishing*

Cut-Off - The length of a print area of a particular type of press that directly relates to the size of the press plate cylinder. *Printing Processes*

Cut Score - A special knife used in die-cutting. The knife makes a slight cut or mark in the paper and folding becomes easier. *Finishing*

Cyan - The bluish color that is one of the four inks that is used in the four-color printing process (magenta, cyan, yellow, and black). *Color Reproduction - Ink*

Cyber Art - Computer art. *Multimedia*

Cylinder - The cylindrical devices on presses for carrying the plate, blanket, and for bringing the press in contact with the paper. *Printing Processes*

Cylinder Gap - The space in the press cylinder where the clamp and gripper devices are located. These devices hold the plates and blankets during the printing process. *Printing Processes*

Cylinder Packing Gauge - A device that indicates the cylinder adjustments necessary for accurate image transfer. *Printing Processes*

DAC (Digital-To-Analog Converter) - A device that converts discrete, digital data to analog data. *Computer Hardware - Digital Photography*

Daisy Chain - The linking of several devices together. *General Computer*

Dampeners - The rollers on a lithographic press that are a part of the entire press dampening system. See Dampening System. *Printing Processes*

Dampening System - The entire system of rollers and devices that spreads the dampening solution onto the offset plate during printing. The function of this system is to keep the non-image areas moist and ink repellent. *Printing Processes*

Dandy Roll - This cylindrical device is used in papermaking to create wove, watermark, and laid effects on the surface of a substrate. *Substrates*

Darkroom - A special room that is free of white light and is used for processing photographic materials. *Graphic Arts Photography*

Dash - A keyboard character that resembles a hyphen, but is longer. See Em Dash and En Dash. *Typography*

DAT - See Digital Audiotape

Database - A collection of information that is stored in computer memory, which can be sorted or reassembled in any number of ways and retrieved to suit the needs of the user. *General Computer*

Database Management - The process of controlling, sorting, storing, updating, and retrieving data in a database. See Database. *General Computer*

Data Communication - Information, data, or files that are sent from a computer to a computer, or to another device, i.e., memory. This usually occurs over networks or modems. *General Computer*

Data Compression - Data or files that have been reduced in size to free memory for additional data. Lossless and Lossy are the most common techniques. See Lossless and Lossy. *General Computer*

Data Rate - The data transfer rate or the number of bits transferred per second. *General Computer*

Day-Glo - A special brand of paint or ink sold in brilliant, eye-catching colors, which creates the illusion that it glows when printed on a surface. *Ink*

DayStar Digital - A pioneer in MacII acceleration. Contact numbers: 5556 Atlanta Hwy., Flowery Branch, GA 30542; (800)962-2077. *Software*

db (Decibel) - 1/10th of a Bel. This is a measurement unit used to compare two powers, voltages, sounds, etc. It is a logarithmical number to keep the numbers manageable. The decibel is frequently used to indicate the ratio of two quantities such as signal and noise voltages. *Digital Photography - General Computer*

DCS (Desktop Color Separation) - A standardized format that is used to encode images as four EPS files and one

PICT file for preview. *Color Reproduction Desktop/Electronic Publishing*

DCS Combine - Enables a RIP to accept DCS files in composite mode. This provides the benefits of trapping, RIP speed, and post-RIP editability. See Scitex Corporation Ltd. *Software*

DDES - See Direct Digital Exchange Standards

Debug - The discovery, removal, and correction of errors that have occurred in computer software and/or hardware. *General Computer*

Decals - Designs and graphics that have been printed on special type of paper and can be easily transferred to other surfaces. *Marketing*

Decalcomania - A highly specialized type of screen printing. Designs are printed on special paper which become decals that can be transferred to another surface. *Printing Processes*

Decibels - A reference to noise level. *Environment - Standards*

Decimal - A system of numbers based on the base 10. Includes the numbers 0, 1, 2, 3, 4, 5, 6, 7, 8, and 9. *General Computer*

Deckle - The actual width of wet paper-sheets that roll off a machine during the manufacture of paper. *Substrates*

Deckle Edge - The edge of a specialty (and often handmade) paper that was manufactured to have an untrimmed, feathery appearance. The feather deckle edge that was created by the older style paper machines is no longer a part of

modern papermaking process and must be created in other ways. *Substrates*

Decompression - The conversion of a compressed file back to its original size. *General Computer - Telecommunications*

Decorative Type - Unique typefaces that draw attention. Also known as novelty type. *Typography*

Dedicated - Computer hardware and/or software that has only one purpose or function. *General Computer*

Deep-Etch Plate - An older style of lithographic printing plate that was traditionally used for long production runs. The image areas on this plate are recessed very slightly, giving the plate greater wear resistance. *Image Carriers*

Default - The condition or instruction that occurs when other instructions are not specified. *General Computer*

Default Drive - The drive (floppy or hard) that will be accessed first by the operating system unless another drive is specified. *Computer Hardware*

Deflected Ink-Jet - Ink-jet printing in which ink droplets are individually controlled and deflected or directed to the proper spot on a substrate through electrostatic charges. Typically used for printing alphanumeric characters. Also known as Drop-On-Demand Ink-Jet. *Printing Processes*

Definition - The sharpness of an image. *Graphic Arts Photography*

De-Inking - The process of removing ink from paper (for recycling) or from the press (or related devices). *Ink - Printing Processes - Substrates*

Demand Assigned Multiple Access (DAMA) - A technique to share channel capacity with idle and unused channels. *Telecommunications*

Demibold Weight - A version of type between bold and roman in thickness. *Typography*

Demographic Finishing - Binding and finishing processes that personalize a publication or other printed media for individuals or target such media for specific geographic regions. A typical process involves the use of ink printing from a subscription database to address publications or direct mail advertising, thus eliminating the need for mailing labels. *Finishing*

Demographic Printing - The personalization of what otherwise would be impersonal print media. Examples include the printing of regional advertisements in national magazines and the targeting of portions of national print media to people having different socio-economic backgrounds and interests. The growth of demographic printing results from the compilation of databases and the computerization of the printing process. *Desktop/Electronic Publishing - Marketing*

Deneba artWORKS - An integrated drawing, painting, and image editing program for the Mac. artWORKS is easy to use and has features that match those of more expensive dedicated drawing, painting, and image editing programs. See Deneba Software. *Software*

Deneba Software - Developer and pub-

lisher of graphics software for Mac and Windows. Best known for its Canvas precision drawing program. Contact numbers: 7400 S.W. 87th Ave., Miama, FL 33173; (305)596-5644. *Software*

Densitometer - A device that measures reflection, transparent density (black and white or color), and dot gain. It is most useful in the measurement of black and shades of gray. An experienced operator can learn a great deal about all types of film, and avoid many potential problems by using a densitometer. *Graphic Arts Photography - Quality/Process Control - Scanning*

Density - The actual weight or degree of blackness of characters and areas as measured with a densitometer. It also refers to an object's ability to stop or absorb light. *Graphic Arts Photography*

Density Range - The density range that exists in a halftone, i.e., from the darkest tones to the lightest tones. *Desktop/Electronic Publishing - Graphic Arts Photography - Scanning*

Desaturated Color - A faded color or a color with excess white ink. *Color Reproduction - Ink*

Descenders - The portion of the lowercase characters that are below the X-Height or baseline.
See Fig. 7.
Typography

Fig. 7 - Descenders

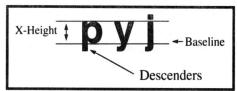

95

Desensitizer - A chemical treatment that converts non-image plate areas from neutrality to being able to repel ink and attract water. *Image Carriers - Printing Processes*

Design - The look of an image that will convey the desired message or feeling. *Art and Copy Preparation*

Design Principles - All design is based on the design concepts of balance, contrast, unity, rhythm, and proportion. See Balance, Contrast, Unity, Rhythm, and Proportion. *Art and Copy Preparation*

Design Science, Inc. - Publisher of MathType, an intelligent mathematical equation editor for the Mac and Windows. Contact numbers: 4028 Broadway, Long Beach, CA 90803; (310)433-0685. *Software*

Desk Accessory - Specialized functions such as a computer or calendar that are available on desktop computers. They can be accessed even when other programs are active. *Software*

Desktop - The opening on-screen window area where various objects and icons are placed, similar to an actual desktop where objects are also placed. *Computer Hardware - Desktop/Electronic Publishing*

Desktop Publishing - A special type of computing that involves the use of special desktop computers (Mac or PC) and software to create flyers, newsletters, ads, and other graphics. Output is typically on laser printers, color proofers, and high-end typesetting equipment or imagesetters. Film or plates are created directly from these electronic files that are suitable for printing. *Desktop/Electronic Publishing - General Computer*

Detail Enhancement - An electronic scanner technique that sharpens image edges. *Scanning*

Developer - The photographic chemical that removes all coatings in the unexposed areas and allows the photographically exposed image to become visible as it is exposed to light. See Processor and Latent Image. *Graphic Arts Photography*

Developing Agent - The chemical agent in the developer that converts the latent image to the visible image on the film, plate, or photo-sensitive paper. *Graphic Arts Photography*

Device Independent - A main feature of PostScript. It means that any information created on a program supported by PostScript can be output on any printer or proofer that supports PostScript at whatever resolution is supported by the printer. *General Computer*

Device-Independent Color - The ability to create color printer output (proofing) that matches the color on the final film output. *Color Reproduction*

Dialog Box - A window in the GUI that presents the user with a series of options, i.e., print a file, set resolution, undo an operation, etc. See GUI. *Software*

Diamond - Linotype-Hell's version of stochastic screening. See Stochastic Screening. *Color Reproduction - Graphic Arts Photography - Scanning*

Diazo - A material which is sensitive to light and is used in platemaking. *Image Carriers*

Diazo Process - A copying process that uses light-sensitive dye. *Proofing*

Die - A sharp tool that is used for cutting an area the size of the tool from a substrate. *Finishing*

Die-Cut - The technique whereby a specially designed steel die is used to cut paper and other substrates into unique shapes and designs. This can be done as a separate operation or as an inline printing operation. *Finishing*

Dielectric Paper - Specially treated paper that is used in electrostatic printing. *Substrates*

Die Press - A special machine that uses a die to perform the die-cutting operation. *Finishing*

Die-Stamping - A process that creates a slightly raised impression from steel or copper intaglio plates. It is used in the printing of letterheads, business cards, and other similar images. *Finishing*

Diffusion - A gray level filtering effect that is used to create special screening effects. *Graphic Arts Photography*

Diffusion Transfer - A Polaroid-like photographic process whereby a light-sensitive emulsion produces a negative, which is then transferred to another sheet to create a positive photograph. *Graphic Arts Photography*

Digital - Numerically discrete signals or values. *General Computer*

Digital Audiotape (DAT) - Cassette tapes that store data in digital form. *Computer Hardware - Multimedia*

Digital Camera - An electronic camera that records digital images direct to disk. *Digital Photography*

Digital Computer - The most common type of computer, which processes all data in discontinuous, discrete elements. *Computer Hardware*

Digital Halftone - Similar to a traditional halftone in that it is comprised of dots of varying shapes and angles. However, digital halftones use halftone cells which contain varying amounts of dots that create the halftone pattern. These varying amounts of dots give the appearance of the gray scale of a halftone. See Dithering. *Graphic Arts Photography - Laser Application - Scanning*

Digital Image - An image that is composed of discrete pixels. Each pixel is characterized by different brightness levels. *Desktop/Electronic Publishing*

Digital Networks - A network that communicates information in digital form. *Telecommunications*

Digital Proofs - Proofs that are produced on special printers or proofing devices and they are a direct output of a digital electronic file which resides on a computer hard drive. *Laser Applications - Proofing*

Digital Signal - A signal that is composed of discontinuous, discrete elements. *Desktop/Electronic Publishing Digital Photography - General Computer*

Digital Signal Processor (DSP) - A hardware image accelerator card. *Digital Photography*

Digital Video Interactive (DVI) - A type of CD used for the storage of digital video data (still and full motion) and other digital information. *Digital Photography - Multimedia*

Digitization - The process of converting analog data to discrete, digital data. *General Computer*

Digitize - The conversion of data to digital formats. The task is performed by digitizers and scanners. See Scanners and Digitizers. *Scanning*

Digitizers - Devices that are used to capture real-life 3-D images, such as a video camera. They produce instant halftone images. Still video cameras, (another type of digitizer), are a major growth area in the graphics field as more photographers begin to capture 3-D information with this new technology. *Digital Photography - General Computer*

Dilatency - The increase in ink viscosity when it is worked or stirred. *Ink*

Diluent - A weak solvent that is used for thinning varnish or ink. *Ink*

Dimensions - A Mac 3-D tool for design professionals. Can create, extrude, revolve, bevel, and manipulate simple 3-D objects. It effects and integrates them with artwork from popular 2-D graphics programs, such as Adobe Illustrator and Deneba Canvas. See Adobe Systems, Inc. *Software*

Dimensional Stability - The resistance of film or a substrate to changes in size when exposed to moisture or humidity. *Substrates*

Diphthong - A character that is a combination of two vowels. See Fig. 8. *Typography*

Fig. 8 - Diphthong

Direct Broadcasting - Using the air-waves to send and receive communication signals between two or more designated points without being able to be picked up by others and without causing general broadcast interference, i.e., two satellite sending and receiving stations can communicate directly with each other. *Telecommunications*

Direct Broadcast TV - The broadcasting of signals (TV) directly from a satellite to a receiver. *Telecommunications*

Direct Digital Color Proofing - A color proof that is digitally generated directly from the color scanning and computerized page make-up program. Dot gain, density, and the other influencing conditions can be controlled digitally by the computer. *Laser Applications - Proofing - Scanning*

Direct Digital Exchange Standards (DDES) - The standards for the communication of digital data within computers and their peripherals. *Standards*

Direct Halftone - A process that directly creates a screened halftone by photographing an original photo through a halftone contact screen. A halftone crossline screen can also be used to complete this process. See Halftone. *Graphic Arts Photography*

Direct Image Plates - An offset plate where the image is produced directly on the surface of the plate. *Image Carriers*

Direct Imaging - Imaging that bypasses the need for film such as imaging from original copy direct to plate or electronic imaging from digital data directly to a proof or printing plate. *Desktop/Electronic Publishing - Image Carriers - Proofing*

Directory - The names and sizes of all the files on a disk or a hard drive. This can often contain the file location. *General Computer*

Direct-To-Plate - A process that creates a plate directly from a computer file. This avoids all traditional graphic arts photography, stripping, and image assembly. *Image Carriers*

Direct-To-Press - Electronic imaging that goes from a computer via a disc or modem directly to a printing press. This technique bypasses the need for typesetting ouput, film, or conventional platemaking. *Desktop/Electronic Publishing Printing Processes*

Disk - A magnetic storage device that contains information, files, programs and data needed by the computer to perform tasks. *Computer Hardware*

Disk Drive - A device that enables the CPU to read and write to and from magnetic disks. See CPU. *Computer Hardware*

Diskette - A flexible magnetic storage medium commonly used on personal computers. *Computer Hardware*

Disk Runner (Mac II, IIx, IIcx, IIvi, IIsi (NuBus), IIci, IIvx, IIfx, Performa 600, all Quadras, Centris 650, DuoDock) - Upgrades old drives and enhances drive speeds. SyQuest's and CD-ROM's are made to run like they do on the fastest hard drives. See DayStar Digital. *Computer Hardware*

Display Ad - An advertisement which usually includes a combination of text, graphics, and photos. It is prepared for some form of print media. *Marketing*

Display Type - All headline fonts and other large, bold fonts. It is often used to command attention in ads, posters, and other advertising pieces. *Typography*

Dissolve - The fading of one shot, scene, frame, or form of media into another. *Digital Photography - Multimedia*

Distortion - The ability to electronically alter images, i.e., stretching or squeezing. *Desktop/Electronic Publishing*

Distributing Rollers - The rollers that are used on presses to distribute the ink from one roller to the next. *Printing Processes*

Dithering - A computer graphics technique that is used by digital output devices to give the illusion of varying shades of gray or shades of color where distinct and different color dots appear in the same area. For example, adjacent white dots and black dots would be dithered to appear as softer shades of gray or where the dot patterns on the edges of lines and curves would be softened to appear to make a smoother transition from the darker to the lighter colors. *Desktop/Electronic Publishing*

Doctor Blade - A blade that is used for the removal of ink from gravure press cylinders in the areas where no printing occurs. *Printing Processes*

Document - A file, of varying sizes, that contains text, graphics, or both. It has a specific name and can be retrieved via inputting of the document name. *General Computer*

Dog-Eared - The ragged edges on any piece of printed material. *Quality/Process Control*

DOS (Disk Operating System) - This is an abbreviation for the operating system MS-DOS or PC-DOS. *Software*

Dot - A tiny spot that is the basic element of digital image creation. It is the foundation for all black and white and four-color halftone images. Plus, all graphics and type are comprised of dots produced on paper and film at various resolutions. See DPI. *Graphic Arts Photography*

Dot Area - The dot size expressed as a percent. *Graphic Arts Photography - Quality/Process Control - Scanning*

Dot Etching - The reduction in the size of a halftone dot, via chemistry, in order to change the amount of image on the film. *Image Carriers*

Dot Formation - The way individual halftone dots are formed on film. *Graphic Arts Photography - Scanning*

Dot Gain - The percentage increase in dot size between the time film is created and the final printing. Conditions that effect dot gain are: type of paper used; the platemaking process; the type of ink; the type of press, and the cylinder pressure used on the press. *Printing Processes*

Dot Loss - Any decrease in dot size that occurs during the prepress process. *Graphic Arts Photography - Quality/Process Control - Scanning*

Dot Matrix - Type characters that are formed by small dots on a computer printer. *General Computer*

Dot Matrix Printer - A special printer that creates characters as dot patterns. *Computer Hardware*

Dots Per Inch (DPI) - The resolution of the images that are output on a printer, imagesetter, or monitor. See Resolution and Figs. 9, 10, and 11 on pages 101, 102, and 103. *Typesetting and Imagesetting*

Dot Percent - See Dot Area.

Dot Shapes - The dots that are created by the various techniques of black and white and four-color halftoning take several distinct shapes. Square, round, and elliptical shapes are the most common. *Graphic Arts Photography*

Double Burn - The process of creating a composite plate or proof. See Composite Plate and Composite Proof. *Image Carriers - Proofing*

Double-Click - The depression of the button on a mouse two times while not moving the position of the mouse. *General Computer*

Double Density - The storage of twice as much information on a magnetic storage medium as is possible on a single density medium. *General Computer*

Double-Sheet Detector - The mechanism that stops a folder if two (or more) sheets are accidently picked up while folding. *Finishing*

Doubling - The overprinting of an image or dots on press, due to a press malfunction causing halftone dots to not transfer to the offset blanket in the same spot during each revolution of the press. This can cause a shift in color and moire patterns. *Printing Processes*

Doughnut - A halftone dot that has lost a portion of its center during printing. *Printing Processes*

This is a sample of 300 d.p.i.

Paper Laser Printer Output

This is a sample of 1, 2, 3, 4, 5, 6, 7, 8, 9, & 10 alphanumeric information that has been set in 12 point type and 15 points of leading.

This is a sample of 1, 2, 3, 4, 5, 6, 7, 8, 9, & 10 alpha-numeric information that has been set in 10 point type and 13 points of leading.

This is a sample of 1, 2, 3, 4, 5, 6, 7, 8, 9, & 10 alpha-numeric information that has been set in 8 point type and 11 points of leading.

This is a sample of 1, 2, 3, 4, 5, 6, 7, 8, 9, & 10 alphanumeric information that has been set in 7 point type and 9 points of leading.

This is a sample of 1, 2, 3, 4, 5, 6, 7, 8, 9, & 10 alphanumeric information that has been set in 6 point type and 8 points of leading.

Large Script Typeface

Large type
and a
screened background.

Black Background
and
White Type

Fig. 9 - 300 DPI Type and Graphics

This is a sample of 1,000 d.p.i.

Paper Laser Printer Output

This is a sample of 1, 2, 3, 4, 5, 6, 7, 8, 9, & 10 alphanumeric information that has been set in 12 point type and 15 points of leading.

This is a sample of 1, 2, 3, 4, 5, 6, 7, 8, 9, & 10 alpha-numeric information that has been set in 10 point type and 13 points of leading.

This is a sample of 1, 2, 3, 4, 5, 6, 7, 8, 9, & 10 alpha-numeric information that has been set in 8 point type and 11 points of leading.

This is a sample of 1, 2, 3, 4, 5, 6, 7, 8, 9, & 10
alphanumeric information that has been set in 7 point type and 9 points of leading.

Large Script Typeface

Large type
and a
screened background.

Black Background.
and
White Type

Fig. 10 - 1000 DPI Type and Graphics

This is a sample of 1270 d.p.i.

High-resolution Output
on Photosensitive RC Paper

This is a sample of 1, 2, 3, 4, 5, 6, 7, 8, 9, & 10
alphanumeric information that has been set in 12 point type
and 15 points of leading.

This is a sample of 1, 2, 3, 4, 5, 6, 7, 8, 9, & 10 alpha-numeric information
that has been set in 10 point type and 13 points of leading.

This is a sample of 1, 2, 3, 4, 5, 6, 7, 8, 9, & 10 alpha-numeric information that has been set in
8 point type and 11 points of leading.

This is a sample of 1, 2, 3, 4, 5, 6, 7, 8, 9, & 10
alphanumeric information that has been set in 7 point type and 9 points of leading.

Large Script Typeface

Large type
and a
screened background.

Black Background
and
White Type

Fig. 11 - 1270 DPI Type and Graphics

103

Down - A period of time when a computer system is not functioning, either due to a malfunction, for testing, or for preventive maintenance. *General Computer*

Downlink - A signal that is transmitted by a satellite to an earth station. *Telecommunications*

Download - To send a file from one computer to another via a network or a modem. *General Computer*

Downtime - See Down.

DPI - See Dots Per Inch, and Figs. 9, 10, and 11 on pages 101,102, and 103.

Drag - To move an object on-screen from one location to another by holding the button on a mouse down as the position of the mouse is moved. This actually moves the object as the mouse moves. *General Computer*

Dragon's Blood - A heat applied powder traditionally used to protect any area against acid damage during printing. *Printing Processes*

DRAM - See Dynamic RAM.

Draw - See Gathering.

Draw-Down - A method of testing ink color by manually spreading the ink on paper to check color match and how well the paper accepts each particular ink. *Ink*

Drawing Tools - The use of draw programs to create images. See Draw Program. *Desktop/Electronic Publishing*

Draw Program - A software program that runs on a computer (Mac, PC, or Unix workstation), that allows the user to create object-oriented illustrations and drawings. *Software*

Dried Process Negative - A special negative film that creates a positive without chemicals. The film is placed in an enclosed contact frame with unexposed film (with the emulsion down). After exposure to light, the positive image is created. *Image Carriers*

Drier - A chemical agent that facilitates ink drying. *Ink*

Drilling - The insertion or placement of various sized holes (usually round) in paper. *Finishing*

Driography - An original process of printing with waterless plates. *Image Carriers - Printing Processes*

Drive - See Hard Disk.

Driver - Software that handles and controls the transfer of data or files from one device to another device. *Software*

Drop Cap - The initial character in a paragraph is enlarged so the top of the letter is even or slightly above the first line and the balance of the letter drops into the body of the paragraph. See Fig. 12 on page 105. *Typography*

Drop Folio - The page number itself, which is not part of the running head, but located in the page's bottom section. *Desktop/Electronic Publishing*

Drop-On-Demand Ink-Jet - See Deflected Ink-Jet.

Drop-Out - The part of an original photograph, illustration, or graphic that cannot be reproduced photographically (i.e., light background area), or parts not wanted when reproducing the original (i.e., certain lines). *Graphic Arts Photography* Areas of a disk in which magnetic particles have fallen away, causing white lines to appear across the screen during playback. *Digital Photography* The condition in a halftone where the smallest highlight dots are lost. *Desktop/Electronic Publishing*

Drop-Out Halftone - The deliberate overexposure of a highlight area to reduce the amount and size of the dots. *Graphic Arts Photography*

Drop Shadow - A special type effect that places a slightly offset shadow behind an image. This creates the illusion that the forward image is popping off the page. *Typography*

Drop Shadow

Drum Imagesetter - A particular type of imagesetter that uses a revolving drum to output film and other media. See Imagesetter. *Laser Applications - Typesetting and Imagesetting*

Drum Scanner - A particular type of scanner that uses a revolving drum to mount media while it is being scanned. See Scanner. *Laser Applications - Scanning*

Dry Back - The lowering of ink density during ink drying, because the gloss of the image surface has been reduced. *Ink - Printing Processes - Substrates*

Drying Oil - Any oil that dries (becomes solid) when exposed to the air. *Ink*

Dry Jet - Similar to bubble jet printing but forms minute dots on a substrate by

N ow is the time for all good men to come to the aid of their party and this is the best time for all of us. This is a good example of one of the drop caps.

Fig. 12 - Drop Cap

projecting dry carbon particles, as opposed to wet ink from an ink-jet orifice. *Printing Processes*

Dry Mount - A quick dry mounting process for affixing artwork to a backing that is less susceptible to blistering and bubbling. This process requires that a special piece of thin paper is placed between the artwork and the backing and then heat is applied. *Art and Copy Preparation*

Drypoint Engraving - A gravure plate which is created by manually scratching the desired design into the plate surface. *Image Carriers*

Dry Trapping - The degree to which a wet ink film adheres to a dry ink film. *Ink - Printing Processes - Quality/Process Control*

Dry-Up - See Catching Up.

DualPort IIsi (Mac IIsi) - A PDS adapter that doubles the expansion capabilities of the IIsi by letting users plug in a DayStar cache card and PDS card at the same time. The on-board 20 MHz 68882 math chip speeds up math functions 500 percent or more. See DayStar Digital. *Computer Hardware*

Ductor Roller - A press roller that is directly involved in the movement of ink from a press' ink fountain to the distributing rollers and onto the plate area. *Printing Processes*

Dull-Coated Paper - A paper with a surface having a dull, flat finish. *Substrates*

Dummy - A representation of where all the elements (photos, copy, illustrations, etc.) of a piece of artwork are to be positioned. *Art and Copy Preparation*

Dummy Folio - The page numbers used on the dummy, but not necessarily on the final book. See Dummy. *Art and Copy Preparation*

Dump - To randomly transfer information from one location in the computer to another. *General Computer*

Duotone - A special technique whereby a black and white (one-color) photo is printed to be a two-color job, thus creating a unique effect. Each of the two colors are printed at different screen angles. *Graphic Arts Photography*

Dupes - Duplicate film or transparencies. *Graphic Arts Photography*

Duplexed - Two fonts that have the same width values, i.e., each character in the font or face is the same width as the same character in the other font. *Typography*

Duplex Paper - A paper that has one type of surface or color on one side and another type of surface or color on the other side. *Substrates*

Duplicate Film - The generation of an additional copy of the negative or positive film. *Graphic Arts Photography - Image Assembly*

Duplicating Film - A film that is designed for film duplication, i.e., positive to negative, positive to positive, etc.

In the color field, this film is used to duplicate any color transparency. *Graphic Arts Photography*

Durometer - A device that will indicate the degree of hardness of various materials and objects. Also known as a hardness tester. *Printing Processes - Quality/Process Control*

Dust Jacket - The paper cover for a case-bound book, which includes front and back flaps that contain additional information about the author and the content of the book. *Finishing*

Dye - A colorant that is soluble. *Ink*

Dye Sublimation - A special type of printer technology used for color reproduction. *Color Reproduction - Printing Processes*

Dye Transfer - A method of color print creation on film or gelatin coated paper that involves the use of photographic emulsions and transfer dyes. *Color Reproduction*

Dylux - A specific brand of paper that is used to create bluelines. *Proofing*

Dynamic RAM (DRAM) - A slower, high capacity RAM, with simpler circuitry. Their capacitors lose power and must be continuously recharged. *Computer Hardware*

Dynamic Range - An indication of gray value spread. The higher the range the wider the gray value spread. *Graphic Arts Photography - Scanning*

Earth Station - Antenna equipment that is located on earth. It is used to send and receive signals from a satellite. *Telecommunications*

Edge Enhancement - A software technique that enhances details on the image's edge. *Software*

Edge Gilding - The application of gold to the outside of a book. *Finishing*

Edit - To make changes to a document or file. *General Computer*

Editing - The manual process of checking a publication of any size for all the necessary corrections before final printing. *Desktop/Electronic Publishing*

Editor - The person responsible for all content and copy editing prior to final publication or printing. See Content Editing and Copy Editing. *Desktop/Electronic Publishing* Special software that can modify text, data, documents, and programs. *Software*

EEPROM (Electrically Erasable Programmable Read-Only Memory) - A computer chip that can be erased or recorded via electrical impulses. *Computer Hardware*

EfiColor Works - An industry standard in color management. It provides fast, accurate, comprehensive color management from scanner to monitor to desktop printer to offset press. It works seamlessly with Photoshop, QuarkXPress, Cachet, Illustrator, Freehand, etc. See Electronics for Imaging, Inc. *Software*

EGA - See Enhanced Graphics Adapter.

Elasticity - The ability of a material to resume its original shape or size after deformation or stretching. *Quality/Process Control*

Electric Image Animation System (EIAS) 2.0 - 3-D graphics system for computer graphics/animation, using higher-end Macs and SGI Computers. Includes: animation choreography interface; VTR control; IMAGE file conversion; digital compositing; and rendering engine. See Electric Image, Inc. *Software*

Electric Image, Inc. - Provides film, video, and other computer graphic professionals with computer animation systems, differentiated by broadcast quality imaging, outstanding performance, and an intuitive, easy to use interface. Contact numbers: 117 E. Colorado Blvd., Suite 300, Pasadena, CA, 91105; (818)577-1627. *Multimedia*

Electronic Airbrushing - The ability to change color tones and values, silhouetting, smoothing, and overall retouching of images on a monitor using electronic methods. *Art and Copy Preparation - Color Reproduction - Desktop/Electronic Publishing*

Electronic Data Interchange (EDI) - The process of electronically exchanging information within a company or between various companies. *Telecommunications*

Electronic Distribution - The process of distributing information by various electronic forms, i.e., TV, computers, telephone, etc. *Telecommunications*

107

Electronic Mail (E-Mail) - Messages that are sent electronically from computer to computer over a network or via a modem. *General Computer*

Electronic Still Camera Standardization Committee (ESCSC) - Committee of over 45 corporations established in the late 70's to create standards for the new still video format. *Digital Photography*

Electronics for Imaging, Inc. - Conceives, develops, and markets products that bring professional quality color to desktop publishing. Contact numbers: 2855 Campus Drive, San Mateo, CA 94403; (415)286-8600. *Computer Hardware - Software*

Electrophotography - A process, based on static electricity, that is used in photocopy machines for the transfer of an image to paper and other surfaces. *Laser Applications - Printing Processes*

Electrostatic Plates - Coated plates that are used in high-speed, state-of-the-art laser printers. *Image Carriers - Laser Applications*

Electrostatic Printer - A special type of printer that places toner onto paper by an electrical charge. *Laser Applications - Printing Processes*

Electrotype - A particular type of plate that is an exact duplicate of its original letterpress plate. *Image Carriers*

Ellipsis - Three dots in a row that denotes more copy should follow except it has been deleted for editorial purposes. See Fig. 13. *Typography*

Fig. 13 - Ellipsis

```
A great book on ...
```

Elliptical Dot - A halftone dot that is mostly used in areas where there are very gradual and subtle changes in the image, i.e., skin tones and vignettes. *Graphic Arts Photography*

Elmendorf Test - A test that is used to determine a paper's resistence to tearing. *Quality/Process Control - Substrates*

E-Mail - See Electronic Mail.

Embossed Finish - A specialty paper with a surface having a textured look. *Substrates*

Embossing - The process of applying a raised image to various types of substrates by using a die with heat and pressure applied on a special letterpress machine. *Finishing*

Embossing Die - A die without sharp edges that is used for the purpose of embossing. *Finishing*

Em Dash - A dash the width of the character "M" in the font and point size that has been selected. *Typography*

EMS (Expanded Memory Spec) - A type of memory used on PC's. *Computer Hardware*

Em Space - A space that is equal in size to the width of the character "M" in the font and point size that has been selected. *Typography*

Emulsion - The light-sensitive coating that is used on most photographic film and plates. See Emulsion Side. *Graphic Arts Photography - Image Carriers*

Emulsion Side - The chemically treated side of photographic film that is light-sensitive and faces the lens during film exposure. *Graphic Arts Photography*

Enamel - An interchangeable term with coated, as in coated paper. *Substrates*

Enamel Proof - A proof that was produced on a coated stock. *Proofing*

Encapsulated PostScript (EPS) - A standarized format that is used to store PostScript images. *Desktop/Electronic Publishing*

End Leaf - The heavy paper that is used to secure the book and its case together. *Finishing*

Endpapers - The sheets of heavy paper that are used to fasten the hardcover book and its cover together. *Finishing*

English Finish - An uncoated book paper that has been manufactured with a smooth, flat finish. *Substrates*

Engrave - To etch an image on metal surfaces for the purpose of printing. *Image Carriers*

Engraver's Proof - The first printed copy from a plate that was created by an engraver. This is used for approval purposes before the remainder of the job is finished. *Image Carriers*

Enhanced Graphics Adapter (EGA) - A color video board for PC's that offers enhanced color over the CGA board. See CGA. *Computer Hardware*

Enlargement - The process of making artwork or copy larger. *Art and Copy Preparation - Graphic Arts Photography*

Enlarger - A device that is used in creating larger photographic prints. *Graphic Arts Photography*

En Dash - A dash the width of the character "N." This space varies with the font and point size that has been selected. See Dash. *Typography*

En Space - A space that is equal in size to half an em space. This space varies with the font and point size that has been selected. *Typography*

Enter Key (Return Key) - A computer input key on the keyboard that causes information to be entered when it is depressed. *Computer Hardware*

Envelope - A paper carrier that holds mail for transportation to its intended address. Envelopes are manufactured in numerous sizes and shapes. *Substrates*

EPROM (Erasable Programmable Read Only Memory) - A programmable computer chip that can be programmed after it is manufactured. Once erased, it can be programmed again. *Computer Hardware*

EPA (Environmental Protection Agency) - Federal agency that regulates federal environmental laws. *Environmental - Standards*

EPS - See Encapsulated PostScript.

Epilogue - The concluding or final part of a publication that represents the parting notes of the author. *Desktop/Electronic Publishing*

Equalization - The enhancement of the shades of gray and/or color to improve picture quality. *Graphic Arts Photography*

Equalizer LC (Mac LC) - The 68030 "LC II upgrade" with optional math chip. Full System 7 compatibility, virtual memory, and 500 percent faster math performance with the optional 16 MHz 68882 math chip. Upgradable to Power-Cache. See DayStar Digital. *Computer Hardware*

Equation Typesetting - The insertion of codes into a software program that causes the machine to output complex, multi-line equations with mathematical symbols. *Typesetting and Imagesetting*

Equivalent Neutral Density - The required densities for magenta, cyan, and yellow to produce a light or neutral gray. *Color Reproduction*

Escape Key - A keyboard key that has different functions, depending on the software being used. However, it usually allows the operator to escape from a specific area in the software, i.e., escape one menu to the next. *Computer Hardware*

ESCOR - Varityper's version of Supercell Screening. See Supercell Screening. *Color Reproduction*

Estimator - The person responsible for the determination of the cost to produce a job. See Quotation. *Printing Processes*

Etch - The process of creating images on plates via chemistry or electrolysis. Also, an acidic solution that can be used to desensitize non-printing areas on the plate from holding ink. *Image Carriers* An on-press solution that is used to keep non-image areas ink free. *Printing Processes*

Etched Plate - An acid-etched metal plate. *Image Carriers*

Ethernet - A popular LAN (Local Area Network) used on many desktop publishing systems. It uses three different connections; thin-net, thick-net, and twisted pair. *Telecommunications*

Execute - To perform or complete the function of any particular instruction or command. *General Computer*

Exposure - The exact moment in photography when light produces an image on the emulsion side of the film. *Graphic Arts Photography*

Expanded Memory Specifications (EMS) - Any RAM over 1MB. Some software packages require 640k system memory and 2MB of EMS. Adding a RAM card means faster working operation. *General Computer*

Expanded Type - Extra-wide type. *Typography*

Extender - A substance that is added to ink to increase its viscosity. *Ink*

Extension - An operating system file name that contains a three-letter extension preceded by a period. Example: DIR.IOS. *General Computer*

Eye Span - The widest line width the human eye can comfortably read. The greater the width, the greater the reading stress. *Desktop/Electronic Publishing*

Face - A particular design of typeface. *Typography*

Facsimile Modem - A computer-based fax for sending files to FAX's. *Computer Hardware*

Fade-In - The movement from a static scene to a moving one. *Multimedia*

Fade-O-Meter - A measuring instrument that will calculate the amount that any particular ink fades with light exposure. *Ink - Quality/Process Control*

Fade-Out - The movement from a moving scene to a static one. *Multimedia*

Fake-Color Process - A manual process whereby a black and white medium is converted to a color medium. *Color Reproduction*

Fanfold - A paper fold that takes the shape of a "Z." *Finishing*

Fan-Out - When moist edges of paper cause the print image to be distorted on press, especially when printing across the grain of the paper. Humidity can also be a consideration on this type of distortion. *Printing Processes*

F.A.S.T. - Mac software utility that accelerates the Finder-level copy function up to 300 percent by using all installed memory as the copy function works. See Newer Technology. *Software*

Fast Cache Family (Mac IIsi, IIci, Centris 610, Quadra 700/800/900/950) - These cache memory cards offer easy installation and boost performance 10

percent to 40 percent. See DayStar Digital. *Computer Hardware*

FAX (Facsimile Machine) - A machine that is capable of sending text and graphics over telephone lines. A document is converted to an electronic signal. The transmission must be from fax to fax or via fax modems in a computer. *Computer Hardware*

FAXGrabber - A fax conversion utility, which allows Microsoft Windows fax card users to convert incoming fax images directly into text. This utility works with virtually any fax software and will automatically convert standard and fine mode faxes into text that can be edited, indexed, or routed via e-mail. See Calera Recognition Systems. *Software*

FCC (Federal Communications Commission) - A governmental regulatory agency that regulates the use of the airwaves and other forms of electronic communications. *Telecommunications*

Feather - A software technique developed for anti-aliasing and to soften the edges of images. *Software*

Feathering - The ragged patterns that appear at the ends of printed areas when ink is applied to a porous substrate. *Printing Processes* The rough edge created by drilling and cutting a substrate. *Finishing*

Feedback - Information that flows into a device and is stored in memory and used later to control future activities. *General Computer*

Feeder - The press device that feeds single, multiple, or continuous sheets of paper into the press. *Printing Processes*

Felt Side - The side of a sheet of paper that is the smoothest and the side that offers the best surface for printing. *Substrates*

F & G's (Folded and Gathered) - Folded book signatures prior to being bound. *Finishing*

Fiber Optics - A cable that carries light instead of electricity. It is used to send massive amounts of information, far more data than possible over other transmission methods. *General Computer*

Fiber Puff - The roughening of the surface of paper that is due to fiber swelling. *Substrates*

Field - A specific area within a record where specific information is located. *General Computer*

Fiery Color Servers - Fiery Color Servers transform color copiers into high speed, high quality, fully networked Adobe PostScript color printers. Fiery's spooling, networking, and sophisticated production utilities provide fast, high quality color. See Electronics for Imaging, Inc. *Computer Hardware*

Figures - The numerical characters 1 through 0 and 9. All have the same width. *Typography*

File - An information block that has a specific name, and is stored on some form of magnetic medium in a computer system. *General Computer*

File Format - A standard specification for storing a certain type of data or file. *Desktop/Electronic Publishing - General Computer*

File Maker Pro 2.0 - Database software for Mac and Windows. See Claris Corporation. *Software*

File Protection - The method used in protecting magnetic media from being erased, either accidently or intentionally. *General Computer*

File Server - A device (usually another computer) that is part of a LAN, and is used to store and manage files. *Computer Hardware*

Filling In (or Up) - An unwanted condition when ink begins to fill in some of the type areas and some spaces that are between the dots in the halftone areas (black and white or color). *Printing Processes*

Film - The polyester material with an emulsion side that is used for the creation of photographs, negatives, positives, and print plates after they have been processed. *Graphic Arts Photography*

Film Assembly - See Stripping.

Film Emulsion - The light-sensitive side of the film. This side of the film is exposed to the light in the camera to create the image on the film. See Emulsion. *Graphic Arts Photography*

Film Negative - See Negative Film.

Film Positive - See Positive Film.

Film Recorder - See Imagesetter.

Film Speed - Refers to photographic film

sensitivity, the greater the sensitivity the greater the speed. *Graphic Arts Photography*

Film Terms - The unique film characteristics of each type of film, i.e., how color is reproduced. *Color Reproduction*

Filter - A colored screen used in a camera that modifies the amount of light and color tonality in a photograph. *Color Reproduction* A software technique that allows image modification by altering specific pixels in the image. *Software*

Final Film - The final film, after all work has been completed, that is ready for the creation of a proof for final approval by a client. *Proofing*

Finder - The Mac operating system interface, which is an information management tool, and GUI. See GUI. *Software*

Fine Etching - A process whereby the dots on metal plates are etched to enhance image tonality. Commonly used in gravure and photoengraving. *Image Carriers*

Fine-Grain - Prints that have a surface free from all types of impurities or irregularities in the tones. *Quality/Process Control*

Fine Lines - The areas in a photo that have the greatest detail and require very high line screens, 150 lines per inch and more, to achieve the best results. *Graphic Arts Photography - Scanning*

Fineness Of Grind - The degree to which a pigment has been dispersed in the ink. *Ink - Quality/Process Control*

Fine Print - A laser printer feature that

enhances the text resolution. *Laser Applications*

Finish - A substrate's surface texture, i.e., coated, glossy, etc. *Substrates*

Finishing - The final enhancements to a printed piece, i.e., die cutting, laminating, coating, punching, drilling, etc. *Finishing*

Finishing Service - A firm that performs finishing services for printers and other companies. See Finishing. *Finishing*

Firmware - Software that has been semi-permanently stored in ROM. See ROM. *Software*

First-Down Color - On a multi-color job, this refers to the first color printed. *Printing Processes*

Fit - The condition when all the register marks on each color of the film are lined up or are "in fit." *Color Reproduction - Image Assembly*

Fixer - A chemical that is used in the development of photographic film negatives. *Graphic Arts Photography*

Fixed Disk - See Hard Disk.

Fixed Pitch - A system where all the characters in all the available typefaces that are used have the identical width, i.e., a typewriter. *General Computer - Typography*

Fixing - The chemical process whereby a photograph becomes permanent and no longer sensitive to light. *Graphic Arts Photography*

Flash Exposure - An additional camera

exposure that enhances detail in the dot patterns of a halftone's shadow areas and lowers contrast. *Graphic Arts Photography*

Flash Point - The point where a substance will ignite. *Environment*

Flat - The assembled film that has been stripped in a carrier and made ready for press plate creation. *Image Assembly*   A photograph without contrast. *Graphic Arts Photography*

Flatbed Scanner - A particular type of scanner that scans images that are placed flat on the scanner glass or carrier, much like a copier operates. See Scanner. *Laser Applications - Scanning*

Flat Color - A color that is printed solid or as a tint without other colors printed over the color (or inks). *Ink*

Flat Etching - A chemical process whereby entire areas on a plate (composed of dots) can be treated and re-etched in order to reduce print image density. The dots are modified in the halftone areas. *Image Carriers*

Flat Proof - A special proof that is created during the make-ready process, in order to see the general look of the piece to be printed. Errors can be located at this point before the piece is printed. *Proofing*

Flat Tint - See Screen Tint.

Flexography - A printing process that uses a thin plastic, photopolymer or synthetic rubber plate, and a raised image on the plate to create the impression. *Printing Processes*

Flier - An unfolded single page (8 1/2" X

11") advertisement or announcement that is created by a graphic artist. *Marketing*

Floating Selection - An item that has been pasted onto a graphic or image. *Desktop/Electronic Publishing*

Flocking - The process whereby cloth fibers have been adhered to the surface of a substrate. *Substrates*

Flocculation - The condition where the ink pigments tend to clump together. *Ink*

Flopped - The reverse or mirror-image of an image, halftone, illustration, or page. *Desktop/Electronic Publishing - Image Assembly*

Flopping - The process whereby a photo, that looks reversed, must be flopped back to its correct position. *Graphic Arts Photography*

Floppy Disk - See Diskette.

Flow - An ink's ability to spread evenly over the plate surface during printing. *Ink*

Fluid Ink - Low viscosity ink. *Ink*

Fluorescent Ink - A very bright ink that has a glowing appearance. *Ink*

Flush Center - The typographic style that centers all text in a paragraph uniformly between the left and right margins. See Fig. 14. *Typography*

Now is the time for all to come home.
Come to the party, even if the
party is held too late at night.
You are not invited to be at home if at

Fig. 14 - Flush Center

114

Flush Cover - When the cover size and the size of the text pages are the same. *Finishing*

Flush Left - See Justified and examples on page 139. *Typography*

Flush Right - See Justified and examples on page 139. *Typography*

Flush Paragraph - A paragraph that has no indention in the initial sentence. *Typography*

Flying Ink - The ink that is thrown off by the rollers on an operating press. *Printing Processes*

Flying Paster - An automatic web press device that splices one roll of paper to another roll as the press is running. This prevents the stoppage of the press to remove the old used-up roll and to install the new full roll. *Printing Processes*

F Keys - See Function Keys.

FM Screening - Frequency Modulated Screeing. See Stochastic Screening. *Color Reproduction - Graphic Arts Photography - Scanning*

Fog - An unwanted silver deposit on a photograph or halftone that looks cloudy. *Graphic Arts Photography*

Foil - A very thin sheet of metal substrate, usually less than .006 of an inch thick. *Substrates*

Foil Blocking - An image on a raised brass surface that is heated and pressed against a roll or sheet of foil. The heat and pressure combine to attach the foil to the sheet of paper. The result is a 3-D

look and the colors can vary with the foil used. *Finishing*

Folder - A type of machine that folds paper, web stock, cardboard and other substrates. See Folding. *Finishing*

Folding - To reduce a large sheet of paper into a smaller size by closing, bending, and making folds in the sheet. *Finishing*

Folding Dummy - A mock-up of an actual folding job that will be used as a guide to completing the job correctly. *Finishing*

Folding Endurance - The number of times a sheet of paper can be folded before the paper will break on the fold. *Finishing*

Folding-To-Paper - Folding a job without consideration for the location and alignment of the printed image. *Finishing*

Folding-To-Print - Folding a job so all the printed images on each signature are properly aligned after folding. *Finishing*

Fold Marks - Indications where the substrate is to be creased. *Finishing*

Folio - Indicates a page number. *Desktop/Electronic Publishing*

Folio Lap - The extra paper over the trim size on a signature that is used to grab each signature during folding and gathering. *Finishing*

Font Family - See Type Family

Font - A complete set of alphabet characters with a specific unique design that include upper and lower case, the numerical figures, and punctuation marks. See Typeface. *Typography*

Font Chameleon - Font portability and type library technology for Mac and Windows. See Ares Software Corporation. *Software*

Font Change - See Change Font.

Font Fiddler - Font utility software for kerning, renaming PostScript and True Type fonts, and printing type specimen sheets under Windows. See Ares Software Corporation. *Software*

Font Hopper - Font conversion software for converting format-specific fonts between Mac and Windows. See Ares Software Corporation. *Software*

Font Metrics - This refers to the width of the characters in a font. *Typography*

Font Minder - PostScript and True Type font management and organization software for Windows. See Ares Software Corporation. *Software*

Font Monger - Font conversion, modification, and creation software for Mac and Windows. See Ares Software Corporation. *Software*

Font Substitution - The automatic substitution of a font if the one requested is not available. *Typesetting and Imagesetting - Typography*

Footer - The publication title or the chapter title, which can include the folio, that is located in the page's bottom section. *Desktop/Electronic Publishing*

Footprint - The desktop space required for a desktop computer. *General Computer* The arc of the earth that one satellite will cover. It typically takes three satellites to cover the entire surface of the earth. *Telecommunications*

Form - When printing with letterpress, this refers to the enclosure of all the type and other materials to be printed in a metal case. The materials are then in the proper form and ready for printing on a letterpress press. *Printing Processes*

Format - The overall arrangement of all the design elements (type, photos, illustrations, etc.) on a page. See Layout. *Art and Copy Preparation*

Formatting - The process of dividing a diskette or hard drive into the system required sectors and tracks. *General Computer*

Form Rollers - The press rollers that make plate contact directly. *Printing Processes*

Forms Printer - A printer that specializes in printing all types of business and computer forms. *Printing Processes*

For Position Only (FPO) - The placement of low-quality and/or low resolution illustrations or photos in the required location and size on the CRC to indicate to the printer where the actual images are to be placed on the final film or plate. "FPO" is normally indicated on the overlay tissue as a guide for the stripper during image assembly. See CRC, Overlay Tissue, and Final Film. *Art and Copy Preparation*

Forward - The initial remarks about a book that are located before the beginning of the main body of the text. *Desktop/Electronic Publishing*

Fountain - The mechanism on a press that provides ink to the rollers or fountain solution to the plate. *Printing Processes*

Fountain Rollers - Rollers that receive the ink from the fountain and move the ink onto the press rollers. Also, the rollers that distribute fountain solution from the dampening fountain to the plate. *Printing Processes*

Fountain Solution - The water and chemical solution that is applied during the lithographic printing process to allow the plate's non-image areas to avoid the acceptance of ink. *Printing Processes*

Four-Color Black/Sepia - The process of separating a black and white photo, and allowing particular colors to create a tinge on the photo. This allows subtle shades of color to produce various interesting effects other than black, gray, or white. *Color Reproduction*

Four-Color Process - This is the basic process for all four-color printing. An electronic scanner creates a color separation of a four-color photo and generates four pieces of film - cyan, magenta, yellow, and black. After plates are prepared and the job is printed this set of films will produce a close approximation of the original photo. Almost all possible colors can be reproduced by the use of these four colors -- magenta, cyan, yellow, and black. Black is added to give detail and extra density in the shadow areas. *Color Reproduction*

Fourdrinier Machine - A paper manufacturing machine that could be as long as 450 feet and makes paper at the rate of approximately 3,000 feet per minute. The paper begins as a stock solution made up of 99 percent water and comes off of the machine as finished paper. *Substrates*

FPO - See For Position Only.

FPS - Frames Per Second. *Digital Photography*

Fractal - An irregular image that has a pattern with a great deal of detail. *Desktop/Electronic Publishing*

Fractal Design Corporation - Developer of multi-platform graphic, paint, photo design, and image processing software for the Mac and Windows. Contact numbers: 335 Spreckels Drive, Ste. F, Aptos, CA 95003; (408)688-5300. *Software*

Fractal Design Painter - Simulates the tools and textures of natural media. The eye actually sees the striated surface of oil paint, the saturated bleed of felt markers, and the nubby richness of charcoal. Includes image retouching, color separations, tear-off tools, visual previews, snap-to and adjustable grid paper, and Type 1 and True Type font support. See Fractal Design Corporation. *Software*

Fractal Design PainterX2 - An expert extension to Fractal Design Painter. Any number of floating images may now be present and images can be moved, layered, scaled, distorted, and skewed. See Fractal Design Corporation. *Software*

Fractal Design Sketcher - For grayscale art and images. Bring natural media and imaging technology to grayscale graphics, by duplicating the expressive line of a soft lead pencil or the luminous glow of oil paints. See Fractal Design Corporation. *Software*

Fractal Terrain Modeler - StrataVision 3-D extension. See Strata, Inc. *Software*

Fragmentation - The process whereby a hard disk will become fragmented due to the creation and deletion of files over an extended time period. The computer operating system spreads portions of a file in different areas to make maximum use of available space. The constant deletion and rewriting of files over the deleted areas causes this fragmentation. The slowing down of disk access time is a typical symptom of this common problem. *General Computer*

Frame - A specific area where text and/or graphics can be placed on a page or document. *Art and Copy Preparation* A unit of data that is composed of two fields that are equal to a 30th of a second. *Digital Photography*

Frame Buffer - A section of memory where graphic images are stored. *Computer Hardware*

Frame Grabber - A device that digitizes a video image. *Computer Hardware - Digital Photography*

Frame/Grabber Board - A computer board that allows the capture of video images, acts as the image buffer and high speed memory, designed to store one or more images, and allows simultaneous video display and CPU access. *Computer Hardware - Digital Photography*

Freedom of Press Classic - PostScript language interpreter for Mac and Windows. Enables users to print PostScript files directly from their software applica-tions on a variety of popular low-cost color and black and white non-PostScript printers. Supports ATM, Type 1 and True Type fonts. See ColorAge, Inc. *Software*

Freedom of Press Pro - Sophisticated software PostScript language interpreter. Available for Mac and DOS, Freedom Pro supports more than 60 high quality non-PostScript devices, including film recorders and color printers. Supports ATM, Type 1 and True Type fonts. See ColorAge, Inc. *Software*

FreeHand - A drawing program that features page design and production tools for the creation of text and graphics. The program allows: a 56" X 56" pasteboard for creating multi-pages; flexible controls of text layout with columns, rows, automatic text wraps, and copyfitting; kerning, drag and drop tabs, hanging punctuation, and other typographic controls; option to export illustrations as either editable or read-only EPS files; and much more. For Mac and Power Mac. See Aldus Corporation. *Software*

Free-Hand Drawings - Drawings that have been created by an artist or illustrator without the use of any drawing aids, templates, or mechanical devices. *Art and Copy Preparation*

Free Lance - Anyone who is operating independently and is paid on a piecework basis. *Art and Copy Preparation*

Free Sheet - Paper that is free of all the fibers found in wood pulp. This quality paper is very durable and is recommended where long life is needed, i.e., catalogs. *Substrates*

Free Software - Public domain software.

Software that can be legally copied and is usually free of charge. *Software*

Freeze-Frame Television - The sending of still video images over narrowband channels, i.e., telephone. *Telecommunications*

French Fold - A fold that is used on four-page jobs and only one side of the sheet is printed. The unprinted side is folded inside. *Finishing*

French Stitch - A binding technique that produces a saddle-stitched magazine from a prestitiched signature. *Finishing*

Frequency - The number of cycles a wave completes in one second. The unit is hertz (Hz). Hertz is the technical term used to measure audio or radio frequencies. *Digital Photography - Telecommunications*

Frequency Domain - A bit-mapped picture that is represented by its various brightness levels. *Digital Photography*

Frequency Transform - The process of segmenting a bit-mapped picture into its basic frequency elements for filtering or analysis. *Digital Photography*

Friction Feed Printer - A typewriter-type printer. The upper and lower rubber rollers and platen move all documents through the printer. *Computer Hardware*

Frisket Paper - A special paper that is used to apply a coating to any area on a piece of artwork. This coating prevents the coated area from being disturbed in any way while working on other areas. This can be very useful for airbrushing. *Art and Copy Preparation*

Frontispiece - The introductory or first illustration in a book, usually next to the initial title page. *Desktop/Electronic Publishing*

Front-End - The computer that is responsible for the processing and manipulation of information before it is sent to another device for further processing or output. See Fig. 15. *Computer Hardware*

Fig. 15 - Typical Front-end

Front Matter - The introductory pages that are in the front of the book before the main body of the text. *Desktop/Electronic Publishing*

F Stops - The fixed settings on a camera which control the opening of the lens, thus controlling the degree of light exposure. *Digital Photography - Graphic Arts Photography*

Full Auto-Frame For the Mac - A professional trapping software for the Mac, which automatically creates traps between color areas on a page. Allows trapping PostScript files from any PostScript generating workstation or desktop application. See Scitex Corporation Ltd. *Software*

Full Bleed - A special printing effect that

:xtends the printed image area beyond he edges of a page. See Bleed. *Printing Processes*

Full-Motion - Video frames that move with enough speed to create motion to the human eye, i.e., 30 frames per second is typical. *Multimedia*

Full-Scale Black - Refers to a plate that will print black halftone dots in all parts of an image. *Color Reproduction*

Full-Service Agency - See Advertising Agency.

FULLtone - Scitex's version of stochastic screening. See Stochastic Screening. *Color Reproduction - Graphic Arts Photography - Scanning*

Function Keys - All keys on a keyboard that are labeled with an F followed by a number. Their use and functionality is determined by application software programs. *Computer Hardware*

Fuzz - Fibers that are on a paper's surface. *Substrates*

Gain - A measurement of signal amplification. *Digital Photography - Telecommunications*

Galley - The initial proof of typeset material that is suitable for proofreading and can often be cut and pasted and used as CRC. *Art and Copy Preparation*

Galley Proof - See Galley.

Gamma - A way of measuring contrast (the difference between the highlight and the shadow areas) in a photograph. *Graphic Arts Photography - Scanning*

Gamma Correction - The process of adjusting the gamma with the Gamma Curve Editor. See Gamma Curve Editor. *Color Reproduction*

Gamma Curve Editor - A software feature that allows one to make gamma adjustments. See Gamma Correction. *Color Reproduction*

Gang - The printed sheet that is part of the gang run. See Gang Run. *Printing Processes*

Ganged Separation - A selection of full-color photographs of the same size or percentage of reduction or enlargement that are produced as one color separation. This greatly reduces the unit cost. *Color Reproduction - Graphic Arts Photography - Scanning*

Gang Run - The running of multiple printing jobs on the press at the same time, however, each job must have a lot of similarities, i.e., same size, acceptable colors, etc. This technique can cut the cost of each job dramatically. A job that is run in this manner is typically called a "ganged" job. *Printing Processes*

Gatefold - A multiple page fold where the inside page on the finished folded product opens on the center of one side. *Finishing*

Gateway - A link or communications device that allows information on one network to be sent to another dissimilar network. The information is converted in the gateway to a form compatible with the receiving network and its protocols. *Computer Hardware*

GATF (Graphic Arts Technical Foundation) - A graphic arts education, consulting, and research organization. Contact numbers: 4615 Forbes Avenue; Pittsburgh, PA 15213; (412) 621-6941.

Gathering - The collection (automatically or manually) of all the signatures that are a part of a job into their correct sequence in order to bind the job into a finished product. All jobs with multiple signatures and separate covers are created by this often highly automated process. See Binding, Signatures, and Bindery. *Finishing*

Gauge Pins - Guides that are used to hold the substrate (paper, etc.) in the required position to create a correct impression. *Printing Processes*

GCA/GATF Proof Comparator - Off-press proofing system. *Proofing - Quality/Process Control*

GCA "T" Ref - A reference that is used to calibrate densitometers. *Quality/ Process Control*

GCR - See Gray Component Replacement.

Gear Streaks - Streaks that appear across the page of a printed piece that coordinate exactly with the gear intervals of the press. *Printing Processes*

GEM (Graphics Environment Manager) - A form of GUI or Graphic User Interface. See GUI. *Software*

General Parametrics Corporation - A manufacturer of multimedia products for business presentations. Offers a line of easy-to-use, high performance presentation hardware and/or software products. For PC and Mac. Contact numbers: 1250 Ninth St., Berkeley, CA 94710; (510)524-3950. *Multimedia*

Generation - Starting from an original, each successive time something is reproduced, i.e., the copy of a copy, the copy quality is reduced. After multiple generations, copy quality is often greatly reduced. *Art and Copy Preparation*

Genlock - A technique that is used to synchronize computer and video signals. *Multimedia*

Geostationary Satellite - A satellite that takes 24 hours to circle earth, thus it appears to be stationary from the earth. See Geosynchronous Orbit. *Telecommunications*

Geosynchronous Orbit - The orbit followed by geostationary satellites. It is 23,300 miles above the earth's surface.

See Geostationary Satellite. *Telecommunications*

Ghost Image - An on-press unwanted image. It can appear in heavily inked areas. *Printing Processes*

Ghosting - The method by which one duplicates an image with less dots. Depending upon the percentage of dots that are reduced, this creates a ghostly or special effect. *Graphic Arts Photography* Ghosting on press is due to uneven ink distribution on rollers from press sheet to press sheet or due to placement of a small image in front of a large image on the same plate. *Printing Processes*

Gigabyte (GB) - Means one billion bytes or characters. *General Computer*

GIGO (Garbage In, Garbage Out) - It means if you input incorrect data you'll get incorrect results. *General Computer*

Glassine - A type of translucent paper. *Substrates*

Glitch - A minor problem in hardware or software. *General Computer*

Gloss - A substrate's ability to reflect all light, however, only at certain angles. *Substrates*

Glossary - Definitions of terms that relate to the material in a publication. It is often included in the back of the book, report, or document. *Desktop/Electronic Publishing*

Gloss Measurement - See Gloss Meter.

Gloss Meter - A device that measures gloss. *Quality/Process Control*

Glossy - Paper that has been manufactured with a smooth surface. *Substrates* A shiny surfaced photograph that is commonly called reflective art. *Graphic Arts Photography*

Glue Lap - The area on a package where glue is applied for fastening a folded carton together. *Finishing*

Glue Line - The area where glue is applied. *Finishing*

Gluing-Off - The process of gluing a book to its hardbound cover. *Finishing*

Goldenrod Paper - A special orange (or sometimes yellowish) masking paper that is used as a carrier sheet when assembling film (stripping) for printing. This approach is not used on the highest quality and most precision type of work because it fails to provide the best level of support for the film. See Stripping. *Image Assembly*

Gouache - An opaque watercolor paint that can be used in color drawings where good opacity is needed. *Art and Copy Preparation*

Grain - The direction most of the fibers run in a paper sheet and the same direction of the paper during manufacture. The grain of a paper will often determine the direction that paper should be fed through a press. *Substrates*

Grain Direction, Across - Printing the opposite of the direction of the grain of the substrate. *Printing Processes*

Grain Direction, Against - Folding along the paper's fibers at a right angle to the grain of the substrate. *Finishing*

Graininess - Emulsion particles that are visual on a print or transparency. *Graphic Arts Photography*

Graining - The traditional process of treating plates with an abrasive that will make the treated areas more porous and more likely to retain water. These areas will reject ink and not accept an image. *Image Carriers*

Grammage - A metric term to express the weight of paper in units of a square meter of paper in grams. *Substrates*

Graphical User Interface (GUI) - An on-screen method of controlling computer operation, by pointing to icons, pictures, or menus with the use of a mouse. *Computer Hardware - Software*

Graphic Arts Camera - A camera that is used for the exposure of black and white type and illustrations onto photographic paper or film. Plus it is used to create black and white halftones with a halftone screen, which converts a photograph into dots. *Graphic Arts Photography*

Graphic Arts Camera Operator - The person who operates the graphic arts camera (process camera) and is highly skilled in the transfer of images to photographic paper and film. The camera operator is usually knowledgeable in the creation of halftones (black and white), duotones, and other special effects. *Graphic Arts Photography*

Graphic Arts Magnifier - A small, hand-held lens that is used to magnify printed images. *Quality/Process Control*

Graphic Communication - The presentation of ideas, feelings, and concepts through visual information, i.e., illustrations, words, photos, etc. *Art and Copy Preparation*

Graphic Designers - Those individuals who determine the placement of all the graphic elements on CRC and who are responsible for the overall look or design of artwork and graphic images. *Art and Copy Preparation*

Graphic Enterprises of Ohio, Inc. Developed the G.U.S.S. publishing output management server and several 18" X 24" laser printers and copiers. Contact numbers: 439 Market Ave; North Canton, OH 44702; (800)321-9874. *Software*

Graphics - Pictures and illustrations that have been created by the hand of a graphic artist. *Art and Copy Preparation*

Graphics (Computer) - Pictures and illustrations that are created on a computer system with sophisticated drawing and graphics software packages, i.e., Illustrator, Freehand, Corel Draw, etc. *Software*

Graphics Card - A computer video board that allows the monitor to display graphics and illustrations. *Computer Hardware*

Graticule - A ruler with such minute increments, that it must be magnified to be viewed with the naked eye. *Quality/Process Control*

Gravure Printing - A unique printing process where the image to be printed is actually sunken or etched into very small and microscopic ink wells that hold the ink for transfer to the paper during printing. Also known as Intaglio. *Printing Processes*

Gray Balance - The different percentage of overlapping cyan, magenta, and yellow colors that are needed to achieve a gray balance. In theory, the overlapping of these three colors will produce black and the overlapping of 50 percent tints of these three colors will produce gray. In practice, gray balance can be more closely achieved by varying the size of the halftone dots for each color, along with color overlapping. *Color Reproduction*

Gray Component Replacement (GCR) A more sophisticated version of Under Color Removal that uses the most modern scanners and digitizing techniques available. This process replaces with black ink those areas where the three colors - magenta, cyan, and yellow - overlap in equal amounts. Because black ink is cheaper and easier to run on press, this technique has reduced the cost of color printing. See Under Color Removal (UCR). *Color Reproduction*

Gray Content - The amount of gray in a process color ink that causes the color to deviate from its saturated hue. *Color Reproduction*

Gray Map Editor - A method of software control over gray levels and shades. *Software*

Gray Level - Each pixel's brightness level. See Brightness Level. *Color Reproduction*

Gray Scale - A scale that shows the full range of gray tones between pure white and solid black. Most computer software used today recognizes 256 levels of gray. The human eye can only see 80 to 100 levels of gray. *Digital Photography - Graphic Arts Photography - Scanning*

Gray Scale Strip - The gray scale strip that is printed along a four-color printed piece that is used to check contrast and tonal range. *Color Reproduction - Digital Photography*

Gray Scale Value - A scale of 0 through 256. Each number indicates the degree of brightness of a single pixel. *Graphic Arts Photography - Scanning*

Greeking - The use of unreadable and meaningless text to create the illusion of text in a specific area. It is most commonly used when creating a rough draft of artwork or a design to show the amount of space to be occupied by the text. *Art and Copy Preparation - General Computer*

Gripper - The metal clamps that hold the substrate in place as it moves through the press. *Printing Processes*

Gripper Edge - The non-image, unprintable paper edge that passes through the press first. This edge, which can be as wide as 3/8 of an inch, is held in place by mechanisms called grippers and is responsible for holding the paper in the press. See Gripper and Gripper Margin. *Printing Processes*

Gripper Margin - The unprintable area on the leading edge of the paper where the grippers hold the paper. See Gripper and Gripper Edge. *Printing Processes*

Groundwood Papers - A lower grade paper that is manufactured from groundwood pulp and is often used for newsprint. *Substrates*

Groundwood Pulp - The wood pulp used to manufacture the lowest grade, and the lowest cost paper. Newspaper and other disposable paper products are created from this type paper. *Substrates*

GTA/Gravure Ink Standard Color Charts - Color proofing references that are used in gravure printing. *Color Reproduction - Quality/Process Control*

GUI - See Graphical User Interface.

Guillotine - The most common large and powerful paper cutter that is used for cutting varying size stacks of paper. The blade requires regular attention in order to be sharp enough to cleanly cut the paper. *Finishing*

Gum Arabic - A material that is applied to non-image lithographic plate areas that make the areas accept water and repel ink. This material is manufactured from the acacia tree. *Printing Processes*

Gummed Holland - Gummed cloth tape which is moistened and is used to cover the stitched spine on a soft paper cover. *Finishing*

Gumming - The application of gum arabic to a non-image area in order to prevent a given area from accepting ink. See Gum Arabic. *Image Carriers*

G. U. S. S. (Graphic Universal Sub System) - A publishing server that is running on Windows NT Advanced Server. This advanced system offers an intelligent publishing oriented print spooler, an OPI server, and a software RIP multiplexer. See Graphic Enterprises of Ohio, Inc. *Software*

Gutter - The white space that is between the edge of the binding and the first printed area. It can also refer to the white space that is between the graphics and photos on a page and the binding. *Art and Copy Preparation - Desktop/Electronic Publishing*

Gutter Margin - See Gutter.

Hairline Register - The alignment or registration of all film in multi-color printing within a ± 1/2 row of dots. *Color Reproduction - Image Assembly*

Hairline - The thinnest line a font or typesetting system can produce. *Typesetting and Imagesetting*

Halation - A halo-like blurry effect on a photograph or developed film in the highlights. *Graphic Arts Photography*

Halftone - A continuous tone photograph that has been screened into patterns of very small dots of different sizes and shapes onto film or photo-sensitive paper. *Graphic Arts Photography - Scanning*

Halftone Cell - A special cell that was developed for computer created halftones. Each cell contains dots of varying sizes and amounts to give the illusion of shades of gray. *Graphic Arts Photography*

Halftone Reproduction - In order to duplicate the many shades of gray in a photograph, the picture is broken up into many dots. Dark areas have larger dots and lighter areas have the smaller dots. These different sized dots give the illusion of gray when it is printed. *Graphic Arts Photography*

Halftone Screen - The screen that is used to convert a continuous tone photograph into halftone dot patterns suitable for printing. *Graphic Arts Photography*

Halftone Tint - A specific area where all the dots are the same size. This creates an even color (or look). *Color Reproduction*

Halo - A halo-like ridge that occurs around an image or letter. *Graphic Arts Photography - Printing Processes*

Hand Correction - The manual reduction of dot sizes to alter color reproduction. *Color Reproduction - Quality/Process Control*

Hand-Cut Film Screening - A type of screen printing that is used when sharp, clean lines and precise detail is needed. See Screen Printing. *Printing Processes*

Hand Lettering - The creation of dense and professional looking characters by hand. They are usually created extra large and reduced to the desired size in order to appear extra sharp. *Art and Copy Preparation*

Hand Scanner - A particular type of small scanner, where the user is required to move the unit manually over the information that is being scanned. See Scanner. *Scanning*

Handshaking - The successful exchange of information or signals between two devices or programs. *General Computer*

Hand Tooling - Handwork on a plate to enhance the detail, contrast, and quality. *Image Carriers*

Hard Copy - Electronic information that has been output from a computer onto paper, plate, film, or other visual media via a printer or an imagesetter. *General Computer*

Hardcover - See Casebound.

Hard Disk - A magnetic storage device. *Computer Hardware*

Hard Dot - A dot that has sharp, smooth edges. See Soft Dot. *Graphic Arts Photography*

Hard Proof - A proof that is produced on paper or other visual media. *Proofing*

Hardness Tester - See Durometer.

Hardware - The actual physical parts of the computer and its peripherals, including the operating manuals. *Computer Hardware*

Harlequin Precision Screening (HPS) Harlequin's version of irrational color screening technology. *Color Reproduction*

Harvard Graphics 2.0 For Windows Presentation graphics software to create more effective presentations and reports. Features: interactive on-line tutorial; thumbnail previews; and an innovative workgroup oriented capabilities. (Harvard Graphics has no connection with Harvard University.) A product of Software Publishing Corporation. *Software*

Hazardous and Toxic Wastes - All materials listed by the EPA that are corrosive, ignitable, reactive, and or toxic. See EPA *Environment*

Haze - A milky appearance on transparent film. *Graphic Arts Photography - Substrates*

HDTV- See High Definition Television.

Head - The mechanism in a hard drive that reads and writes the data. *Computer Hardware* The top of a page. *Finishing*

Headband - The reinforcing material (usually cloth) on both ends of a casebound book. *Finishing*

Head Gap - The effective distance between the poles of a magnetic recording head. The width has a direct bearing on the range of frequencies that can be recorded. *Digital Photography*

Headline - The extra large opening statement used by graphic artists in an ad. For maximum effectiveness it should be designed to grab the reader's attention. *Marketing*

Head Margin - All white space that is at the top of each page above the text or image elements. *Art and Copy Preparation - Desktop/Electronic Publishing*

Head-To-Head Imposition - The assembly of a job so the top of each page butt up against each other. See Fig. 16 on page 129. *Finishing - Image Assembly*

Head-To-Tail Imposition - The assembly of a job so the top of the page and the bottom of the back page butt against each other. See Fig. 17 on page 129. *Finishing - Image Assembly*

Head Trim - Paper that is removed (or cut-off) from the top of a page. *Finishing*

Heat Sealing - The process of joining multiple surfaces together by heat and pressure. *Finishing*

Helium-Neon Laser - A specific type of laser that is used on the highest quality capstan and drum imagesetters. *Laser Applications*

Help - On-screen answers to the correct operation of the keyboard functions and most of the less complex software functions. *Software*

He/Ne - An abbreviation for helium-neon laser. See Helium-Neon Laser. *Laser Applications*

Hercules - A monochrome video board for the PC. See VGA, CGA, and EGA. *Computer Hardware*

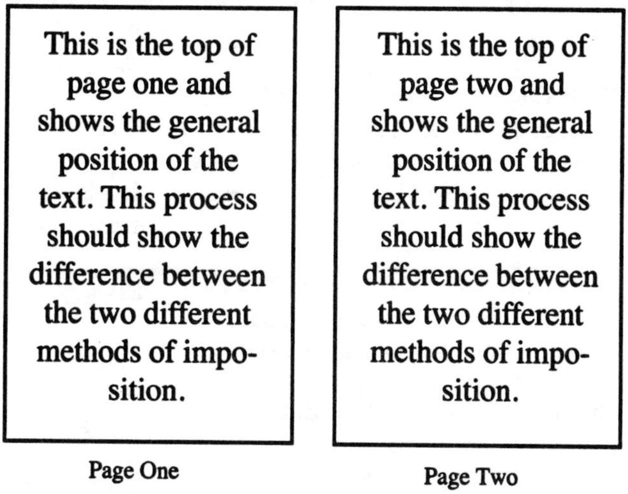

Hertz (HZ) - The unit of frequency equal to one cycle per second. One kilohertz (KHz) equals 1,000 cps; one megahertz (MHz) equals 1,000,000 cps. *Digital Photography - Telecommunications*

Hewlett-Packard Graphics Language (HPGL) - A Hewlett-Packard language for the storage of graphic images. *Desktop/Electronic Publishing*

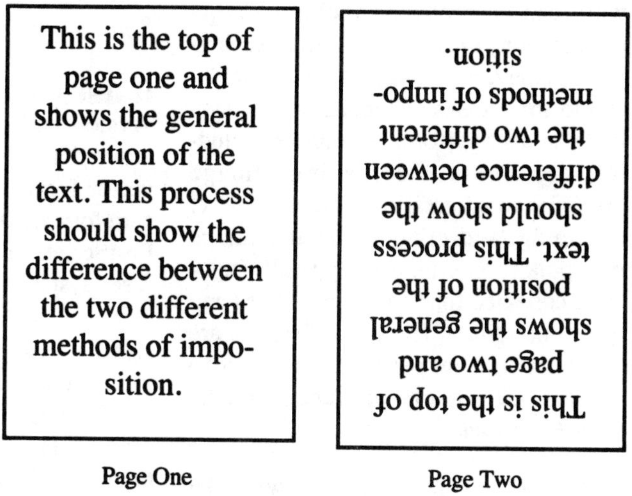

Hickey - A blemish on a printed piece that has occurred while printing. *Printing Processes*

High Band Recording Format - A new

This is the top of page one and shows the general position of the text. This process should show the difference between the two different methods of imposition.

Page One

This is the top of page two and shows the general position of the text. This process should show the difference between the two different methods of imposition.

Page Two

Fig. 16 - Head to Head Imposition

This is the top of page one and shows the general position of the text. This process should show the difference between the two different methods of imposition.

Page One

Page Two

Fig. 17 - Head to Tail Imposition

standard recording format for still video which allows greater horizontal resolution. New recording heads and processing circuits are used to improve the

129

luminance frequency response. *Digital Photography*

High Contrast - The reproduction of a photograph which has greater contrast between the lightest and the darkest areas than in the original. See Gamma. *Graphic Arts Photography*

High-Definition Television (HDTV) - A very high resolution TV standard for video systems. *Telecommunications*

High-Density - A disk or diskette that can store more information than a standard or double-density one. *Computer Hardware*

High-End System - Typically refers to an integrated color electronic prepress system (CEPS) on which all prepress work can be produced including copy preparation, typesetting, graphics arts photography, scanning, image assembly, and in some cases platemaking. The system can also perform operations including electronic airbrushing, image distortions and rotations, cloning, pixel swapping, and other color and image manipulations. Output is typically fully color corrected four-color separations and sometimes plates. High-End Systems are typically very expensive and used to accommodate heavy production loads. *Color Reproduction*

High Fidelity Color - Also known as Hi Fi color. A technique for creating precise color by using more than the traditional four plates (usually 6 or more) and stochastic or FM screening. See Stochastic Screening and FM Screening *Color Reproduction*

High Frequency Image - An image (picture) with excess complex detail or an excess of different brightness level changes. See Brightness Levels. *Digital Photography*

High Key Transparency - A light, overexposed transparency with highlight details. *Art and Copy Preparation - Graphic Arts Photography*

Highlight - That portion of a photograph that is the lightest. In a halftone, these highlight areas have the tiniest dots or no dots at all in some areas. *Graphic Arts Photography*

Highlight Dots - The very smallest halftone dots. *Graphic Arts Photography*

High Quality Screening (HQS) - Linotype-Hell's version of Supercell Screening. See Supercell Screening. *Color Reproduction*

HiJaak For DOS 2.1 - A graphics conversion and capture tool that converts more than 60 formats. Support for 16 vector formats, 24 raster formats, 24 fax card formats, and all supported formats to PostScript. For DOS and Windows. See Inset Systems. *Software*

HiJaak Pro - Conversion technology for virtually any image: vector; raster; and fax formats. Captures Windows or DOS screens. Has image processing to adjust tonal ranges, and perform color remapping and color reduction. Supports OLE, JPEG, PhotoCD, TWAIN, cross-platform conversion to Mac, SUN, and Amiga. See Inset Systems. *Software*

HiJaak PS 2.1 - All the conversion and capture technology of HiJaak 2.1 plus the ability to convert PostScript language print-to-disk files into any of the supported raster and fax card formats. See Inset Systems. *Software*

Hinting - A series of software techniques that improve type quality on low resolution laser printers. *Laser Applications*

Histogram - A special graph that illustrates the amount of gray level and color level pixels that are in a specific image. *Desktop/Electronic Publishing*

Holdout - Ink that has dried on the paper's surface and has not penetrated the fibers of the substrate. This is determined by the paper's absorption characteristics. Coated or glossy paper exhibit the most holdout. *Ink - Substrates*

Holograms - Images that create a 3-D look on a 2-D plane with the aid of special lighting conditions. *Laser Applications - Multimedia*

Horizontal Process Camera - A graphic arts camera that was designed to operate in a horizontal position. See Graphic Arts Camera. *Graphic Arts Photography*

Horizontal Resolution - A measure of the finest detail that can be viewed on the screen. Horizontal Resolution is determined by photographing a test chart and visually checking how many vertical lines can be distinguished on the screen. *Digital Photography* The amount of pixels in each horizontal scan line. *Scanning*

Hot Composition - See Hot Type.

Hot Type - Metal type made from hot molten metal and formed in a special machine and output as a line of type. The original hot type machine was called the Linotype. The name was derived from the result "a line of type." *Typesetting and Imagesetting*

HPGL - See Hewlett-Packard Graphics Language.

Hue - That quality of a color that allows it to be classified as the actual color, i.e., its redness, its greenness, its blueness, etc., without regard to saturation or brightness. *Color Reproduction*

Hue Error - The amount a process color deviates from perfect hue. *Color Reproduction*

Hydrophilic - The characteristic of a substrate to attract or absorb water. *Printing Processes*

Hydrophobic - The characteristic of a substrate to reject or repel water. *Printing Processes*

Hygrometer - A device that measures the relative humidity. *Environment - Quality/Process Control*

Hygroscopic - A material's tendency to absorb or pick-up moisture. *Substrates*

Hysteresis - The inability of a wet substrate, once it is dry, to return to its original size and shape. *Substrates*

Hypercard - A data and information management program designed for the Mac. *Software*

Hypertext - An electronic database where documents and information can be quickly linked to each other. *Desktop/Electronic Publishing - Software*

Hyphenation - Where the word is divided with a hyphen and the last part of the divided word is advanced to the next line. The words are divided at the syllable level automatically by the type-setting/word processing program. *Desk-top/Electronic Publishing*

Hyphenation Program - A computer program that is part of most word pro-cessing and publishing software. It auto-matically hyphenates multiple syllable words that must be broken at the end of a line due to a lack of room on that line. *Software*

IC - See Integrated Circuit.

Icon - Software related on-screen pictures that allow the user to initiate functions or control operations. A mouse is usually used to control the icon. *Software*

IGES - See Initial Graphics Exchange Specification.

Illustration - A drawing and/or design that have been hand created by a graphic artist. See Art and Artwork *Art and Copy Preparation*

Illustration Program - See Draw Program and Object-Oriented Program.

Illustrator - The person (usually referred to as a graphic artist) who creates illustrations. See Illustration, Art, and Artwork. *Art and Copy Preparation*

Illustrator - A powerful illustration and page-design tool that combines precise illustration and single-page design capabilities in one package. It allows creating, manipulating and refining artwork, drawing from scratch, autotracing scanned images, or entering precise object dimensions. It allows editing in preview mode; adding and selecting points on curves, lines, and objects; snapping to any point; placing text along any path; and works with text blocks of any shape. Generates separations automatically. For Mac, Windows, DEC, Silicon Graphics, and NeXT. See Adobe Systems, Inc. *Software*

Image 040-Quadra and Centris Imaging Accelerator (Mac Centris 610/650/660AV and Quadra 700/800/900/950) -

Turns fast Macs into faster Mac imaging workstations. Features a 40 MHz 68040 CPU, a 128K Static RAM secondary cache, and twin DSP's for imaging acceleration. See DayStar Digital. *Computer Hardware*

Image Area - The area on a page that is printed. *Printing Processes*

Image Assembly - See Stripping.

Image Carrier - The plate, screen, or cylinder that is responsible for placing the image on the substrate. *Image Carriers - Printing Processes*

Image Operation - The conversion to bit-mapped or image data. *Digital Photography*

Imager - A light-sensitive mechanism, i.e., photomultipliers used in high-end scanners. *Scanning*

Image Regeneration - The creation of a quality reproduction of an image. *Image Assembly - Printing Processes*

Imagesetter - A sophisticated laser device that is capable of creating high-resolution text and graphics on film, paper, and on plates. *Laser Applications - Typesetting and Imagesetting*

Imaging Accelerators (Mac II, IIx, IIcx, IIvi, IIsi (NuBus), IIci, IIvx, IIfx, Performa 600, all Quadras, Centris 610 NuBus/650, DuoDock) - Accelerates all applications up to 300 percent and Adobe Photoshop and other imaging applications up to 500 percent. See DayStar Digital. *Computer Hardware*

IMG - A file format used on bit-mapped images in GEM programs. *Desktop/Electronic Publishing*

Impactless Printing - See Non-Impact Printing.

Impedance - A measure of the resistance to AC current flow in a circuit. Impedance is expressed in ohms. *Digital Photography*

Imposition - The correct layout or placement of each page of a multi-page job, so that every page is positioned in the exact location needed to correctly print and fold the job to achieve the correct pagination or paging sequence. *Image Assembly - Printing Processes*

Imposition Layout - The guide that is used to indicate the correct folding sequence of each signature, how the signatures are to be arranged, and indications for all needed cuts and scores. *Finishing - Image Assembly*

Impression - The pressure that occurs when the plate (or type in letterpress) touches the paper (or other substrate) and creates the printed image. *Printing Processes*

Impression Counter - The meter that indicates the number of impressions that have been created during any interval. *Printing Processes*

Impression Cylinder - A cylindrical press device that causes the impression to occur during printing. See Impression. *Printing Processes*

Impressions Per Hour (IPH) - A term that indicates press speed. *Printing Processes*

Imprinting - The process of affixing or stamping information or symbols onto different forms of substrates. *Finishing*

Impulse Jet - Ink-jet printing in which pressure on the ink reservoir is not maintained continuously. Appropriate pressure is applied when a droplet is needed to form part of a character or image. *Printing Processes*

Indent - The placement of copy or graphics to the right or to the left of the margin. See Fig. 19 on page 135. *Typography*

Index - The alphabetical listing of all the key words in a book with the appropriate page numbers of where further information on each word is located in the text. *Desktop/Electronic Publishing*

Indexing - The printing of index tabs that protrude from a book or binder to indicate subdivisions of the total piece. *Printing Processes - Substrates*

Inferiors - Characters that are dramatically smaller than the point size of the characters next to them. They sit below the adjacent character. See Fig. 18. *Typography*

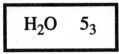

Fig. 18 - Inferiors

Information Superhighway - A telecommunication and networking concept for government, business, education, and all other public and private institutions to send and receive information electronically. The concept was designed for expediting and simplifying the flow of information. *Multimedia - Telecommunications*

```
┌─────────────────────────────────────────────────────┐
│                Commonly Used Indents                  │
│   Hanging Indent              First Line Indent       │
│                                                        │
│   This is this an example of a      This is a example of the most │
│   very unique type of indentation   common type of indentation that │
│   that can be used in magazines and can be used in any type of publi- │
│   newsletters.                      caiton.           │
│                                                        │
│           Left/Right Indent - Flush Center            │
│                                                        │
│   This is the first paragraph that will have the      │
│   standard indentation.                               │
│                                                        │
│   This next paragraph is indented with                │
│   the Left/Right Indent to create a spe-              │
│   cial emphasis.                                      │
│                                                        │
│   The next paragraph returns to the style of the      │
│   previous paragraph.                                 │
└─────────────────────────────────────────────────────┘
```

Fig. 19 - Commonly used indentations.

Information Time Value - The length of time that information remains useful. *General Computer*

Infrared Laser - A specific type of laser that is used in all varieties of imagesetters. *Laser Applications*

Inheritance - An aspect of object-oriented software that allows one object (i.e., a subheading) to inherit its attributes (i.e., typeface, point size, etc.) from another object (i.e., a header). *Desktop/Electronic Publishing*

Initial Graphics Exchange Specifications (IGES) - A standardized graphics file format. *Desktop/Electronic Publishing - Standards*

Initial Cap - A style that sets the first letter in the beginning sentence of a paragraph in an extra large, bold mode. See Fig. 20. *Typography*

```
┌─────────────────────────────────────┐
│  Any old time is a good              │
│  time for all parties concerned.     │
└─────────────────────────────────────┘
```

Fig. 20 - Initial Cap

Initialize - The process of formatting a diskette or hard drive. See Formatting. *General Computer*

Ink Channel - Areas within the printed section, but outside the crop marks of the main image where on-press ink adjustments can be made. *Printing Processes - Quality/Process Control*

Ink Film Thickness - The exact thickness of the ink used on press. *Ink - Quality/Process Control*

Ink Film Thickness Gauge - A device that is used on the press that will show the exact ink film thickness. *Ink - Quality/Process Control*

Ink Fineness of Grind Gauge - A device that is used for the measurement of the size of pigment particles in the ink. *Ink - Quality/Process Control*

Ink Flying - See Ink Mist.

Ink Fountain - A press storage device that provides the ink for the rollers, which transport the ink to the plate to create the printed impression. *Ink*

Ink Gloss - The gloss or shine that is reflected at specific angles by the ink itself. *Ink - Quality/Process Control*

Ink-Jet Printer - A printer that places characters on paper by minute dots of ink. *Computer Hardware - Printing Processes*

Ink-Jet Printing - The process of printing with an ink-jet printer. See Ink-Jet Printer. *General Computer*

Ink Mist - The mist of minute ink particles that are created while printing. This mist tends to collect on the press and on all materials surrounding the press. *Ink*

Inkometer - A device that measures ink tackiness. Ink that is too sticky or tacky can harm the paper and cause poor printing. *Ink - Quality/Process Control*

Ink Opacity - An ink's ability to cover another ink and prevent any showthrough. *Ink - Quality/Process Control*

Ink Sequence - See Color Sequence.

Ink Splitting - The ink rupturing as it leaves the nip on press. *Printing Processes*

Ink Trapping - A condition that occurs when inks in multi-color printing do not adhere to each other and the result is color distortion and related problems. *Ink*

In-Line Finishing - Binding and finishing operations that are integrated with printing presses and take place as a continuous operation when the substrate leaves the printing press. Such operations include trimming, slitting, and all other finishing operations. *Finishing*

In-Line Position - Images that print in the same direction as the paper moves in the press. *Printing Processes*

In-Plant Printer - A company that owns and operates its own printing presses and only prints jobs for internal use. *Printing Processes*

In-Point - The section of a multimedia project where the editing process begins. *Multimedia*

Input - The entering of data into a computer. *General Computer*

Insert - An extra page or printed piece that is included or inserted in another publication during the finishing process, i.e., an order form or special flyer in a catalog. *Desktop/Electronic Publishing - Finishing*

Insertion Point - The on-screen (Mac or

PC) line or blinking object that marks the beginning location for the entry of text. See Cursor. *Software*

Inset Systems - A software developer dedicated to a broad range of inter-applications graphic solutions, and a major company in graphics file conversion technology. Contact numbers: 71 Commerce Drive, Brookfield, CT 06804; (203)740-2400. *Software*

Intaglio Printing - See Gravure Printing.

Integrated Circuit (IC) - A silicon chip that houses many resistors and transistors (from as few as 60 to over 100,000 or more per chip). *Computer Hardware*

Integrated Color Removal - A less popular term that is synonymous with Gray Component Replacement. See Gray Component Replacement. *Color Reproduction*

Integrated Services Digital Network (ISDN) - The standards that have been established for communicating audio and digital data over international telephone networks. *Standards - Telecommunications*

Integrated System - A computerized system combining two or more operations that typically would be performed separately. For example, copy preparation, typesetting, and image assembly would be combined into one operation. See Desktop Publishing and High-End System. *Desktop/Electronic Publishing - General Computer*

Integrated Technology - A technology that integrates a fax, printer, copier, and a scanner in one unit. *Laser Applications - Telecommunications*

Intel - The company that creates and manufactures the 286, 386, 486, and Pentium chips for the PC. *Computer Hardware*

INTELSAT (International Satellite Telecommunications Organization) An international consortium that provides global satellite communications services and participates in recommendations regarding the placement of communication satellites in orbit. Contact numbers: 3400 International Drive, N.W., Washington, D.C. 20008; (202)944-6800. *Telecommunications*

Intensity - See Chroma.

Interactive - Software that can react immediately to user commands or choices. *Software*

Interactive Media - Media applications that allow the user to interact with the information presented, i.e., video games. *Multimedia*

Interactive Multimedia - See Interactive Media.

Interactive System - A computer system that reacts immediately to data that is entered into the system and produces results from that data. *General Computer*

Interlace - A video technique where old fields (lines) are immediately followed by even fields (lines) in order to reduce display flickering. *Digital Photography*

Interlaced Scanning - The scanning system used in most TV systems where one field containing one half of the lines for a complete frame is scanned and then the next field is interlaced between the first field to form the complete frame. This system lowers flicker in the TV picture. The scanning rate is 60 fields (30 frames) per second. See Frame/Field Recording and Interlace. *Digital Photography*

Interleaving - The rerouting of the various amounts of data within the different files on the CD-ROM disc while it is playing. *Multimedia*

Internal Font - A font that is stored permanently in the printer ROM chips. *Typography*

Internal Storage - The primary storage or central memory in the computer's CPU. *Computer Hardware*

Interpolation - The estimation of intermediate values, resolutions, and dot patterns between known values, resolutions, and dot patterns. *Desktop/Electronic Publishing*

Interpolated Scanner Resolution - Software that is included with most scanners that can actually create additional pixels when they are needed to increase the visible and reproducible resolution. *Scanning*

Interpress - Xerox's page description language. See Page Description Language. *Desktop/Electronic Publishing*

Interpreter - A software program or hardware unit that converts the PDL into codes understandable by the output printer or proofer. See PDL. *Desktop/Electronic Publishing - Proofing - Typesetting and Imagesetting*

Interpretor Software - Software that interprets the computer language of one system so it can be used or understood by another system, i.e., a page description software that allows a computer's software to be compatible with an imagesetter's or laser printer's software. *Software*

Inter-Satellite Links - A system that allows satellites to be able to communicate directly with each other. *Telecommunications*

I/O - Input/Output. *General Computer*

IR - See Infrared Laser.

Iris - That portion of a lens that expands or contracts to allow light to pass through to the film. *Graphic Arts Photography* An ink-jet color proofing system. *Proofing*

Irrational Tangent Screening (IT) - A powerful color separation or screening method that was used on the expensive high-end color systems. *Color Reproduction*

ISDN - See Integrated Services Digital Network.

Italic - Type or characters that slant to the right. They are used when a greater emphasis is needed to be placed on certain words, phrases, quotations, and titles. See Fig. 21. *Typography*

Fig. 21 - Italic Type

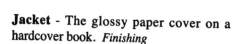

Jacket - The glossy paper cover on a hardcover book. *Finishing*

Jaw Folder - A folder on the web press that is responsible for folding the printed web into a finished job. *Printing Processes*

Jitter - A distortion in the television picture. Slight horizontal and vertical unsteadiness appears. *Digital Photography Telecommunications*

Job Case - See California Job Case.

Job Printer - A company that does printing only. *Printing Processes*

Job Ticket - An order that describes the work to be done. *Printing Processes*

Jog - Alignment of uneven paper stacks into neat and even stacks. *Finishing*

Joint - The flexible area on a book's hardcover that folds when it is opened. *Finishing*

Joint Photographic Experts Group (JPEG) - Set the standards for image compression/decompression commonly called lossy. See Lossy and Lossless. *General Computer - Standards*

JPEG - See Joint Photographic Experts Group and Lossy.

Jumbo Roll - An extra large web roll. *Substrates*

Justified (Justify or Justification) - The arrangement of copy so that each line is set to a predetermined line length. In most cases, both the right and left sides or margins are even. This dictionary is justified. See Fig. 22. *Typography*
 Other forms of margin alignment:
 Flush left - All the lines on the left side are even.
 Flush right - All the lines on the right side are even.

Additional forms continued on next page.

Justified
This is a good example of justified copy and is often used in books and other publications. See how both margins are even, and it looks very

Flush Left/Ragged Right
This is a good example of flush left and ragged right copy and is often used in brochures and other publications. See how both margins look dif-

Ragged Left/ Flush Right
This is a good example of ragged left and flush right copy and is often used in brochures and other publications. See how both margins look different.

Ragged Left/Ragged Right
This is a good example of ragged left and ragged right copy and is often used in brochures and other publications. See how both margins look

Fig. 22 - Most common margin alignment.

Ragged right - All the lines on the right side are of uneven lengths.
Ragged left - All the lines on the left side are of uneven lengths.
Ragged left/Ragged right - Every line is of uneven length, and neither side is flush.

K - A unit of measurement for computer memory. 1K is 1,024 characters, but in practice, 32K means slightly more than 32,000 characters. *General Computer*

Kanji - Japanese characters. *Typography*

KB (Kilobyte) - See K.

Kelvin - A measurement standard for color illumination and it is primarily used in monitors and for evaluating color jobs. *Standards*

Kermit - A software program for sending files from one device to another. *Software*

Kerning - The reduced spacing between various combinations of two characters to enhance their visual appeal. Certain combinations of characters have a greater need for kerning than others. See Fig. 23. *Typography*

Kerning Table - A storage area that holds all the necessary information on the control of needed character spacing. These controls automatically make character spacing adjustments as required by the text that is used. *Typography*

Key - Certain letter or number combinations that are codes, which trigger certain typesetting functions. *Typesetting and Imagesetting*   The keyboard buttons. *Computer Hardware*

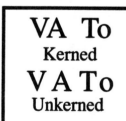

VA To
Kerned
V A To
Unkerned

Fig. 23 - Kerning

Keyboard - The device for inputting information into a computer or front-end. *Computer Hardware*

Keyboard Template - A specially cut piece of plastic that fits around the keys on the keyboard to indicate in writing the functions of each key. Typically, there would be a different template for each software program. *General Computer*

Key Frame - The main animation frame that controls the action in upcoming frames. *Multimedia*

Keyline - A drawing that shows only the outside edges of all the elements that are to be included in the finished CRC. Their exact position and size must be indicated. See CRC. *Art and Copy Preparation*

Key Plate - The guide plate that is used for the precise registration of all four plates on a multi-color job. *Color Reproduction*

Kilobyte - See K.

Kiosk - A small display unit that is used to inform the public of events or the location of stores. *Multimedia*

Kiss Impression - The lightest impression that can be made on the press and still produce a complete impression. See Impression. *Printing Processes*

Knife - A blade that assists in the process of folding paper. *Finishing*

Knock Out - The removal (or knock out) of the color in an area, and it usually refers to white. In fact, the term "knock out white" means to convert an area to white. *Color Reproduction*

Kraft - A brown (can be dyed other colors) paper that contains wood pulp. The stronger version of this paper is used in paper grocery bags and large mailing envelopes. *Substrates*

Label - A special gummed paper of various sizes that can be adhered to any item for purposes of identification or to provide information about the item. The label information can be preprinted, machine typed or handwritten onto the label. *Substrates*

Lacquer - A clear (dull or glossy) coating that is applied to a substrate to protect the printed surface, to enhance overall appearance, or to draw attention to certain areas on the printed piece. *Printing Processes*

Laid Paper - A high-quality paper that is manufactured with a parallel line pattern on the surface. This ribbed look was created to project sophistication and style to the reader of the printed piece. *Substrates*

Laminate - The process of lamination. See Lamination. *Finishing*

Lamination - The bonding (with heat and steady pressure) of clear plastic onto a printed piece to enhance appearance and provide protection. *Finishing*

LAN - See Local Area Network.

Lands - The non-image areas on gravure cylinders. *Image Carriers*

Landscape Mode - The capability of a printer to output computer images that are wider than they are tall. See Fig. 24. *Desktop/Electronic Publishing*

Laptop - A small portable computer. *Computer Hardware*

Laser (Light Amplification by Stimulated Emission of Radiation) - A low power, highly concentrated, narrow-band light beam that creates images through the use of impulses. These electronic impulses can be received by computers, printers, FAX's and other such devices. *Laser Applications*

Laser Color Separations - The creation of color separations via laser techniques. *Laser Applications*

Laser Paper - Paper having surface char-

> This is an example of text that has been prepared for your instruction in landscape mode. It is wider than it is tall.

> This is an example of text that has been prepared for your instruction in portrait mode.
>
> It is taller than it is wide.

Fig. 24 - Landscape and Portrait Modes

143

acteristics such as smoothness and adhesion properties that are desirable for the dry toners used in imaging on laser printers. *Laser Applications - Substrates*

Laser Platemaking - The creation of plates via state-of-the-art laser techniques. This technique can be tied into electronic impulses over telephone lines and the creation of the plates at a remote location or locally. *Image Carriers - Laser Applications*

Laser Printer - Printers that operate on the electrophotographic principle. An image is created by laser beam from digital data, and then it is transferred to the paper electrostatically. *Laser Applications*

Laser Printing - The process of printing on a laser printer. *Laser Applications*

Laser Writer - A low-cost PostScript printer that is used primarily with the Mac. *Laser Applications*

Laser Writer 13 - The original 13 resident fonts in the first Laser Writer. They include Times Roman, Helvetica (normal, bold, italic, and bold italic), Courier (4 styles) and Symbol. *Laser Applications*

Laser Writer 35 - The 35 resident fonts in the upgraded Laser Writer Plus. They include the Laser Writer 13 plus Palatino, Avant Garde, Bookman, New Century Schoolbook, Helvetica Narrow (roman, bold, italic, and bold italic), Zapf Chancery, and Zapf Dingbats. These fonts are all standard issue on all new PostScript printers. *Laser Applications*

Latent Image - A non-visible image on light sensitive paper or film. Once that latent image is developed, the finished image will appear. *Graphics Arts Photography - Image Carriers*

Layout - A proposed piece of artwork indicating the location of all the elements (copy, photos, illustrations, etc.) that are to be included in the piece. This will become the finished CRC. See Thumbnail Sketch, CRC, Rough Layout and Comprehensive Layout. *Art and Copy Preparation*

LCD - See Liquid Crystal Display.

Leaders - Many characters (usually dots, periods or dashes) between two widely spaced characters that are used to control eye movement from the one character to the other more distant character. This enhances readability. See Fig. 25. *Typography*

<table>
<tr><td>Chapter One ....23</td></tr>
<tr><td>Chapter Two ....35</td></tr>
<tr><td>Chapter Three ....47</td></tr>
<tr><td>Chapter Four ....59</td></tr>
</table>

Fir. 25 - Leaders

Leading - The amount of space that is below a typeset character and expressed in points. A 10 point character could have 3 points of leading, thus a line would occupy 13 points of space and is called 10/13 type. Leading effects readability. Extra leading makes copy more readable. See Figs. 26 & 27 on pages 145. *Typography*

LED - See Light-Emitting Diode.

Ledger Paper - A very durable grade of paper that is used were long-term paper life is required, i.e., file cards and accounting records. *Substrates*

Fig. 26 - Leading

Legend - The descriptive text that appears below photos and illustrations. *Desktop/Electronic Publishing*

Letterfold- A sheet of paper that is folded to appear as a folded letter, which is then inserted into an envelope. Hence the name, letterfold. *Finishing*

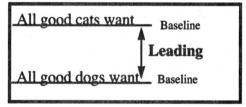

Fig. 27 - Leading

Letterhead - Specially printed business stationery that is unique to a company. *Substrates*

Lettering - Hand drawn letters. *Art and Copy Preparation*

Letterpress Printing - A printing process that uses a raised metal surface on the plate. This surface carries the ink to the substrate to be printed. *Printing Processes*

Letter Quality - Computer output that is equal to top-quality typewriter output. *General Computer*

Letterset - A printing process where a blanket transfers the information onto the plate and then onto the paper. This creates the impression. *Printing Processes*

Letterspacing - The amount of space that is between each word is changed or modified. This can be done to create text that has more visual appeal and is easier to read. It also aids in the justification of text where text has wide spaces between words. *Typography*

Library - The user's collection of programs, subroutines, files, and electronic documents. This includes all archived material. *General Computer*

Library Edition - An edition with extra rugged binding. *Finishing*

145

Ligature - A character consisting of two or more letters joined by a stroke or tie. See Fig. 28. *Typography*

Fig. 28
Ligature

Light - The electromagnetic waves that humans can see. It is called visible radiation, and is a very small range between infrared and ultraviolet. *Color Reproduction*

Light Box - A box with built-in lights and a translucent cover which allows the light to shine through for viewing items, and for working with transparent copy. *Art and Copy Preparation*

Light-Emitting Diode (LED) - A particular type of display that is commonly used in the graphics field. Current is passed through diodes to produce visible images and letters. *Computer Hardware*

Lightfastness - A substrate's ability to resist color change or fading when exposed to light. *Quality/Process Control - Substrates*

Lightness - The brightness of an image of any color. *Color Reproduction*

Light Pen - A pen-like device that is attached to the computer. It is used to select items on the screen and is faster than a mouse. *Computer Hardware*

Light Source Color - This is where the object itself emits light and the range of that light determines the color. *Color Reproduction*

Light Typestyle - A thinner version of the basic plain or roman typestyle. *Typography*

Line Art - Drawings, illustrations, or graphics that contain solids and lines placed on a white background suitable for CRC or reproduction, i.e., clip art, preprinted type, graphics, etc. *Art and Copy Preparation*

Linear Array - A specific type of a charged coupled device (CCD) that is used in scanners. See Charged Coupled Device. *Scanning*

Linearize - The adjustment of the grayscale on a PostScript imagesetter in order to reproduce the most accurate tints and halftones. *Color Reproduction - Typesetting and Imagesetting*

Line Copy - See Line Art.

Line Gauge - See Printer's Rule.

Line Length - The width of a row of text. *Desktop/Electronic Publishing - Typography*

Line Negatives - Negatives reproduced as black line copy, totally without gradations, with a white background. The line negative is created on film or photo sensitized paper. *Graphic Arts Photography*

Line Original - A special graphic or illustration created in a black and white format with all crop marks and placement specifications. *Art and Copy Preparation*

Line Screen - The lines per inch (lpi) that are used in halftone creation. Dot size is effected by the screen rulings. The standard screen rulings are 65, 85, 100, 120, 133, 150, 200, and 300. Each number refers to the number of lines per inch and the decision to use one size over another is most often the type of paper used and the quality of the results that are desired. Newspapers typically use 65 and 85 line screens because newsprint is very coarse, whereas, magazines use high quality paper and need the better results of a 133 or 150 line screen. See Examples of Coarse Screens in Fig. 4 on page 81. *Color Reproduction - Graphic Arts Photography - Scanning*

Line Spacing - See Leading.

Line Cut - An etched plate that is used for the reproduction of line artwork. See Line Art. *Image Carriers*

Linen Tester - A magnifier that is specifically designed to inspect printing, to check shadow areas, and to be sure all the colors are printing in the highlight areas. *Color Reproduction*

Line Shot - A photographic technique that is used for reproducing line artwork. *Graphics Arts Photography*

Line Width - The exact distance between either side of a line. *Desktop/Electronic Publishing - Typography*

Lining - A reinforcing material between the spine and the book itself. *Finishing*

Linotronic - An original brand of imagesetters by Linotype Hell Company. The Linotronic was the first PostScript high-resolution imagesetter. *Laser Applications Typesetting and Imagesetting*

Lithographic - See Offset Lithographic Press.

Liquid Crystal Display (LCD) - A special type of display system using non-illuminated reflective numerals and characters. LCD's require very little power. *Computer Hardware*

List - A compilation of the names and addresses of people or companies with common needs or interests. *Marketing* A list of items that can be increased, deleted, or rearranged. *General Computer*

List Box - See Dialog Box.

Lithographic Printing - See Offset Lithographic Press.

Lithography - See Offset Lithographic Press.

Live Matter - The image area on the plate. *Image Carriers*

Load - The process of sending information from secondary storage into main memory. *General Computer*

Local-Area Network (LAN) - A series of computers and peripherals that are connected within a small geographic area by a common communications network. *General Computer*

Lock-Up - The enclosure of all the elements (type, etc.) of the job, which are in plate form, into a metal frame (chase). This makes the job ready to be printed on a letterpress. *Printing Processes*

Login - See Logon.

Logo - A combination of characters and or graphics to create a single design that is used to identify a company. It is often trademarked and is always included on all company printed material. *Marketing*

Logon (Login) - A personal identification code or word that recognizes the user

147

as being authorized to enter and use the computer system. *General Computer*

Logotype - See Logo.

Long Ink - A flow characteristic of ink. A more fluid ink will breakup and tend to "mist" on press. See Ink Mist. *Ink*

Loose-Color Proofs - See Scatter Proofs.

Loose-Leaf Binding - See Binding (Mechanical or Manual).

Lossless (LZW) - A compression/-decompression technique that compresses images up to 50 percent but decompresses them to the exact original. *General Computer*

Lossy (JPEG) - A compression/decompression technique that compresses images to a minimum of 25 percent but where decompressed portions of the original are lost. *General Computer*

Loupe (Lupe) - See Graphics Arts Magnifier.

Low-End System - A basic desktop publishing system involving an inexpensive computer, printer, and software which allows simple routines for page layout, typesetting, word processing, and image assembly. *Desktop/Electronic Publishing*

Lower Case - The smaller version of a character. See Upper Case for example. *Typography*

Low Frequency Image - An image (picture) with little detail, or a few changes in the brightness levels. See Brightness Level. *Digital Photography*

Low Key Transparency - A dark, underexposed transparency with shadow details. *Art and Copy Preparation - Graphic Arts Photography*

LPI - Lines Per Inch. It refers to the resolution of halftones. See Line Screen. *Graphic Arts Photography - Scanning*

Lucy - A device used for scaling artwork to be larger or smaller than the original. This allows the image to be copied at the desired size. *Art and Copy Preparation*

Ludlow - A machine that creates lines of metal characters called slugs that are used for display type. *Typesetting and Imagesetting*

Luminance - The brightness level in video signals. See Brightness Level. *Digital Photography*

Lux - The measurement of illumination in metric. *Standards*

LZW - See Lossless.

M - A capital letter character that is used in printing which refers to 1000, as in 1,000 finished printed pieces, or some multiple of 1,000 as in 5M, meaning 5,000. *Standards*

Machine Address - See Absolute Address.

Machine-Coated - Paper that has been coated on one or both sides while the paper was manufactured. *Substrates*

Machine Composition - Type that has been created on a specially designed mechanical machine or electronic system. *Typesetting and Imagesetting*

Machine Cycle - The fastest time a computer can perform an operation. *General Computer*

Machine Direction - The direction of the grain in the paper. *Substrates*

MacDraw II - See MacDraw Pro.

MacDraw Pro - A Mac graphics package. See Claris Corporation. *Software*

Machine Guarding - A safety feature. The placement of guards around hazardous machinery in companies to protect workers from harm. *Environmental*

Machine Readable - Any information that can be input directly into a computer. *General Computer*

Mac PowerBook Memory Modules - A line of memory modules for PowerBook computers available in capacities from 2MB to 28MB. See Newer Technology. *Computer Hardware*

MacPaint - A Mac-based paint program. See Claris Corporation. *Software*

Macro - A series of instructions or keystrokes that can be activated by the depression of a single key or a specific sequence of several keys. *General Computer*

MacWrite Pro - A Mac word processor. See Claris Corporation. *Software*

Magenta - A reddish color process ink that is used in full-color printing. Also refers to the red color of the ink. *Color Reproduction - Ink*

Magenta Screen - A dyed screen that is used in the creation of halftones. *Graphic Arts Photography*

Magnetic Disk - A magnetic computer storage medium. See Hard Disk and Floppy Disk. *Computer Hardware*

Magnetic Recording - The memorizing of some condition by converting it to an analogous amount of magnetic flux on a magnetic medium. *Digital Photography*

Mailer - Durable containers of varying sizes that are used for mailing items. *Marketing*

Mail-Merge - Word processing software that was designed to produce personalized mailings. *Software*

Mainframe Computer - The highest

level computers that handle the most complex jobs and control the greatest amount of peripherals. *Computer Hardware*

Make-Over - The process of remaking a plate in order to make corrections before a job is printed. *Image Carriers*

Make-Ready - The steps necessary to prepare a press for a job to be printed. It involves checking for the right ink, the image position, plate and blanket operation, the correct paper, etc. *Printing Processes*

Make-Up - The process of combining typeset copy, graphics, illustrations, and photos to create a finished page. *Art and Copy Preparation - Image Assembly*

Management Graphics, Inc. - Manufacturer of high quality film recorders, networking systems, turnkey graphics workstations, and graphics software. Contact numbers: 1401 E. 79th St., Minneapolis, MN 55425; (612)854-1220. *Computer Hardware - Software*

Managing Editor Software, Inc. - Software to facilitate a publication's workflow. Help in publication management and in addressing particular functions, like ad dummying, forms management, and pagination. Contact numbers: 101 Greenwood Ave., Suite 550, Jenkintown, PA 19046; (215)886-5662. *Software*

Managing Editor XT - This program was formerly called "The Gatherer" and it automatically rounds up text and graphic files from specified folders on a network or hard disk and lists them in an items palette. See Managing Editor Software, Inc. *Software*

Manuscript - A book or any body of text in handwritten, typed or electronic form prior to final preparation for typesetting and creation of the CRC. See CRC. *Desktop/Electronic Publishing*

Margin - The top, bottom, and side spaces on a printed page that is between the page's edge and the image area. *Art and Copy Preparation - Desktop/Electronic Publishing*

Markers (Color) - Special markers that are available in a multitude of colors. They are used to create a full-color layout of suggested artwork or a design in order to secure customer approval of the concepts presented. *Art and Copy Preparation*

Marking Up - See Mark-Up.

Mark-Up - The notations, on copy that is to be typeset, of certain markings that tell the typesetter how to create the finished typeset material. For example, the word stet next to some copy tells the typesetter to ignore the corrections indicated. See Proofreaders Symbols. *Art and Copy Preparation - Typesetting and Imagesetting*

Mask - Intermediate film that is used in photographic color correction. *Color Reproduction - Graphic Arts Photography* The material that is used to block certain portions of an image area from light exposure during the creation of the printing plate. See Mask Out. *Image Assembly - Image Carriers*

Masking - The process of localizing a particular area in a photo and making specific corrections, such as making an apple in a fruit bowl darker or lighter. *Color Reproduction - Graphic Arts Photography - Scanning*

Mask Out - To block certain portions of an image area from light exposure during the creation of the printing plate. *Image Assembly - Image Carriers*

Master - The primary element (film, file, tape, etc.) from which all copies are created. *Art and Copy Preparation - Image Assembly*

Mastering - An element in the process of duplicating CD's. *Multimedia*

Matchprint - A color proofing system by 3M. Colored film (magenta, cyan, yellow, and black), instead of toners, is laminated to a white sheet of paper. This combination of all four colors produces a very close representation of the final printed job. Each of the four colors must be processed in the correct order to achieve the desired results. *Proofing*

MathType - A program that builds complex mathematical equations by using simple point-and-click techniques. You can import the equations into most word processing and page layout applications. For Mac and Windows. See Design Science, Inc. *Software*

Matrix - A plate mold that is made of paper and is used when a low-cost duplicate is needed. *Image Carriers* The small mold of a character that is used in hot metal typesetting. *Typesetting and Imagesetting*

Matte Finish - A paper with a dull surface, i.e., zero gloss. *Substrates*

Matte Print - A dull surfaced print, i.e., zero gloss. *Graphic Arts Photography*

MB - See Megabyte.

Mealiness - See Snowflaking.

Measure (or Line Length) - The overall width (stated in points and picas) of a line, i.e., the distance between the left and right margins of the body of text. *Desktop/Electronic Publishing - Typography*

Mechanical - See Camera-Ready Copy.

Mechanical Dot Gain - See Dot Gain.

Mechanical Drawings - Drawings by a person with a basic knowledge of drafting techniques and the use of drafting tools. *Art and Copy Preparation*

Mechanical Pulp - Groundwood pulp that is used for newsprint and other lower grade paper applications, and is manufactured by grinding wood chips. *Substrates*

Mechanical Separation - The preparation of color separations by hand. Separate overlays are created for each color. *Art and Copy Preparation - Color Reproduction*

Media - The type of vehicle chosen for final delivery of a message, i.e., radio, newspaper, magazine, etc. *Art and Copy Preparation - Marketing*

Megabyte (MB) - Means one million bytes or characters. *General Computer*

Megahertz (MHz) - A frequency measurement that is equal to one million cycles a second. *General Computer - Telecommunications*

Memory - A chip were data and information is stored for later retrieval. *Computer Hardware*

Memory Colors - Colors that are readily

recognized, i.e., blue sky, human flesh, etc. *Color Reproduction*

Menu - An on-screen series of options that allow the user to select a specific activity or action from the available choices. *Software*

Menu-Driven - A computer program that is operated by a series of option choices on a menu. See Menu. *Software*

Menu Item - An individual item on a menu that can be selected by a keyboard command or mouse. See Menu. *Software*

Metameric Colors - See Metamerism.

Metamerism - The condition that occurs where color appears differently under different lighting. *Color Reproduction - Quality/Process Control*

Metric System - A system of measurement based on decimal. See Grammage. *Standards*

Mezzo Screen - Produces a mezzotint pattern. See Mezzotint. *Graphic Arts Photography*

Mezzotint - An special type of engraving that has been created on textured copper. *Image Carriers*

Micron - A term for a millionth of one meter. *Standards*

Microfiche Card - Card-sized film that stores large amounts of information for easy and inexpensive retrieval. *Computer Hardware*

Micrometer - A precision instrument for determining substrate, plate, or blanket

thickness. See Caliper. *Quality/Process Control*

Microprocessor - A chip that contains an entire CPU and is a part of all Mac's and PC's. *Computer Hardware*

Microsoft - A leading software company. Offer a wide range of products and services for business and personal use, each designed with the mission of making it easier to take advantage of the full power of computing. Contact numbers: One Microsoft Way, Redmond, WA 98052-6399; 1-800-426-9400. *Software*

Microsoft Publisher - A full-featured desktop publishing program. For Windows. See Microsoft. *Software*

Microsoft Windows - A PC based program that creates an easy-to-use user-interface on most popular graphic arts programs. See Microsoft. *Software*

Microsoft Word - A powerful and popular word processing program. For Mac and Windows. See Microsoft. *Software*

Microwave - A term used to describe very high frequencies or short wavelengths used for point-to-point transmission and for satellite transmission. The wavelengths usually range from 1 GHz to 30 GHz. Satellite signals are microwaves. *Telecommunications*

Microwave Relay - The sending of microwave signals from a low powered broadcasting station, which allows a weak signal from a distance to control a more powerful local signal. Otherwise, the sending of information via microwaves from one point to another. *Telecommunications*

Mid-Range System - A desktop or electronic publishing system of sufficent complexity and expense that it falls somewhere between low-end systems and high-end systems. It typically allows fairly sophisticated color computer graphics and image manipulation routines but is not designed for the heavy production capabilities of high-end systems. *Desktop/Electronic Publishing*

Mid-Tones - A photograph's tonal range that is between the lightest and the darkest areas, i.e., the tones in the middle (hence "mid" tones). *Graphic Arts Photography*

Migration - An ink's penetration through the various layers of ink, varnish, and substrate. *Ink*

Mimeograph Duplication - A form of printing that uses a stencil as a master (plate) and produces an image or impression by a method that is similar to screen printing. See Screen Printing. *Printing Processes*

Minimize - The process of making a window very small, i.e., converting it to an icon. *General Computer*

MIPS (**M**illion **I**nstructions **P**er **S**econd) - A computer speed reference tool. *General Computer*

Misregister - A condition where two images are overprinted or placed next to each other and they are visually not in alignment. *Printing Processes*

Mixed Mode CD-ROM - A CD that contains both the audio and the digital data in CD-Audio (Red Book) format. *Multimedia*

Mixer - A board (video or audio) that can mix different signals into a single signal. *Multimedia*

MM - A combination of two capital letters that is used in printing to refer to the quantity of one million, i.e., 1,000,000. For example, 5MM means 5,000,000 *Standards*

ModelPRO - A high level 3-D modeling/sculpting package offering powerful and intuitive spline-based modeling, rendering, and animation for the Mac. See Visual Information Development, Inc. *Software*

Modem - A device that allows users to send information and data to and from their computers over standard telephone lines. *Computer Hardware - Telecommunications*

Modulation - The process by which some characteristic of one wave is modified in accordance with another wave. The wave which is modified is called the carrier wave and the modifier, the signal wave. Amplitude Modulation (AM) changes the height (amplitude) of the carrier wave and Frequency Modulation (FM) varies the frequency of the carrier. *Digital Photography - Telecommunications*

Moire - This is a pattern that can occur in four-color printing when one or more of the colors (in the film) is created during the separation process at a wrong angle. This creates a visually objectionable pattern of dots which are called moire patterns. *Color Reproduction - Graphic Arts Photography - Scanning*

Moire Patterns - See Moire.

Molleton - The heavy cotton material

153

that is used on the press' dampening rollers. *Printing Processes*

Monitor - A high quality television set without a tuner, used to display the composite video signal from a still video camera, VCR, computer or separate tuner. Since monitors lack a tuner, they cannot receive broadcast pictures. *Digital Photography - Telecommunications*

Monochrome - A one color image or monitor. *Color Reproduction*

Monochrome Monitor (Display) - A monitor with one color capability only. Usually refers to a gray-scale monitor. *Computer Hardware*

Monograph - A treatise or report that is focused to a specific subject or a single area. *Desktop/Electronic Publishing*

Monospaced Characters - Typefaces where the space allotted for each character is the same width regardless of the character. See Fixed Pitch. *Typography*

Monospaced Font - See Fixed Pitch.

Monotone - Printing or reproduction in only one color, usually black. One color or one tone, i.e., a black and white photograph. *Printing Processes*

Montage - A collection of drawings and photographs in one art piece that have been creatively arranged to show a specific story or impression. *Art and Copy Preparation*

Montage FR2 - A desktop film recorder. Compatible with all Windows, Mac, and PostScript applications. See Presentation Technologies, Inc. *Computer Hardware*

Montaging - The creation of a single electronic image by combining different graphic elements, i.e., scanned images with computer created art or illustrations. *Desktop/Electronic Publishing*

Morphing - The gradual or the rapid transition of one shape or scene into another shape or scene. *Desktop/Electronic Publishing*

Mortise - A slot in a printing plate that allows for the insertion of another plate. Both plates are then printed simultaneously. *Image Carriers*

MOS-Photodiodes - A new type of technology centered around sensors. *Digital Photography*

Mouse - A pointing mechanism for a computer. It allows the user, by depressing the buttons, to choose commands or items on-screen. It is also used to control where data is entered. *Computer Hardware*

MPEG (Motion Picture Experts Group) - The standard protocols that are used to decompress and compress sound and digital video. *Multimedia*

MS-DOS - The operating system for the IBM-PC computers and their clones. See DOS. *Software*

MOS (Metal-Oxide Semiconductor) - A solid-state image pick-up device that is very similar to a CCD unit. However, the MOS type uses a different method of transferring the signal from the image pick-up. This MOS electronic chip typically contains more noise, has a low sensitivity to the color blue, and offers more complicated signal processing. *Digital Photography*

Mottle - A spotty printed pattern (or appearance) that is used to create a special effect or it could be the result of some printing error. *Printing Processes*

M/Series - OCR systems with powerful Windows software for real-time foreground and background document conversion and index creation. See Calera Recognition Systems. *Computer Hardware*

M/Series Professional Software - Realtime document processing and manipulation, and it enables hardware to serve as network peripherals for office-wide document conversion. For Windows. See Calera Recognition Systems. *Software*

MSP - A Microsoft graphics format used in Windows Paint. *Software*

Mullen Tester - A device that measures any particular paper's bursting strength. *Quality/Process Control - Substrates*

Multi-Ad CAMS 3 (Classified Advertising Management System) - A comprehensive Mac classified advertising management system, which incorporates accounting, billing, reporting, and design features into one program. See Multi-Ad Services, Inc. *Software*

Multi-Ad Creator 3.6 - Display advertisement design and production capabilities with color, masking capability, and printing support. Includes rotation and editing of graphics and text, copyfitting, kerning, multiple special text effects, advanced drawing tools, gradient fills, and a custom font menu. See Multi-Ad Services, Inc. *Software*

Multi-Ad Search - A Mac graphic cataloging and retrieval system. Provides thumbnail previews for EPS, TIFF, RIFF, PICT, MacPaint, JPEG, and Multi-Ad Creator formats. Views and prints images by thumbnail, text list, or actual image. See Multi-Ad Services, Inc. *Software*

Multi-Ad Services, Inc. - Providing state-of-the-art Mac products and services to facilitate product advertising and promotion. Contact numbers: 1720 West Detweiller Drive, Peoria, IL 61615; (309)692-1530. *Software*

Multi-Function Device - A state-of-the-art device that performs multiple tasks, i.e., faxing, copying, printing, networking, etc. *Computer Hardware*

Multimedia - A presentation that combines text, graphics, sound, video and animation. *Multimedia*

Multiple Internal Reflections - A condition that occurs when light strikes paper and the light is absorbed (not reflected) by the paper. *Color Reproduction*

Multiplexed - Three or more fonts that have the same width values, character for character, in each font. *Typography*

Multitasking - An operating system that allows more than one task to be executing simultaneously. *Software*

Multithreading - A computer program that allows more than one task or process to be executed simultaneously. *Software*

Munsell-Foss Color Chart - A color production aid that shows the color capability of specific combinations of ink, press, and different substrates. *Color Reproduction*

155

Mylar - A strong and stable polyester
film that was developed by DuPont.
Image Carriers

National Television Standards Committee (NTSC) - A group that establishes all the TV standards for telecasting now used in the U.S. and other countries. NTSC designates video signals which conform to the 525 scanning line, 60 field/30 frames per second format. *Digital Photography - Standards - Telecommunications*

Near Letter Quality (NLQ) - The next level of quality on computer printers above the dot matrix printer. The characters are not as fully formed as high-quality electric typewriters. See Dot Matrix Printer. *General Computer*

Negative Film - Film that contains the reverse of an original image, i.e., the light areas appear dark and the dark areas are light. *Graphic Arts Photography*

Network - A communications link that connects a series of computers together. This allows them to share files and send files to other computers and to peripherals, i.e., printers. *General Computer*

Neutral Gray - An overprint of the three process colors. *Color Reproduction*

Newer Technology - Engineered the first Mac 4MB, 8MB, and 16 MB SIMM's and 32-bit SIMM memory. Line of CPU accelerators and variable speed overdrives for Mac and a speed improvement using the Mac's existing CPU. Contact numbers: 7803 E. Osie St., Suite 105; Wichita, KS 67207; (800)678-3726. *Computer Hardware*

Newspaper Printer - A printer specializing in news and newspaper print production. *Printing Processes*

Newsprint - Low-cost paper manufactured from groundwood and chemical pulp. Newspapers are most commonly printed on this type of paper, hence the name of newsprint. *Substrates*

Newton Rings - A pattern of concentric, colored circles that can occur between smooth, polished surfaces and is caused when light is reflected off these surfaces. *Quality/Process Control*

Nikon, Inc., Electronic Imaging Div. Products designed for image management; from capture and transmission, to processing, storage, retrieval, output, and distribution. Contact numbers: 1300 Walt Whitman Road, Melville, New York, 11747; (516)547-4200. *Computer Hardware - Graphic Arts Photography - Software*

Nikon Image Access - A database software application for the rapid archival, retrieval, and display of digital images. For Windows and Mac. See Nikon, Inc. *Software*

Nip - A crease located on a hardcover book's joint. *Finishing* The point where two cylinders come together. *Printing Processes*

Nippers - The irons that join the hardcover to the book by clamping them together under pressure with heat applied. *Finishing*

Nipping - The process of squeezing a book before the hardcover is attached to remove all the excess air caused during binding and stitching. *Finishing*

Noise - Any undesired random voltage. It can be produced by any electronic part or component, or may occur naturally. Appears on a TV set as grain, snow, or other disturbances in the picture. *Digital Photography - Telecommunications*

Non-Impact Printing - A printing process where there is no contact between the paper (or other substrate) in transferring the image to be printed, i.e., ink-jet printing, electrostatic printing, etc. *Printing Processes*

Non-Metallic Composition - A composition technique that uses paper or film carriers instead of metal carriers. This method lends itself to a more rapid makeready. *Typesetting and Imagesetting*

Non-Photo Blue - A marking instrument with light blue coloring that cannot be seen by a graphic arts camera when photostats, plates, or negatives are created. *Art and Copy Preparation*

Non-Reproducible Colors - Specific colors that occur in nature (certain flowers) and in photography that are not reproducible by the four-color printing process. *Color Reproduction*

Non-Reproducing Blue - See Non-Photo Blue.

North Atlantic Publishing Systems Develops software products to enhance the off-the-shelf components and bring the power of professional high-end publishing systems to desktop publishing users. Contact numbers: 9 Acton Rd., Chelmsford, MA 01824; (508)250-8080. *Software*

Notch Binding - The process of making small cuts to the spine of a book, prior to perfect binding, to hold the glue when the cover and the book are bound together. *Finishing*

Notebook - A very small and portable computer. *Computer Hardware*

Novell NetWare - A LAN (Local Area Network) designed and developed by Novell, Inc. for PC's, Mac's, and other computers and their peripherals. *Software*

Nozzle - The device that ejects the ink on an ink-jet printer. *Computer Hardware - Printing Processes*

NTSC - See National Television Standards Committee.

NuBus Adapter IIsi (Mac IIsi) - Provides an accelerator slot for a Universal PowerCache or Turbo 040 and a NuBus slot for your NuBus-based cards. See DayStar Digital. *Computer Hardware*

Numbering - The process of placing numbers on printed business forms that are in consecutive order. The operation is frequently performed during the time of printing, i.e., immediately after or before the creation of an impression. *Printing Processes*

Numeric Keypad - That portion of the keyboard where the numbers (0-9) and the decimal point are located. It is usually on the right side. *Computer Hardware*

NyQuist Criterion - The criteria used in the definition of image sampling rates. *Digital Photography*

Object-Oriented Graphics - A system of computer graphics that is based on the graphic primaries - lines, squares, circles, and curves. These graphics are created mathematically and can be easily altered by changing their mathematical descriptions. See Draw Program. *Desktop/Electronic Publishing*

Oblique Typestyle - Roman characters that are computer slanted. *Typography*

Oblong - Publications that are bound at the shorter length. *Finishing*

OCR - See Optical Character Recognition.

OCR Scanner - A mechanism that can read and identify typed or typeset characters and convert these characters to electronic data that is stored and can be used at a later date. *Scanning*

Off-Color - A color that is different from the desired color. *Color Reproduction*

Off-Line Converting - The groups of different machines that perform all the binding and finishing operations, i.e., cutting, folding, imprinting, etc. *Finishing*

Off-Machine Proofs - Proofs that are not created on a press. See Matchprint (3M) and Cromalin (DuPont). *Proofing*

Off-Press Proofs - See Off-Machine Proofs and Pre-Press Proofs.

Offset - See Offset Lithographic Press.

Offset Duplicator - A small printing press based on the principles of the offset lithographic process. *Printing Processes*

Offset Gravure - A press that combines the basic principles of gravure and offset technology. *Printing Processes*

Offset/Gravure Conversions - The process of converting offset film to gravure cylinders. *Printing Processes*

Offset Lithographic Press - A printing press on which the plate is dampened and then it is inked. This newly inked image is immediately transferred to the blanket. This freshly inked blanket will immediately transfer the image to the paper (or any other acceptable substrate) and create the impression. This whole process is designed to attract water to non-image areas and ink to the image areas. *Printing Processes*

Ohm - The basic unit of resistance (impedance) or the opposition to the flow of an electrical current. *Digital Photography - Telecommunications*

OK Sheet - A proof or printed sheet that has been OK'd, and is used as a guide for the press run. *Proofing*

Oleophilic - See Hydrophilic.

Oleophobic - See Hydrophobic.

Omnifont - An OCR scanner feature that allows accurate scanning of most fonts without the need for learning all the font's characteristics prior to the actual scanning. *Scanning*

OmniPage - Optical character recognition (OCR) software. Allows the recognition of documents with any mix of text, numbers or graphics, and the creation of files in any popular word processing, spreadsheet, image, or database file format. See Caere Corporation. *Software*

OmniScan - An integrated scanner. Combines a hand-held scanner, OCR, image editing, and fax capabilities in one unit. Provides tools needed to manage, share, and enhance information. See Caere Corporation. *Scanning*

One-Point Perspective - A perspective drawing where all the parallel lines appear to converge on one point. *Art and Copy Preparation*

On-Line Information and Database Services - Computerized information databases that share their contents with customers via a modem and another computer. *Telecommunications*

On-Off - A writable CD. It is often used for testing a CD production. *Multimedia*

Onyx Plates - Special polyester plates developed by 3M that were designed to run in imagesetters. *Image Carriers*

Opacity - The degree to which one can see the printed image through the paper. Generally, thickness enhances opacity. *Substrates*

Opaquing - The process of applying opaque ink. See Opaque Ink. *Image Assembly*

Opaque Ink - The fast drying ink material that is used to cover unwanted areas on negative film. This prevents these unwanted areas from appearing on the final plate. *Image Assembly - Ink*

Opaquer - The person who corrects all the film imperfections with opaquing material and removes the unwanted images prior to final platemaking. *Image Assembly*

Open Prepress ENvironment (OPEN) - A program that orchestrates the production workflow among all prepress applications, sets the parameters for a job, executes the job, then passes it into the next application, while automatically monitoring the progress of all tasks, i.e., trapping, imposition, etc. See Aldus Corporation. *Software*

Operator Side - The side of the press where the printing adjustments are made. *Printing Processes*

Operating System - A software program that controls the operations of the computer. This allows the computer to recognize user and software commands, complete input and output functions, and recognize any necessary built-in operations. *Software*

Optical Character Recognition (OCR) An electronic scanner that can read and identify typed or typeset characters and convert these characters into electronic data files on magnetic disks or other types of media. The data can be used at a later date. *General Computer - Scanning*

Optical Density - A material's ability for light absorptance. *Color Reproduction*

Optical Disk - A high-capacity magnetic computer storage medium. *Computer Hardware*

Optical Dot Gain - The shadow that is projected onto the paper from a printed dot. *Printing Processes*

Optical Fiber - An extremely thin glass fiber, often the diameter of a typical human hair, that is capable of transmitting vast amounts of data via light waves. *Telecommunications*

Optical Scanner Resolution - The actual hardware determined resolution of a scanner as expressed in the horizontal and vertical directions, i.e., a 1200 X 600 scanner. This optical resolution can be optimized via interpolated scanning software. See Interpolated Scanner Resolution. *Scanning*

Optical Storage - The magnetic storage of data on optical media (disks). See Optical Disk. *Computer Hardware*

Opticopy - An electronic imposition system. See Imposition. *Image Assembly*

Original - The initial black and white or color art, photos, or artwork with no alterations of any kind. It should be sharp, have a good density range, and have acceptable contrast. *Art and Copy Preparation*

Orphan - The first or last line of a paragraph that is printed by itself at the top or the bottom of a page. This is considered improper design. *Typography*

Orthochromatic - A film that is only sensitive to the ultraviolet rays (blue, green, and yellow), and is not responsive to red. *Graphic Arts Photography*

OS/2 - An IBM/Microsoft operating system. *Software*

Outline (or Scalable) Fonts - Typefaces that are stored as mathematical expressions. These formulas create the outline of a type character, which can be scaled to any point size and output at whatever resolution the printer is capable of printing. *Typography*

Out Of Fit - When the register marks in each color of film on a multi-color job do not line-up. *Image Assembly*

Out-Point - The section of a multimedia project where the editing process ends. *Multimedia*

Output - Information that is produced by computer application programs on printers, monitors, or stored on external storage devices. *General Computer*

Over-Exposure - Areas on film that are weak and appear to be breaking-up. *Graphic Arts Photography*

Overhang Cover - The cover of a publication that exceeds the size of its inside pages (in length and width), except on the bound side. *Finishing*

Overlay Tissue - The cover or tissue (semi-transparent) that is placed over CRC that provides an area for writing all the instructions and notations that must be followed by the printer and color separation vendor to produce a finished product. *Art and Copy Preparation*

Overprinting - Printing over the same area twice, usually with a lacquer to provide emphasis or protection. Sometimes overprinted colors are used for special effects. *Printing Processes*

Over-Run - When the amount that was actually printed exceeds the amount originally requested, the excess portion is called the over-run. *Printing Processes*

Overset - Copy that exceeds the available space. *Typesetting and Imagesetting*

Overset! - Fits text into boxes using QuarkXpress when the overset mark is clicked. Temporary text box immediately shows the overset material. Once the copy, design, or typography is edited so the copy fits the design, the temporary box automatically vanishes. For Mac or PC. See North Atlantic Publishing Systems. *Software*

Oversewing - A process that repairs damaged hardcover books. *Finishing*

Package Design - The actual design of the appearance, the color, the most compelling copy, and the size and form of the product's package. *Marketing*

Packing - Paper or other material that is added under the offset plate or the blanket to achieve the required pressure. *Printing Processes*

Padding - A form of perfect binding that is produced by a manual process. It is used in short-run binding only. *Finishing*

Page Flex - The stress a casebound book is able to withstand before the book will break away from its binding. *Finishing - Quality/Process Control*

PageKeeper - An information management tool that turns paper documents and existing word processing files into intelligent electronic filing systems with text, graphics, and halftone images. See Caere Corporation. *Software*

Page Description Language (PDL) - A computer language that controls page layout. It commands the output device to print in a precise manner. PostScript is the most popular PDL, along with HPGL, Interpress, etc. *Software*

Page Director - Accelerates publication layout and controls issue management. Gathers text, graphics, and advertising for page placement. Headlines, cutlines, and credit lines are formatted and glued to stories and graphics. Color can be applied and jumplines and folio styles are automatic. See Managing Editor Software, Inc. *Software*

Page Director Classified - Page dummying and paste-up is automated. Reads advertising text files, measures them, and flows multiple elements onto pages. Offers page squaring options, vertical justification of elements within a column, and insertion of filler elements. See Managing Editor Software, Inc. *Software*

Page-Layout Program - See Page Make-Up and Page Make-Up, Electronic.

PageMaker - A full featured page layout program that enables users to combine text and graphics to produce professional-level publications. The program allows: rotation and skewing of text and graphics in 0.01^0 increments; horizontal and vertical reflection of objects; positioning, scaling, or cropping of objects; selecting the type attributes of individual characters or whole paragraphs; sophisticated kerning and track editing; incrementally rotated inline graphics; numeric kerning; non-consecutive page-range printing; printing scalable up to 1600%; process-color separations of PageMaker text and graphics, as well as imported CMYK, TIFF, DCS, and EPS images without leaving PageMaker; cropping of rotated objects; numerically exact positioning and rotation of any object, from its center or any handle; and much more. For Mac, Windows, and Power Mac. See Aldus Corporation. *Software*

Page Make-Up - The process of assembling the various elements (type/copy, graphics, and photos) that need to be combined to create a finished page or CRC. This can either be accomplished on a computer monitor with the appropriate software or on an art board. See CRC. *Art and Copy Preparation*

Page Make-Up, Electronic - Computerized systems that can create complete pages of text, graphics, and scanned photos that are ready to be output to film or plate for printing. See Page Makeup. *Art and Copy Preparation - Desktop/Electronic Publishing*

Page Printer - An output printer that prints a full page once it has been fully processed. *Computer Hardware - Printing Processes*

Page Proofs - A representation of a page as it will appear printed, including all the elements: type, graphics, and photos, in the actual correct colors. *Proofing*

Pages Per Inch (PPI) - Paper thickness, i.e., the exact number of pages in an inch. *Substrates*

Pagination - A computer technique that automatically breaks all the pages in a document into their correct page sequence. *Desktop/Electronic Publishing*

Paint Program - An application program that allows the user to create drawings, graphics, and illustrations by manipulating various pixels. *Software*

Palette - A group of colors that have been selected from a larger set of colors which can be shown on-screen. *Color Reproduction*

Panchromatic - A type of photographic film that is sensitive to all the wavelengths of the visible spectrum (the full range of all the visible colors). *Graphic Arts Photography*

Panning - Moving an image, page, or document that is larger than the monitor or frame around to view all sections. *Desktop/Electronic Publishing*

Pantone Matching System (PMS) - A worldwide standard for color. Each unique color has a PMS Number, which is used by printers and all other individuals in the graphics field to specify the exact colors required on each job. *Color Reproduction - Ink*

Paper - A sheet or roll usually made of cellulose and other materials, less than .006th of an inch in thickness, that is used as a printing substrate. *Substrates*

Paperback - Any book with a soft cover. *Desktop/Electronic Publishing*

Paperboard - A thick sheet usually made of cellulose and other materials, that is over .010th of an inch thick. *Substrates*

Paper Cutters - A device that has been designed to precisely cut paper sheets into the desired sizes. *Finishing*

Paper Master - A paper plate used in some aspects of printing, i.e., offset-duplicator, etc. *Image Carriers*

Paper Stencil Screening - An inexpensive method of screen printing that uses a paper stencil. See Screen Printing. *Printing Processes*

Parallel - The sending of data, side by side (at the same time), over different wires in the same cable. *General Computer*

Parallel Port - The computer connection that accepts parallel communication. *Computer Hardware*

Park - Setting the head on the hard drive in a rigid position so as not to damage information on the drive if it is moved or jarred. *General Computer*

Password - A character string or code that is a part of a computer security system. The user cannot log onto the computer without entering a private code. This limits access to computer usage. *General Computer*

Paste Drier - A material that is compounded into ink to quicken the drying time. *Ink*

Paste Ink - An ink that has a high viscosity. *Ink*

Paste-Up - The manual process of assembling all the copy, graphics, and photos onto a board in preparation for the creation of the CRC. See CRC. *Art and Copy Preparation*

Paste-Up Artist - The person who manually adheres the copy and graphic elements onto boards to create CRC. See CRC. *Art and Copy Preparation*

Patch - A last minute change or revision to a plate. *Image Carriers*

PC-Compatible - Computer hardware and software that is compatible with MS-DOS and PC-DOS operating systems. *General Computer*

PC-DOS - See MS-DOS.

PCM (Pulse Code Modulation) - A standard format for the compression of analog voice signals. *Multimedia*

PCX - A PC Paint Brush format for storage of graphic images. *Desktop/Electronic Publishing*

PDL - See Page Description Language.

PE - See Printer's Error.

Peaking - A scanner technique for edge enhancement. *Scanning*

Pebbling - The embossing of paper after printing is completed to create this special effect. *Finishing*

Pel - See Pixel.

Penetration - The amount of ink that is absorbed by the substrate. See Migration. *Ink*

Pentium Chips - A computer chip produced by Intel that offers greater speeds than the fastest 486 chips. *Computer Hardware*

Perfect Binding - A specific type of binding that is used on books and a few magazines or catalogs. This method is most often used when the number of pages exceeds 96 and when it is required to have a publication with a spine-side edge that is square. *Finishing*

Perfecting Press (Perfector) - A press that can print on either side of a sheet or roll of paper in one pass through the press. *Printing Processes*

Perforate - See Perforating.

Perforating - A process that creates a line of tiny slits in a substrate to make tearing apart easier. *Printing Processes*

Perforation - See Perforating.

Periodical - A publication that is issued monthly, bimonthly, weekly, biweekly or quarterly, such as a magazine or newsletter. *Desktop/Electronic Publishing*

Periodical Printer - A printer specializing in magazine production. *Printing Processes*

Peripheral - A device that is attached externally to a computer to achieve specific conditions, i.e., secondary memory, etc. *Computer Hardware*

Personal Computers (PC's) - Powerful, self-contained desktop computers with limited peripherals, not part of a network, and usually used by one person. In fact, PC's are now becoming so powerful they are being used on networks and as a part of work groups *Computer Hardware*

Personalized Media - Information that is specially packaged to meet the interests of a single person or of small groups of people. *Multimedia - Printing Processes*

Perspective Drawings - Drawings that show the most distant objects as smaller than the closer objects. See One-point Perspective. *Art and Copy Preparation*

pH - A symbol that is used when indicating acidity and alkalinity. *Quality/Process Control*

pH Meter - A device that measures acidity and alkalinity. *Quality/Process Control*

Phosphor - A material which converts part of absorbed primary energy into emitted luminescent radiation. Phosphors are coated on the CRT of the television set. When they are struck by the electron beam they glow causing the picture. *Digital Photography - Telecommunications*

Photo CD - A file format (which includes color standards) that holds images on a compact disc that are scanned from 35 mm negatives and/or slides. *Computer Hardware*

Photocomposing - Image creation through the merger of light, the image, and light-sensitive film, paper, or plates. See Phototypesetting, Photomechanical, and Photo Direct. *Typesetting and Imagesetting*

Photoconductor - Materials that become light-sensitive by being charged by a visible discharge, like a corona. *Graphic Arts Photography - Printing Processes*

Photoconversion - See Photocomposing.

Photo Direct - The direct exposure of an image to light-sensitive material. *Graphic Arts Photography*

Photo-Direct Plate - A type of paper offset plate that is created photographically. The image is exposed directly onto the plate without the need for an intermediate negative. *Image Carriers*

Photoengraver - The person who creates letterpress plates. See Photoengraving. *Image Carriers*

Photoengraving - The process of creating letterpress plates. See Photoengraver. *Image Carriers*

Photo Grade - A laser printer feature that enhances halftone quality. *Laser Applications*

Photographer - The individual who takes photographs on a freelance basis for their personal clients or for the companies who employ their services. *Graphic Arts Photography*

Photographic Blotters - These blotters are placed between prints as they dry in order to create a matte finish. *Art and Copy Preparation*

Photographic Stencil Screening - A type of screen printing that uses a photographic process (an image is exposed to the sensitized screen) in the creation of the stencils. See Screen Printing. *Printing Processes*

Photography - The process of placing images on a sensitized material by exposure to light. *Graphic Arts Photography*

Photomechanical - Any process that involves film or CRC being exposed onto sensitized paper or metal plates that have a special photographically sensitive material on their surface. *Image Carriers*

Photomechanical Transfer - See PMT.

Photo-Optics - Systems requiring the use of lenses for enlarging, reducing, or distorting images, i.e., a graphic arts camera or a phototypesetter using zoom lenses for enlarging or reducing type size. *Graphic Arts Photography - Typesetting and Imagesetting*

Photopolymer Coating - A special coating that is applied to a plate to toughen the surface for long printing runs. This plastic coating can also be changed by chemistry to alter any area's receptivity to ink. *Image Carriers*

Photopolymer Plate - This is a flexible plate that is used when printing on a letterpress or a flexographic press. *Image Carriers*

Photorealism - The creation of images on a computer that are close to real life or photographic realism. *Desktop/Electronic Publishing - Multimedia*

Photoresist - A material that hardens when exposed to ultraviolet light and cannot be washed away. It can be used to create the image area on a plate. *Image Carriers*

Photoshop - Photo design and production tool for creating original artwork, retouching photographic images, and producing high-quality color separations and output. It allows designing electronic artwork with powerful painting and selection tools; retouching and correcting true color or black and white scanned images with image processing tools and filters; and adding or correcting color, or executing delicate retouching. The user can create duotones, tritones, and quadtones. For Mac and Windows. See Adobe Systems, Inc. *Software*

Photostat - See Stat.

Phototypesetting - The process of setting professional looking type onto photographic film and/or paper on any type of phototypesetter. *Typesetting and Imagesetting*

Phototypesetter - A device that produces high resolution text. They traditionally use negative film containing the character shapes through which light is shined onto photo-sensitive paper to form the character images. This paper is developed into galleys and the resulting copy is used as a part of the camera-ready copy. *Typesetting and Imagesetting*

Pica - The basic measurement unit that is

167

used in the graphic arts field. A pica is about .166 of an inch, and this makes six picas per inch. Picas are further broken down into points. There are 12 points per pica; 6 picas per inch; and 72 points per inch. *Typography*

Picking - Paper fiber or surface that lifts during printing, due to the tackiness or stickiness of the ink. *Ink - Substrates*

PICT - A standardized format that is used to store and manipulate graphic images. *Desktop/Electronic Publishing*

Pied Type (PI) - Individual hot type characters that have become accidently scrambled out of order. *Typesetting and Imagesetting*

Pigments - Substances that give color or body to ink. *Ink*

Piling - Ink build-up on press blankets, plates, and rollers. *Ink*

Pinfeed Holes - The holes along the edges of the continuous computer forms that hold and guide the paper in the printer. *Substrates*

Pinholes - Unwanted holes or transparent areas in film negatives which must be opaqued before plates are created. *Image Carriers*

Pin Register - A stripping and image assembly technique that is used to achieve accurate and precise registration with multiple sheets of film. This method involves the use of pins and holes punched in paper and film, which are aligned for precise registration. A pin register system can also be used in platemaking and can be installed on print-

ing presses and imagesetters. *Image Assembly - Image Carriers*

Pitch - The amount of characters in an inch on a printer. *Computer Hardware*

Pitch Gauge - A device that measures a wire's diameter. *Quality/Process Control*

Pixar Company - Computer animation services and design software for generating realistic high-quality images. The RenderMan software products allow the creation of pictures that have all the qualities of real life. Contact numbers: 1001 West Cutting Blvd., Richmond, CA 94804; (510)236-4000. *Multimedia*

Pixar One Twenty Eight CD - Collection of 128 high-quality, photographic textures specifically designed for use in computer graphics on CD. Can be read by any application that can read TIFF files on Windows, Mac, and UNIX workstations. See Pixar Company. *Software*

Pixar Showplace - Mac software that allows the creation of realistic 3-D scenes. The user picks and places predesigned objects, sets lights, and views the scene from any angle and processes a high-impact, realistic looking picture using RenderMan technology. See Pixar Company. *Software*

Pixar Typestry - Turns Type I and True-Type fonts into 3-D images that can be rotated, moved, and scaled. Extrudes any word or individual letter either uniformly or non-uniformly. Offers motion blur, patterns, shadows, embossing, cut-outs, and simple animations. See Pixar Company. *Software*

Pixel - The smallest picture element or

amount of data where color and brightness can be independently assigned and a computer software can manipulate. *Desktop/Electronic Publishing - General Computer* The image pick-up device (the CCD) in a still video camera that is composed of thousands of light-sensitive picture elements. These pixels are the smallest elements which comprise the image and react to the brightness variations produced by the image from the lens by producing electrical charges. *Digital Photography*

Pixel Burst - A product developed by Adobe Systems that greatly boosts the processing of halftones, i.e., an accelerator for four-color separations. *Color Reproduction*

Pixellation - The method by which the actual number of pixels are reduced in an image. Then the remaining pixels can be enlarged or modified to create a special effect. *Desktop/Electronic Publishing*

Pixel Swapping - The electronic replacement of pixels in one area of an image with pixels from another area of an image. This feature can be used to correct image defects and for cloning. See Clone. *Color Reproduction - Desktop/Electronic Publishing - Digital Photography*

Pixo Arts - A graphic software company that develops and distributes color image editing and processing systems for PC platforms. Contact numbers: 2570 W. El Camino Real, #105, Mountain View, CA 94040; (415)949-2578. *Software*

PixoFoto - DOS software that allows bit-mapped images to be manipulated as floating objects. Offers a variety of advanced features that allow scanning, editing, photo corrections, and prepares images for printing and color separations. See Pixo Arts. *Software*

PixoFoto PRO - Inherits all powerful features of PixoFoto and PixoNova, in addition, it provides all functions necessary for Nova Jet Color reproductions, such as printing replicate copies, continuous printing, batch mode printing, etc. See Pixo Arts. *Software*

PixoNova - The scanning, color correcting, and printing DOS software for Nova-Jet users to produce wide-format posters using error diffusion algorithms. See Pixo Arts. *Software*

Plain or Roman Typestyle - The basic version of a typestyle which is used for body text. *Typography*

Planographic Printing - See Lithography.

Plasticizer - A material that makes products, such as film, more flexible. *Graphic Arts Photography - Image Carriers*

Plate - The metal, plastic, or other surface that holds an image that will be printed. The plate striking the substrate creates the printed image. *Image Carriers*

Plate Cylinder - The mechanism that holds the plate during printing on rotary presses. *Printing Processes*

Plate Finish - Paper with a hard, smooth finish. It is produced by a process called calendering. See Calendering and Supercalendering. *Substrates*

Platemaker - The person who completes the platemaking process. See Platemaking. *Image Carriers*

Platemaking - The steps involved in creating press plates from images on a negative or positive. *Image Carriers*

Platen - The large rubber cylinder in a printer. The paper rolls around the platen and provides a cushion for the striking keys. *Computer Hardware* The surface that presses the paper and the type together on a letterpress to produce the printed impression. *Printing Processes*

Playback Head - The device that makes contact with the magnetic diskette to convert magnetism to electrical signals or vice versa. They are used to record, erase, or play video signals. *Digital Photography*

Plug - See Plugging.

Plugging - A printing problem when halftones and/or copy receive excess ink and begin to fill in. *Printing Processes*

PMS - See Pantone Matching System.

PMT - A photomechanical transfer process. See Photomechanical. *Graphic Arts Photography*

Point - The standard measurement used in the graphic arts field for type size designation, i.e., 12 points to a pica. See Pica. *Typography*

Point-Of-Purchase Display (POP) - A specialty display or rack that is designed by graphic artists which holds products for sale, in order to enhance their salability. *Art and Copy Preparation - Marketing*

Point Size - All type is expressed in point sizes - 72 point type is one inch high and 36 point type is 1/2 inch in height. See Fig. 29 on page 171. *Typography*

Point-To-Multipoint Service - One signal that travels from its point of origin to many other points, i.e., a television signal transmits from a satellite to many different homes or television sets. *Telecommunications*

Point-To-Point Service - One signal travels from its originating point to another point. *Telecommunications*

Polybag - A polyethylene bag. *Finishing*

Poor Trapping - See Undertrapping.

POP - See Point-Of-Purchase Display.

Pop Test - See Mullen Test.

Pop-Up - A special printed and finished product that becomes 3-D when opened. *Finishing*

Porosity - The degree to which paper will allow the permeation of liquids (i.e., ink) and vapors, (i.e., air). The minute holes in the surface of these substrates allow this permeation. *Substrates*

Porous - The degree to which a substrate exhibits porosity. *Substrates*

Port - A connection on the computer where data can be sent to and from the computer. *Computer Hardware* The process of modifying a program to run on a different computer. *General Computer*

Portable - A software program that can be run on many different computers. *Software* A small laptop or notebook computer. *Computer Hardware*

Portrait Mode - The capability of a printer to output computer images that

Fig. 29 - Different Point Sizes

are taller than they are wide. See Landscape Mode for example. *Desktop/Electronic Publishing*

Position Stat - A reproduction of artwork, halftones, or photos that is used on CRC to indicate its actual location and size on final film and plates. *Art and Copy Preparation*

Positive - An image where both light and dark areas correspond to the original image. *Graphic Arts Photography*

Positive Films - An image on film where light and dark areas correspond to the original optical image. The opposite of a negative. *Graphic Arts Photography*

Posterization - A special effect where the gray levels or color pixels are reduced. This produces an effect where changes in color and shading is abrupt and noticeably visible. See Pixellation

Color Reproduction The reproduction of continuous tones, in black and white and color plates, as flat solid colors. *Graphic Arts Photography*

Post Binder - A method of binding loose pages together with a rod. *Finishing*

Post-House - See Post-Production Company.

Post-Press - All activities after printing, i.e., finishing services. See Finishing. *Finishing*

Post-Processing Device - A combination finishing and printing system that is capable of creating completed documents, i.e., proposal, booklets, etc. *Finishing - Printing Processes*

Post-Production Company - A company that processes all sound and video data after it is produced. *Multimedia*

PostScript - A page description language that was developed by Adobe Systems, Inc. It allows fully scalable text (fonts) to be combined on a single page with high level graphics and output on a wide range of printers. PostScript has become a standard in the graphic arts industry for printers, imagesetters, and graphics software. See PostScript Level 1, PostScript Level 2, PDL, and Page Description Language. *Software*

PostScript Clone - A page description language that closely emulates the licensed Adobe PostScript product. *Computer Hardware - Software*

PostScript Level 1 - The initial implementation of PostScript and most commonly known as "PostScript," a product of Adobe Systems, Inc. See Adobe Systems, Inc. and PostScript. *Software*

PostScript Level 2 - A superset of PS Level 1, with all the features of Level 1 plus some excellent enhancements, i.e., data decompression and compression, enhanced halftoning, printer-specific functions, and device-independent color. *Software*

PowerMath (LC, LC II, Performa 400 405/430) - A math chip board that speeds up math/science and spreadsheet applications 500 percent or more. Includes a 16 MHz 68882 math chip, and is upgradable to the PowerCache. See DayStar Digital. *Software*

PowerPC - A family of computer processors built on reduced instruction-set computing (RISC) technology and developed as part of an alliance between Apple Computer, IBM, and Motorola. In addition to its greater processing speed, this system allows cross-platforming, thus permitting different computer systems to work together. *Computer Hardware*

Power To Go - See Retrieve It!

P-P (Peak To Peak) - The total difference between the most positive and most negative peaks of a waveform. *Telecommunications*

PPI - Pixels Per Inch. See Pages Per Inch. *Desktop/Electronic Publishing*

PQET (Print Quality Enhancement Technology) - A type of technology for resolution enhancement. *Quality/Process Control*

Preemptive Multi-Tasking - Ability to stop an operating process during program execution to begin another process and be able to keep track of the interruption in order to begin the interrupted process again. *Software*

Preface - An author's remarks that generally define the goals and aims of the book. It is normally located within the first 10 to 12 pages of the book and is a part of what is termed as front matter. *Desktop/Electronic Publishing*

Pre-Mastering - The process of combining all the various files in a multimedia project into a single file in preparation for the final mastering operation. *Multimedia*

Premiere - A digital movie-making and video production tool. Allows easy combination of video, audio, animation, still images, and graphics to bring ideas to the screen. Has ability to export work to professional production equipment. For Mac. See Adobe Systems, Inc. *Multimedia - Software*

Pre-Press - All the processes that occur to a job to be printed prior to the printing, i.e., creation of CRC, image assembly, platemaking, etc. *Art and Copy Preparation - Graphic Arts Photography - Image Assembly - Image Carriers - Scanning*

Pre-Press Proof - A proof that was created photographically without the use of a press itself. It is usually produced for the customer's approval of the job before the actual printing occurs. *Proofing*

Pre-Publishing - The publisher's or print buyer's involvement in electronic graphic arts production and multimedia and all those operations required before publishing. This includes art and copy preparation, text preparation and typesetting, scanning, imagesetting, image assembly, audio, animations, and video preparations. *Desktop/Electronic Publishing - Digital Photography - Multimedia*

Presensitized Plate - A plate that has a coating of light-sensitive material. *Image Carriers*

Presentation Software - Programs that are used to create slide shows and transparency presentations. *Multimedia - Software*

Presentation Technologies - Desktop slide making solutions. Designs, manufactures, and markets the Montage Presentation Series of products which are based around the Montage FR2 digital film recorder. Contact numbers: 779 Palomar Ave., Sunnyvale, CA 94086; (408)730-3700. *Computer Hardware*

Presenter Professional - Powerful and intuitive spline-based modeling, rendering, and animation package. Combines free-form modeling and "Digital Clay" sculpting, path/object animation, and RenderMan interface. For Mac. See Visual Information Development Inc. *Software*

Press - A machine that places inked images onto paper or other similar substrates. *Printing Processes*

Press Operator - The person who operates a printing press. These individuals must have extensive knowledge of the operation of the press, the paper (and other substrates), and the inks. *Printing Processes*

Press Proofs - An actual printing of a few pieces of a job on press prior to full production for customer approval. This is typically the final check and the last chance to make changes. If the customer is present for a press proof, once it is OK'd, the full job will be completed immediately. *Proofing*

Press Run - See Run

Pressureless Printing - See Non-impact Printing.

Pressure-Sensitive Paper - A special paper product that will adhere to other surfaces without the need for moisture once the protective back sheet is removed. This type of paper is used to produce labels. *Substrates*

Press Varnish - The varnish that is applied on press by the press inking system. *Printing Processes*

PressWise - A page imposition program that enables users to quickly prepare accurate, plate-ready signatures of multi-page documents for web-fed presses and up to 40 inch sheet-fed presses. For Mac, Windows, or UNIX. See Aldus Corporation. *Software*

Presswork - The process of running a printing press and doing all necessary adjustments during printing. *Printing Processes*

Preventive Maintenance - Adjustments that are performed on machines to avoid unexpected mechanical breakdowns. *Quality/Process Control*

Primary Colors - The three primary colors - red, green, and blue - of light which can be added together to create white light. These three colors are often known as additive color and are the basic technology in all TV monitors. In four-color process printing yellow, magenta, and cyan are the primary colors and red, green, and blue are the secondary colors in this subtractive color process. *Color Reproduction*

Printability - A substrate's ability to accept a printed image. *Substrates*

Printer - Person or company that has a printing press or runs a printing press as a business for customers. *Printing Processes* A device that outputs data from a computer onto paper. *Computer Hardware*

Print Driver - Software that allows an application program to output on specific printers. *Software*

Printer's Errors - Printer's errors that are not chargeable to the customer. *Quality/Process Control*

Printer's Helper - Those individuals

who assist the press operators, especially on larger presses. *Printing Processes*

Printer's Rule - A short, (1 foot or less) two-sided metal or clear plastic ruler that has inch measurements on one side and pica and point gradations on the other side. *Art and Copy Preparation - Quality/Process Control*

Print Image - The image created on the printing press. *Printing Processes*

Printing Plate - The metal or paper surface that contains and carries the complete image that will be printed on the press. *Image Carriers*

Printing Press - See Press.

Printing Surface - The actual printing plate surface. It is flat in lithography, raised in letterpress and flexography, and recessed in gravure. *Printing Processes*

Print Quality - The final quality of the material that has been printed. It should match the proof and meet the customer's expectations. *Quality/Process Control*

Print Rub Resistence - See Rub Resistence.

Print Run - See Run

Print Server - A computer device (or workstation), having the primary function of management of all the printers on a network. *Computer Hardware*

Print Shop - Traditionally a small neighborhood store in which printing would take place. See Printer. *Printing Processes*

Print Spooler - Software running on a

computer or file server that holds documents in memory until the printer can accept and process the files. *Software*

ProArt Professional Art Library - A comprehensive, easy-to-use art collection where all images are created in Illustrator and saved in EPS format. See Multi-Ad Services, Inc. *Software*

Processor - A special device or unit that converts, through chemistry, the latent image on light-sensitive film or paper to a permanent, visible image. See Developer. *Graphic Arts Photography*

Process Camera - See Graphic Arts Camera.

Process Colors - There are four process colors - magenta, cyan, yellow, and black. See Subtractive Primaries. *Color Reproduction - Ink*

Process Lens - A photographic lens that is used in the graphics field to produce color and black and white halftones (by using a screen), plus line artwork. *Graphic Arts Photography*

Process Plate - The color plates that are used in four-color printing - yellow, magenta, cyan, and black. When all four are combined together, full-color printing is produced. *Image Carriers*

Process Color Printing - Printing from the color plates that are used in four-color printing: yellow, magenta, cyan, and black. When all four are combined together full-color printing is produced. See Process Plate. *Color Reproduction*

Producer - The person responsible for an entire multimedia product. *Multimedia*

Productivity Enhancement, Inc. - Software development firm that specializes in Mac, Windows, and cross-platform application development. Contact Numbers: 5806 Glenn Hollow Lane, Norcross, GA, 30071; (404)446-8866 . *Software*

Program - See Software.

Programmable Function Key - A keyboard key having a function controlled by a software program. *Computer Hardware*

Programmer - The person who writes the codes or instructions which constitute a computer program. *General Computer*

Programming - The process of writing the codes or instructions of a computer program. *General Computer*

Progressives - See Progressive Proofs.

Progressive Proofs (PROGS) - A series of seven proofs that include the individual printing of each of the four basic colors - yellow, magenta, cyan and black, and various combinations of these four as a final look of the printed job. They are rarely used anymore and have been replaced with more efficient and economical pre-press proofs. *Proofing*

Projection Printing - The creation of enlarged prints from a small negative. *Printing Processes*

Proof - A copy of any galleys, rough proofs, or pages that allow corrections to be made by the customer or client before final output of the job is printed. *Proofing*

Proof Copy - A representative sample of the material before it is printed. The proof gives the customer a final chance to

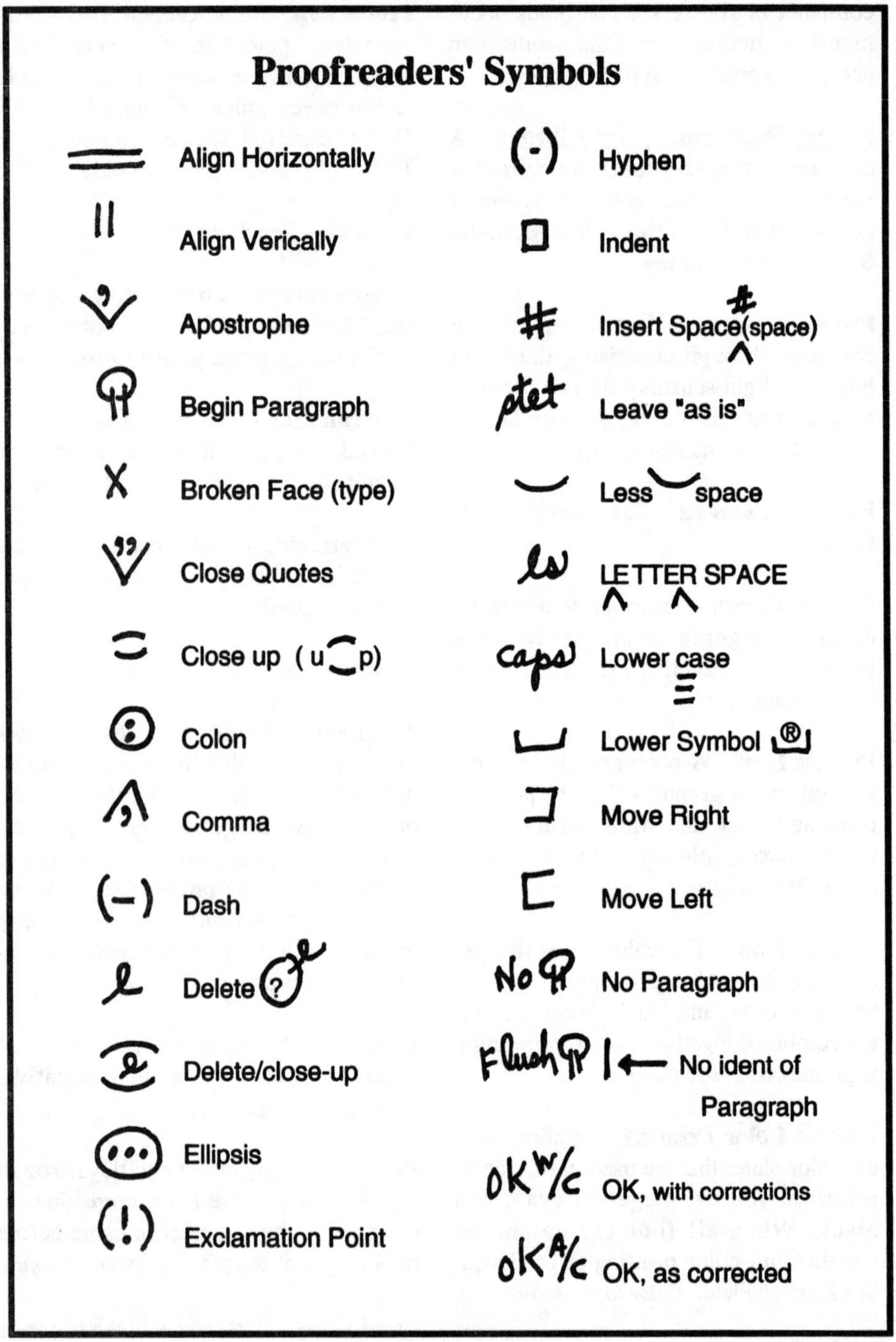

Proofreaders' Symbols

☰	Align Horizontally	(·)	Hyphen
‖	Align Verically	☐	Indent
⌄	Apostrophe	#	Insert Space(space)
¶	Begin Paragraph	*stet*	Leave "as is"
X	Broken Face (type)	⌣	Less space
⌄	Close Quotes	*la*	LETTER SPACE
⌒	Close up (u⌒p)	*caps*	Lower case
⊙	Colon	⊔	Lower Symbol ®
⋀	Comma	⊐	Move Right
(–)	Dash	⊏	Move Left
l	Delete ⊘	No ¶	No Paragraph
⊘	Delete/close-up	Flush ¶ ←	No ident of Paragraph
⊙⋯	Ellipsis	OK w/c	OK, with corrections
(!)	Exclamation Point	OK A/c	OK, as corrected

Fig. 30 - Proofreaders' Symbols

Proofreaders' Symbols - continued

V̎	Open Quotes	**Caps**	Use capitals
(I)	Parenthesis		or (capitals)
⊙	Period	**SC**	Use small capitals
(?)	Question Mark		or (small capitals)
⌐¬	Raise symbol ®̄	**ital**	Use italic or
No ¶	Run in together		(italic)
⨀	Semicolon	**lf**	Use light face or
sp	Spell Out (Lt.)		(light face)
tr	Transpose word	**bf**	Use bold face or
tr	Transpose word (a)		(bold face)
lc	Use LOWER case	**wf**	Wrong face (type)
	or (LOWER) case		

Fig. 30 - Cont'd

make changes before the full production. *Proofing*

Proofreaders' Symbols - The indications made by the copy editor in the text that define the necessary corrections. See Fig. 30 on pages 176 and 177. *Desktop/Electronic Publishing*

PROM (Programmable Read-Only Memory) - Computer chips that, once they have been programmed, cannot be altered. *Computer Hardware*

Prompt - An on-screen indicator which signals that the user can begin inputting information and data. *Computer Hardware*

Proportion - The relationship between all the elements in a design. It creates balance, unity, and contrast. Proportion allows the elements to have life and to generate interest. See Design Principles. *Art and Copy Preparation*

Proportional Scale - Typicallly, a circular scale that is used to compute the percentage of reduction or enlargement of photos, line drawings, and other graphic elements. *Art and Copy Preparation*

Proportional Spaced Characters - Typeface or fonts where the characters differ in width, depending on the character and its size. An "m" space is wider than a "i" space. *Typography*

Protocol - The set of instructions that govern and control the exchange of information over different networks. Each network, like Ethernet or AppleTalk, has its own set of protocols. *Software*

PSE (Paper Surface Efficiency) - Describes the ink/paper relationship. The amount of gloss of the paper in relation to the amount of the absorptance of the ink. *Ink - Quality/Process Control - Substrates*

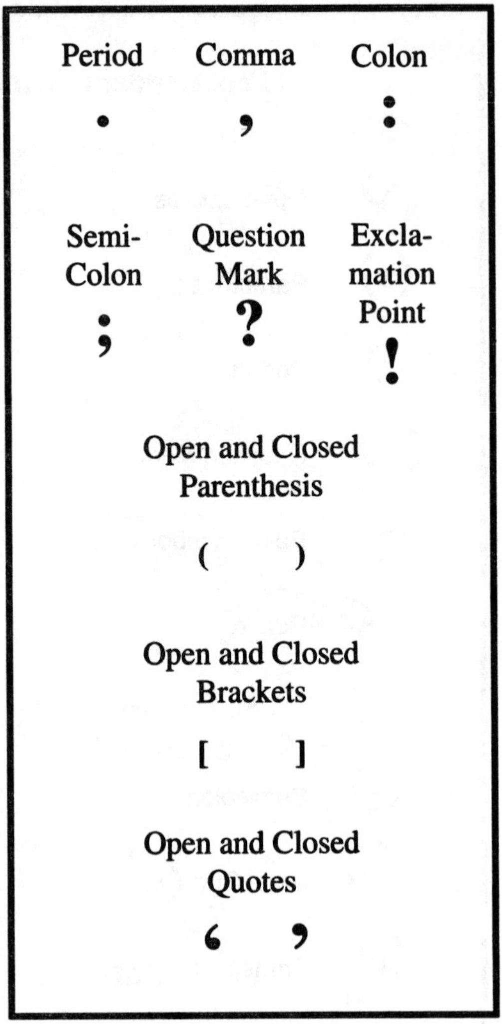

Period	Comma	Colon
•	,	:

Semi-Colon	Question Mark	Exclamation Point
;	?	!

Open and Closed Parenthesis

(   )

Open and Closed Brackets

[   ]

Open and Closed Quotes

'   '

Fig. 31 - Punctuation

Psychrometer - A device that is used for the measurement of relative humidity. *Environment - Quality/Process Control - Substrates*

Publication - A complete body of written material that is distributed to others free of charge or for a fee, i.e., a magazine, book, report, etc. *Desktop/Electronic Publishing*

Publication Administrator 2.0 - A client-server database for managing QuarkXPress documents. Monitors the creation and editing of an XPress document, updates the publication status of text and art box elements, and controls access to documents. See North Atlantic Publishing Systems. *Software*

Public Domain - Information and/or computer software that is not copyrighted and can be used by anyone. This material is usually free or it is very inexpensive. *Software*

Publish It! 3.0 - Complete page layout, word processing, and graphics tools. Features: an improved graphical user interface; On-The-Fly-Font Scaling with 20 scalable fonts; 150 clip art illustrations; spell checker; and Power Text for creating special text effects. See Timeworks, Inc. *Software*

Publish It! Easy - Page layout, word processing, ad graphics tools, a database/mail-merge program, and slide show feature. Supports: expanded drawing tools; graduated fills for rectangles; color TIFF images; image control for gray scale; color PICT; and TIFF images. See Timeworks, Inc. *Software*

Publish It! Lite - Designed for the beginning user. Includes built-in word processing and drawing tools, nine sample layouts, 40 clip art images, and over 140 possible font combinations. See Timeworks, Inc. *Software*

Publish It! For Windows - A full-featured, easy-to-learn desktop publisher with page layout, word processing, typesetting, and graphics tools. Features a spell checker, over 150 clip art illustrations, Adobe Type Manager with 25 scalable fonts, and a feature for creating special text effects. See Timeworks, Inc. *Software*

Puck - A device similar in look and application to a mouse, except the puck is usually used in conjunction with a tablet. See Mouse. *Computer Hardware*

Pull-Down Menu - A list of options which appear at the point a main menu option or bar is opened. *Software*

Pulsed Laser - A laser that produces a very intense, non-continuous, burst of white light from stored-up energy and is used for cutting solid material. *Laser Applications*

Pulsed Xenon Light - An exposure light source that is often used in graphic arts photography and lithographic platemaking, It is a gas filled lamp that provides a continuous emission of light of a little over 5000K. *Graphic Arts Photography - Image Carriers*

Punching - See Drilling.

Punctuation - That portion of a font that includes the standard punctuation used in the language, i.e., comma, period, colon, semi-colon, open and closed quotes, question mark, open and closed parentheses, open and closed brackets, and the exclamation point. See Fig. 31 on page 178. *Typography*

Purge - The elimination of all the unneeded data and files from a database or a memory bank. *General Computer*

Quad - A blank spacing slug used in traditional metal typesetting for the creation of indentations and spaces. *Typesetting and Imagesetting*

Quad 040 - Quadra and Centris Accelerator (Mac Centris 610/650/660AV and Quadra 700/800/900/950) - Boosts the Quadra or Centris beyond speed of Quadra 840AV. Features a 40 MHz 68040 CPU and a superfast 128K Static Photoshop without taking up an additional slot. See DayStar Digital. *Computer Hardware*

Quality - A measure of flawless work. *Quality/Process Control*

Quality Assurance - A program that is designed to produce quality. See Quality. *Quality/Process Control*

Quality Control - The procedures within a company that produce and control quality. See Quality. *Quality/Process Control*

Quality Paperback - A trade paperback, usually 5" X 8" to 6" X 9" in size. See Paperback. *Desktop/Electronic Publishing*

Quantity Prints - Multiple prints made from an original that are produced at one time. *Art and Copy Preparation*

Quantization - The conversion from analog signals (cycles) to digital signals (bits). *Digital Photography*

Quark, Inc. - A leading producer of publishing software for desktop publishing. QuarkXPress, QuarkXPress Passport, and Quark Publishing System are their prima-

ry products. Contact numbers: 1800 Grant St., Denver, CO 80203; (303)894-8888. *Software*

QuarkXPress - A full range of word processing, typographic, and page layout features that enables users to combine text and graphics to create high-quality publications. Superior typographic, design, and color capabilities. The program accommodates type size from 2 points to 720 points in .001 point increments; tracking and kerning to a tolerance of .000005 of an em space; and full text and graphic rotation to .001°. The program's interface includes six interactive palettes and numerous keyboard commands enabling users to create sophisticated pages quickly and easily. Enables users to import all popular text and picture formats. Users can style text using the program's text-formatting capabilities and can modify imported pictures by cropping, rotating, scaling, or skewing. For Mac and Windows platforms with complete file compatibility between the platforms. See Quark, Inc. *Software*

QuarkXPress Passport - Combines the features and capabilities of the single language program with the ability to create multilingual publications. The 13 languages supported are: Danish, Dutch, English (U.S. and Intl.), Finnish, French, German, Greek, Italian, Norwegian, Spanish, Swedish and Swiss-German. See Quark, Inc. *Software*

Quark Publishing System - The Quark Publishing System is an editorial management system for work-group publishing environments that integrates with

QuarkXPress. See Quark, Inc. *Software*

Quarter Fold - See Chopper Fold.

Quarter Tone - Dot percentages in the 25 percent dot size range. *Graphic Arts Photography*

Quarto - A single sheet of paper that is folded into eight pages. *Finishing*

Quick Draw - The operating system software that governs Mac screen display. *Software*

Quick Printer - A printer that specializes in small and short run jobs. *Printing Processes*

Quick Time - Software for the Mac and Windows that allows the display of animation and video. Sound and moving images can be manipulated and synchronized. *Software*

Quotation - A form that states the estimate of the cost to produce a particular printing job or other graphic arts service. See Estimator. *Printing Processes*

Quote - See Quotation.

Rachwal - An electronic imposition system. See Imposition. *Image Assembly*

Radio Frequency (RF) - An extremely wide band of frequencies that can be used to send signals through the atmosphere. They range from under 30 KHz to 300,000 MHz and are divided into bands and allocated for certain uses. Commercial TV uses parts of the VHF (30-300 MHz) and UHF (300-3,000 MHz) bands. *Telecommunications*

Radio Frequency (RF) Converter - A device that modulates a radio frequency carrier signal to the video signal so that images recorded on the floppy disk can be played back on a normal TV through the antenna terminals. *Digital Photography - Telecommunications*

Ragged Left - See Fig. 22 on page 139.

Ragged Right - See Fig. 22 on page 139.

Ragged Left/Ragged Right - See Fig. 22 on page 139.

RAM (Random Access Memory) - A read/write memory, which is the CPU's main memory. *Computer Hardware*

RAM PowerCard (Mac II, IIx, IIcx, IIvi, IIsi (NuBus), IIci, IIvx, IIfx, Performa 600, all Quadras, Centris 650, DuoDock) - Accelerates Photoshop and other applications up to 300 percent. Includes software to copy files between the hard drive and RAM disk automatically. See DayStar Digital. *Computer Hardware*

Random Access Memory - See RAM.

Raster - Scanned or bit-mapped data. *Scanning*

Raster Display - The division of a raster image into dots along each scan line. *Desktop/Electronic Publishing - Digital Photography - Scanning*

Raster Graphics - The representation of an image as a pattern of dots. Scanned images are raster graphics. *Scanning*

Raster Image Processor - See RIP.

Rational Tangent Screening (RTS) - A color separation or screening method that was used on the original desktop systems. It often produced moire patterns and hampered the creation of color separations on the desktop. *Color Reproduction - Desktop/Electronic Publishing*

Raw Stock - A substrate before coatings or ink is applied. *Substrates*

Read - The process of a computer reading or copying data from a secondary memory source (hard drive, diskette, etc.) to its main memory. *General Computer*

Read-Only Memory - See ROM.

Real Time - An image capturing feature that allows switching between live images from a video camera and captured images. *Digital Photography*

Ream - 500 sheets of paper. One of the basic ways of packaging paper for sale in the marketplace. *Substrates*

Re-Boot - To turn a computer off and restart. *General Computer*

183

Record - Entire groups of related data or fields, where each field has a unique name. *General Computer*

Recto - The odd-numbered pages, i.e., 1, 3, 5, etc. *Desktop/Electronic Publishing*

Red Book - See CD (Compact Disk).

Reduced Instruction Set Computer - See RISC.

Reducers - Compounds used in printing to reduce ink consistency. *Ink* In photography these chemicals are used in the reduction of image density on film. *Graphic Arts Photography*

Reduction - The process of making artwork or copy smaller. *Art and Copy Preparation - Graphic Arts Photography - Scanning*

Re-Etch - To continue to etch a halftone plate for improved contrast. *Image Carriers*

Reflectance - The amount (or percentage) of light that is reflected from a surface. *Color Reproduction*

Reflection Copy - Copy that must be viewed and/or photographed by a special light that is reflected from the surface of the copy, i.e., oil paintings and glossy photographs. *Art and Copy Preparation*

Reflection Density - A reading with a densitometer of the reflected light off a surface. *Quality/Process Control*

Reflective Media - Any media where the image is visible because light reflects off the surface of the media towards the naked eye. *Art and Copy Preparation - Graphic Arts Photography*

Register - A specific section of main memory that is used to hold or store binary digits that are needed by the system, i.e., a memory location. *Computer Hardware* The placement of one image in the precise position over the next image to achieve correct alignment. See Registration. *Image Assembly - Printing Processes*

Register Marks - See Registration Marks, Crop Marks.

Registration - The alignment of color separations and all other types of artwork that are being assembled in preparation for printing by using the crop marks as guides. See Registration Marks. *Color Reproduction - Image Assembly*

Registration Marks - The marks that are used for the alignment of color separations and all other artwork that are being assembled in preparation for printing. *Color Reproduction - Image Assembly*

Relative Humidity (RH) - The ratio of the actual amount of moisture in the air as compared to the amount needed to saturate the air, expressed as a percentage. *Standards - Substrates*

Relief - The distance from the plate's surface to the top of the image on the plate. *Image Carriers*

Relief Plate - Plates where the image to be printed is raised above the surface of the plate. *Image Carriers*

Relief Printing - See Letterpress Printing.

Relink - Prevents the user from having to go back into QuarkXPress and use the chain tool to relink boxes in a new order, when the order of the text boxes have been modified. See North Atlantic Publishing Systems. *Software*

Rendering - The final process of creating a 3-D image. *Multimedia*

Rendering Style - See Camut Style.

Render Man Technology - See Pixar Company.

RenderPro - Distributed rendering engine that divides StrataVision 3-D rendering jobs among networked Macs. See Strata, Inc. *Software*

Rend-X - Extension for exporting Strata StudioPro and StrataVision 3-D files to RenderMan. See Strata, Inc. *Software*

Repeater - A mechanism that was designed to amplify a signal over distances, because signal quality decreases over a long distance. *Telecommunications*

Reprint - To print the same job or item once again, either without any changes or with only very minor changes. *Printing Processes*

Reproduction Proof - A camera-ready type of proof that was created from black and white text (copy), illustrations, or photographs. *Proofing*

Reprography - The process of duplicating materials. *Printing Processes*

Re-Proofing - When a new proof is needed to be generated, usually because of unacceptable results on the initial proofs. *Proofing*

Re-Scale - See Scaling, Re-Size, Enlargement, and Reduction.

Re-Scanning - When a scanning job is completely redone, usually because changes need to be made to any one or all of the four different colors. *Scanning*

Re-Screening - The halftone screening of an existing halftone or screened copy. Re-screening is typically done when original continuous tone copy is not available. If this technique is not handled properly it can lead to some objectionable moire patterns in the final reproduction. *Graphic Arts Photography*

Resin - A binder that is used in ink and varnish. *Ink*

Resident Fonts - Fonts that are a part of a printer and permanently reside in the unit. *Typography*

Resist - A material that is used for the protection from exposure of the non-image plate areas to etching solutions. *Image Carriers*

Re-Size - To reduce or enlarge the size of artwork or copy. *Art and Copy Preparation*

Resolution - The degree of detail visible on a monitor (number of pixels) or on output (dots per inch). *Graphic Arts Photography - Scanning* A measure of the finest detail visible in an image, or supported by a display device or printer. Usually horizontal resolution in video. For scanned images and printers, the number of scan dots, printer dots, or halftone lines per inch is the measure of resolution, i.e., a 1000 dpi. For frame buffer and stored digital images, the total number of pixels horizontally and vertically is commonly stated, i.e., as a 512 X 512 image. *Digital Photography - General Computer*

Resolution Enhancement Technology A laser printer that enhances the resolution of images and text. See Fine Print, Photo Grade and TurboRes. *Laser Applications*

Respi Screen - A special contact screen that has large amounts (up to 220 lpi) of tiny halftone dots. It produces smooth tonal gradations on halftones. *Graphic Arts Photography*

Retouching - Changes that are made to photographs and other copy, such as for improving contrast and detail, or for correcting imperfections, or to improve quality. *Art and Copy Preparation*

Retouching, Electronic - Computer software that allows for the correction or alteration of a color photo or illustration at the dot or pixel level. *Color Reproduction - Software*

Retrieve It! - Mac utilities. See Claris Clear Choice and Claris Corporation. *Software*

Return Key - See Enter Key.

Reverse - To change the color of an image from white to black, or black to white. *Art and Copy Preparation - Graphic Arts Photography*

Reverse Printing - See Back Printing.

Reverse Leading - The creation of type (characters) where the size of the type is greater than the line spacing, i.e., set 24/20. *Typography*

Reverse Type - A typeface where the characters are white with a solid black (or other color) background. *Typography*

RGB - An acronym for the red, green, and blue primary colors used in computer monitors. *Computer Hardware*

RGB > CMYK - Conversion from a RGB format to a CMYK format or an indication of the ability to perform this conversion. *Color Reproduction*

RGB Monitor - A color computer monitor having a design and operation based on the three additive primary colors - red, green, and blue. See Additive Color. *Computer Hardware*

RGBI Monitor - See RGB Monitor.

RGB Video Signal - The red, green, and blue colors that make up the three additive primary colors. They are used in combination to reproduce all natural colors. *Color Reproduction*

Rhythm - The combining of various elements in order to suggest movement and direction. This often relates directly to the control of eye movement over a page, so the reader can follow all the key points. See Design Principles. *Art and Copy Preparation*

RIFF (Raster Image File Format) - A file format for storing gray scales that are most commonly used in Letraset software. *Desktop/Electronic Publishing*

Right-Angle Fold - A paper folding technique that features a series of folds that are at right angles to one another. See Chopper Fold. *Finishing*

Right-Reading - Type and images that are in their normal reading or viewing position on film and plates. *Image Assembly - Image Carriers*

Rigid Artwork - This is artwork that has been created on a rigid board, and cannot be wrapped around a drum scanner in order to produce a separation. *Art and Copy Preparation*

RIP (Raster Image Processor) - A device that receives data from a Mac or PC, then converts the information according to its PostScript interpreter, then rasterizes the data (converts it to dot patterns) and then sends the rasterized data to a recording device (imagesetter) for output on photo-sensitive paper, film, or plates. *Computer Hardware - Software*

RISC (Reduced Instruction Set Computer) - A computer chip that produces rapid processing of a limited set of computer instructions. *Computer Hardware*

RIT/T&E (Rochester Institute of Technology/Technical and Education Center) - An organization that is dedicated to upgrading the graphic arts profession via seminars and other educational tools.

Robotics - The science or field of creating working robots. *General Computer - Quality/Process Control - Software*

Robots - Reprogrammable, multifunctional manipulators which are designed to move material, ports, tools, and to assemble. This process is done through programmable motions to perform a variety of tasks that simulate human motion. *Computer Hardware - Quality/Process Control - Software*

Roller Stripping - A printing problem where the ink is repelled from the ink rollers. *Printing Processes*

Roll-To-Roll Printing - A printing technique that prints on a roll or web and ends as a printed roll by winding onto the roll while printing. *Printing Processes*

ROM (Read Only Memory) - Memory chips, which cannot be modified, and can only read their contents to other memory areas. *Computer Hardware*

Rosettes - The circular patterns that are created with four-color halftone dots when the job is in registration. *Printing Processes*

Rotary Press - A press that prints from cylinders, i.e., each revolution of the plate creates an impression. Suitable for high-speed and high volume production runs. *Printing Processes*

Rotogravure - A web-fed rotary gravure printing press that uses gravure cylinders. *Printing Processes*

Rough Layout - A layout created in actual size that shows the position of all elements (copy, illustrations, photos, etc.), but lacking in details. *Art and Copy Preparation*

Round Dot - A halftone dot that is recommended for use in areas that require a high degree of definition. *Graphic Arts Photography*

Routing - The process of removing the non-image areas on a letterpress plate. *Image Carriers*

RS-170 Video Signal - The recommended standard for video signals sent by video cameras and other video sources, which has a 15.75 KHz horizontal scan rate and a 30 KHz interlaced vertical refresh rate. *Digital Photography - Telecommunications*

Rub-Off and Marking - The failure of ink to stick and its tendency to smear or scratch when dry. *Ink - Quality/Process Control*

Rub-Proof - Ink that is dry enough so it will not smear under normal handling. *Ink - Quality/Process Control*

Rub Resistance - A surface's resistance to abrasion, i.e., handling. *Image Carriers - Quality/Process Control*

Ruby Laser - A laser that produces a very intense beam for cutting. It uses a solid crystal instead of a gas to create its energy. Specific applications are for cutting solid materials. *Laser Applications*

Rubylith - A masking film. See Amberlith. *Art and Copy Preparation - Image Assembly*

Ruling - The placement of lines and dimensions onto sheets of paper, illustration boards, film, and other substrates. *Art and Copy Preparation - Image Assembly*

Run - Actual program execution. *General Computer* The actual number of printed pieces that were ordered or requested for a particular print job. *Printing Processes*

Run-Around - An indented space or hole in the copy to make room for a photo or other graphics. The copy will appear to run-around the object. *Art and Copy Preparation*

Runability - This refers to how well a specific paper runs on press. *Substrates*

Running Head - The same heading or title that runs along the top of every page in the main body of a book, magazine, or other similar publications. *Desktop/Electronic Publishing*

Saddle Sewing - A binding process similar to saddle stitching, except that thread is used on the full length of the spine instead of the few wire stitches used in saddle stitching. *Finishing*

Saddle Stitch - A binding technique that is used on small books or booklets (usually less than 96 pages and when using 50 lb. offset paper or lighter). The pages are stitched together with wire from the center fold to the outside of the book or booklet. The stitches look like staples. This method allows the book to lie flat when opened. *Finishing*

Saddle Wire - A wire that is used in saddle stitch binding. *Finishing*

Safelight - The special light that is used in darkrooms which will not adversely affect the film being processed in the darkroom. It is important to coordinate the correct type of safelight with the matching film type to prevent film damage. *Graphic Arts Photography*

Sampling - The process of converting audio signals (analog) into digital signals. *Multimedia - Telecommunications*

Sampling Rate - The measurement of the frequency of the sampling. See Sampling. *Multimedia - Telecommunications*

Sans Serif - A font or typeface in which all the characters lack serifs (the short lines at the tops and bottoms of letters). See Fig. 32 on page 193. *Typography*

Sapphire - A desktop precision color slide recorder from Management Graphics, Inc. *Computer Hardware*

Satellite - See Communication Satellite.

Satellite Dish - The main reflector used to send and receive signals from satellites. The antenna is parabolic and shaped like a dish. *Telecommunications*

Satellite Transmission - The sending of signals from one point to another using satellites. *Telecommunications*

Saturation - The intenseness of a color and the extent to which any color is pure and free of grays, whites, and blacks. *Color Reproduction*

Scatter Proofs - The placement on one proof sheet as many color separations as possible. Each is corrected, sized, and no text material is included. This can be a good check on color quality before final make-up of each page. *Proofing*

Scalable - The ability to transmit a finished video product to a variety of different quality receivers, i.e., each could have a different resolution. *Multimedia - Telecommunications*

Scalable Fonts - See Outline Fonts.

Scale - See Scaling.

Scaling - An image enlargement or reduction in order to fit the image into a specific area. *Art and Copy Preparation*

Scan-A-Web - A mirror that is used on a high-speed web press to be able to view and inspect the job while it is being printed. *Printing Processes - Quality/Process Control*

Scanner Operator - The person who performs the scanning operations on a scanner. See Scanners and Scanning. *Scanning*

Scanners (Color) - Color scanners have the ability to separate a color photograph or image into its yellow, cyan, and magenta components and then create the black image (or component) for the details and shadow areas. These four components are used in four-color printing. *Scanning*

Scanners (Gray Scale) - A device that can recognize multiple shades of gray and is used to capture images for the creation of digital halftones. *Scanning*

Scanners (OCR) - See Optical Character Recognition.

Scanning - The process of breaking an image into its many elements and to reproduce the image as a whole. The light energy of each pixel is converted into an electric signal and the number of lines and their dimensions determines the details of the image. *Desktop/Electronic Publishing - Digital Photography - Scanning*

Scitex Corporation Ltd. - A world leader in four-color electronic prepress. Offers creative layout and design systems, image digitizing scanners, color workstations for page assembly and retouching, digital proofers, and a full line of imagesetters. Contact numbers: Eight Oak Park Drive, Bedford, MA 01730; (617)275-5150. *Computer Hardware - Software*

Scitex ColorFill - Mac application dedicated to automating time-consuming line work coloring. Scanned line work is quickly colored with flat tints and radial or linear vignettes at any angle. See Scitex Corporation Ltd. *Software*

Scitex Cornerstone - A Mac software kit for packaging design and layout, communications for remote visual or verbal reviews, as well as a management and control system. See Scitex Corporation Ltd. *Software*

Scitex Document Reports - Extracts information from QuarkXPress documents on over three dozen document attributes, including page geometry, style sheets, fonts, text, pictures, colors, and trapping. Reports can be saved, printed, exported, or may be cataloged. See Scitex Corporation Ltd. *Software*

Scitex Fractions - Provides typographic control over the appearance of fractions in text. Users can specify numerators and denominators up to three characters and independently adjust the size and vertical position of the numerator, denominator, and divisor. See Scitex Corporation Ltd. *Software*

Scitex Grids and Guides - A powerful set of tools for designing and editing grids and guidelines. Grids can also be copied and pasted from one page to another, and saved for use in other documents. See Scitex Corporation Ltd. *Software*

Scitex Image Tools - Four QuarkXPress extensions that provide multiple color blends, straight line or smooth silhouetting, on-screen picture scaling, and fast proofing of image-intensive documents. Produces high-quality vignettes with "noise" to eliminate banding. See Scitex Corporation Ltd. *Software*

Scitex Layers - Creates and names up to 31 layers for viewing and printing. Layers may be displayed or hidden and selected layers printed. See Scitex Corporation Ltd. *Software*

Scitex Precision Tools - Four QuarkXPress extensions that precisely align, center and offset page elements, measure the distance between any two points on a page, move items in user-definable increments, lock boxes, and zoom up to 1600 percent. See Scitex Corporation Ltd. *Software*

Scitex Visionary Echo - A Mac-to-Mac proofing system capable of dramatically reducing proofing times. Using telecommunications data links, pages are transmitted to any remote site in a compressed state where files can be proofed. See Scitex Corporation Ltd. *Software*

Score - A slight indentation made on a sheet of paper along the line where it is to be folded. It is used on heavier paper because it makes the process of folding the paper easier. *Finishing*

Scoring - See Score.

Scrambling - A technique that alters signals so an unauthorized person cannot receive the information or data. *Telecommunications*

Screen - A sheet of film having a screen-like pattern that is used in preparation of halftones. It converts a continuous-tone photograph to a printable dot pattern. *Graphic Arts Photography*

Screen Angle Indicator - See Screen Tester.

Screen Angles - The mathematically cor-rect angles of the halftone screens that are required for each of the four colors - yellow, magenta, cyan, and black - to avoid moire patterns would be the following: cyan is 105 degrees, magenta is 75 degrees, yellow is 90 degrees, and black is 45 degrees. See Moire. *Color Reproduction*

Screen Fonts - Fonts that have been designed to display on a computer monitor. *Typography*

Screenless Printing - A printing technique that does not use halftone screens or conventional halftone dots. *Printing Processes*

Screen Percentage - Refers to the percentage of an area that is covered by dots, i.e., a 20 percent screen covers about a 20 percent of the area, and a 50 percent screen covers about 50 percent of the area. See Fig. 35 on page 203. *Graphic Arts Photography - Printing Processes*

Screen Process Printing - See Screen Printing.

Screened Photo - Continuous tone photo that has been converted to a halftone. See Halftone. *Graphic Arts Photography*

Screened Print - A photographic print that was created from a halftone screen and is also known as a screen negative. *Graphic Arts Photography*

Screen Printing - A special color printing process where an ink is pushed through a mesh screen to create images. Each color has its own stencil which defines the image. This technique is most useful for printing on fabrics, wood, glass, plastic, metal, and many other non-flat surfaces like bottles and hats. *Printing Processes*

Screen Rulings - See Line Screen.

Screen Tester - A uniquely designed piece of film that allows one to check the screen angle on each one of the pieces of four-color film. *Color Reproduction*

Screen Tint - See Tint.

Script Typeface - A typeface that resembles cursive handwriting. *Typography*

Scroll Bar - The on-screen bars (horizontal or vertical) which are mouse controlled. This allows the user to view larger portions of a document not visible on the monitor by controlling these bars. *Software*

SCSI (Small Computer System Interface) - The standard interface on a computer (Mac or PC) that is used for connecting peripheral devices to the computer itself. *Computer Hardware*

Scum - Ink that is incorrectly adhering to the non-image plate areas. *Image Carriers - Ink*

Scumming - The condition when scum occurs. See Scum. *Ink*

SE/30 PowerCache Accelerator (Mac SE/30) - A 68030 accelerator that provides the same performance and compatibility as the Universal PowerCache, plus it leaves the PDS slot open for video or Ethernet boards. See DayStar Digital. *Computer Hardware*

Search And Replace - A software feature which gives the user the ability to

searching for a specific word, series of characters, or typeface and then replacing them with another word, series of characters, or typeface. *Software*

SECAM - A European television standard. *Standards - Telecommunications*

Secondary Color - The color that results from the mixing (in equal parts) of two different primary colors. *Color Reproduction*

Self Cover - A publication's cover that is printed on paper which is identical to the inside pages. *Finishing*

Self-Mailer - A single sheet advertising piece that includes the message and the response tool (envelope or reply card). *Marketing*

Semi-Chemical Pulp - A chemical pulp that contains mechanical pulp but has all the characteristics of a chemical pulp. *Substrates*

Sensitivity Guide - A guide that can be used to determine if a plate, film, or proof was properly exposed and developed. *Quality/Process Control*

Sensitometer - A device that measures light sensitivity of different film, plates, and photographic paper. *Graphic Arts Photography - Quality/Process Control*

Separation Vendor - A company traditionally called a separation house or a trade house, that is devoted primarily to the creation of four-color separations for printing. *Color Reproduction - Graphic Arts Photography - Scanning*

Separations - See Color Separations.

192

Sepia - A photograph that has brown tones instead of gray tones. *Art and Copy Preparation - Graphic Arts Photography*

Serial - The sending of data via a serial port network or phone line at the rate of one bit per send or impulse. *General Computer*

Serial Port - The computer connection that accepts serial communication. *Computer Hardware*

Serif - The short lines that are added to the tops and bottoms of a typeface. See Fig. 32. *Typography*

Serigraphy - See Screen Printing.

Set - The setting of type, as in typesetting. *Typesetting and Imagesetting*

Set-Off - The condition where the ink on a sheet that is being printed rubs off onto the incoming sheet during printing, i.e., the smudging of the ink while printing. *Printing Processes*

Setprint Plates - Special polyester plates developed by Agfa that were designed to run in imagesetters. *Image Carriers*

Set Solid - The creation of type (characters) where the size of the type is the same as the line spacing or leading, i.e., set 12/12. *Typography*

Sans Serif Fonts

This font is Helvetica, the most commonly used typeface in the world. These are excellent examples for your review.

I H

Serif Fonts

This font is Times, a commonly used typeface throughout the world. These are excellent examples for your review.

I H

As you can see, the serif font has little tails and the sans serif has no tails.

Fig. 32 - Serif and Sans Serif Fonts

Set-Width - The width of a type character. *Typography*

Sewing - The process of sewing signatures together by needle and a thin cord. *Finishing*

SGML (Standard Generalized Markup Language) - A document coding system for page layout. *Desktop/Electronic Publishing - Standards*

Shadow - The areas on photographic images that are the darkest. On halftones, the shadows have the largest and the greatest density of dots. *Graphic Arts Photography - Printing Processes*

Shadow Dots - The larger size dots in the shadow areas of a halftone. *Graphic Arts Photography - Printing Processes*

Sharpen - To enhance the contrast around an image's edges. *Scanning*

Shapes Libraries - Collections of ready-to-use 3-D objects to be used with StudioPro, Strata Vision 3d and Strata Type 3d. See Strata, Inc. *Software*

Sheet - Paper suitable for printing. Also, cutting roll paper to various size sheets. *Substrates*

Sheet-Fed - The use of printing presses that print paper sheets of varying sizes instead of using presses that print on rolls of paper. *Printing Processes*

Sheetwise - This method prints one image on one side and another image is printed on the opposite side (in registration), using the identical gripper and guide edge on the press. For multiple pages see imposition. *Printing Processes*

Short Ink - Ink that flows poorly and has a creamy consistency. *Ink*

Show-Through - This is when a printed image shows through on the opposite side. It looks like a shadow. *Substrates*

Shrinkage - A reduction in a mold's original size. See Matrix. *Image Carriers*

Shrink Wrap - A tight-fitting, transparent, protective covering of plastic that is used in product packaging. *Finishing*

Side Bearing - The amount of space that has been designed on either side of a character, in order to prevent any of the bordering characters from touching. *Typography*

Side Guide - A device used for paper alignment. It works as the particular paper or substrate feeds automatically through a press. *Printing Processes*

Side Sewing - A technique of sewing an entire book together in one operation versus sewing in separate units. *Finishing*

Side Stitching - Large wire stitches that are inserted into the side of a publication to bind it together. It will not lie flat when opened with this method. *Finishing*

Side Wire - A method of binding that stitches a book or booklet together with wire stitches that are along the edge on one side. *Finishing*

Signal Wave - See Modulation.

Signature - A sheet of paper that will produce a correctly paginated series of pages after it is folded. Multiple signatures are gathered together in correct page sequence and then bound by whatever binding process chosen to produce a finished book, booklet, or other publication. *Finishing*

Silhouette Halftone - A halftone image where the background around the main image is eliminated, either by masking or by etching. *Graphic Arts Photography*

Silk - Fabric traditionally used for screen printing stencils. Today, other synthetic fabrics are used. See Screen Printing. *Printing Processes*

Silk Screening - See Screen Printing.

Silicon - A semiconductor that is used in the manufacture of silicon chips or integrated circuits. *Computer Hardware*

Silicon Chip - An integrated circuit where silicon is the semiconductor material. *Computer Hardware*

Silver Halide - A chemical component of the emulsion side on the film. It will respond to light and becomes dark when processed. *Graphic Arts Photography*

SIMM (Single In-Line Memory Module) - A circuit board that holds memory chips. *Computer Hardware*

Simulation - Computerized multimedia that creates an illusion of movement. *Multimedia*

Single Color Press - A press that is only capable of printing one color per pass through the press. *Printing Processes*

Single In-Line Memory Module - See SIMM.

Site License - The right granted to an organization or to a specific location of an organization to copy a specific number (could be unlimited) of copies of a software program. *Software*

Sizing - The process of applying chemicals or compounds to paper that make the paper more resistant against damage by vapors or moisture (typically water). *Substrates*

Skelton Black - The printing of the color black in full-color printing to add more detail and contrast. *Color Reproduction*

Skew - The bending, left or right of a TV picture. *Digital Photography - Telecommunications*

Skid - A platform that holds piles of printed or unprinted paper and allows for greater portability of heavy goods. Also known as a pallet. *Substrates*

Skinny - See Chokes.

Slick - High gloss camera-ready ad. *Art and Copy Preparation*

Slide - 35 mm positive film that is mounted in a special slide mount. Slides can be in color or black and white. See Positive Film and Transparencies. *Art and Copy Preparation - Graphic Arts Photography*

Slide Scanner - A particular type of scanner that scans images on 35 mm slides. *Scanning*

SlideScript - A PostScript RIP (raster image processor) and controller for the Montage Series film recorders. See Presentation Technologies, Inc. *Computer Hardware*

Slitting - The various paper cutting techniques. See Slitting Equipment. *Finishing*

Slitting Equipment - Special paper cutting devices that are attached to presses and to various types of folding equipment. They cut the printed paper after is has been printed and/or folded. See Slitting. *Finishing*

Slow-Scan Television - See Freeze-Frame Television.

Slur - See Slurring.

Slurring - An on-press condition where halftone dots become elongated and lose sharpness. *Printing Processes*

Slug - A single line of hot-metal type. *Typesetting and Imagesetting*

Small Caps - The uppercase version of each character that has been reduced to the X-Height. See Fig. 33. *Typography*

Small-Quantity Generation Exemptions - Special exceptions to environmental laws where the quantities of pollution is small. *Environment*

Smash - See Nipping.

Smudged Print - The indication of excess ink or inks that do not dry properly. *Ink*

Smythe Sewn - A bookbinding technique that sews signatures together before the book cover is installed. Most commonly used on casebound (hardcover) books. *Finishing*

Snowflaking - A press condition where halftone dots are missing. *Printing Processes*

S/N Ratio - The ratio of the video signal to the noise contained in the signal usually expressed in db. Noise gives the picture a grainy, snowy look. Depending on the camera, this property may vary with scene luminance. The higher the S/N ratio, the better. *Digital Photography*

THESE ARE 12 POINT UPPERCASE CHARACTERS.

THESE ARE 12 POINT SMALL CAPS

Fig. 33 - Small Caps

Soft Copy - Copy, text, or data in electronic form, that is usually stored on some computer media, i.e., hard disk, diskette, etc., and viewed on a CRT. *Proofing*

Soft Dot - A dot that has poorly determined and fuzzy edges. See Hard Dot. *Graphic Arts Photography*

Soften - To decrease the contrast around an image. *Graphic Arts Photography - Scanning*

Soft Ink - A term that describes the consistency of inks. *Ink*

Software - A series of codes or instructions that cause the computer to perform specific functions, i.e., accounting, word processing, mail list management, etc. *General Computer*

Software Developer's Kit - Allows system integrators and VAR's to integrate software into customized applications. *Software*

Software Publishing Corporation Business productivity software for the PC. Currently develops and markets the Harvard Graphics and Superbase product lines. Contact numbers: 3165 Kifer Rd., P.O. Box 54983, Santa Clara, CA 95056; (408)986-8000. *Software*

Solarization - A special photographic effect where some areas of the photo's negative are underexposed and other areas the reverse. This is accomplished by excess exposure to light. *Graphic Arts Photography*

Solid - Type that has been set without leading. See Set Solid. *Typography*

Solitaire - A professional series of recorders from Management Graphics, Inc. They produce full-color slides, overhead transparencies, prints, 4" x 5" transparencies, film animation, and other film requirements of a photo lab. See Management Graphics, Inc. *Computer Hardware*

Sort - The process of arranging a list of items into either alphabetical or numerical sequence, i.e., A, B, C, etc. or 1, 2, 3, etc. *General Computer*

Space Station - A space facility that transmits telecommunication signals. *Telecommunications*

SPARC (Scalar Processor Architecture) - A high-speed workstation (microprocessor) that is manufactured by Sun Microsystems. *Computer Hardware*

Spatial Domain - A bit-mapped picture that is represented by its various pixels. *Desktop/Electronic Publishing - Digital Photography*

Spatial Resolution - The representation of an image (picture) by the number of its discrete pixels, i.e., 512 pixels X 512 pixels. *Desktop/Electronic Publishing - Digital Photography*

Specifications - The guidelines that are used in the determination of the cost of a print job, i.e., number of color separations, quantity, paper type, page size, etc. *Printing Processes*

Spectracell - Hyphen's version of Supercell Screening. See Supercell Screening. *Color Reproduction*

Spectrophotometer - An instrument used to measure the intensities of light in various segments of the color spectrum when reflected from or transmitted through a medium. *Color Reproduction - Quality/Process Control*

Spectrum - The full range of all the visible colors or wavelenghts - from blue (short) to red (long) wavelengths. *Color Reproduction*

Spell Checker - Software that checks a document for possible misspelled words. The user is given the option to change or ignore the words that are selected for review by the program. *Software*

Spelling Coach Professional - Document and interactive spell checker and a reference thesaurus for all popular Mac software programs. See Deneba Software. *Software*

Spillover - Satellite signals that unintentionally transmit to unwanted receivers. *Telecommunications*

Spine - The side of a book that has the binding and is between the front and back cover. *Finishing*

Spine-See Binding - A binding technique that uses a wire running through a series of holes on the edge of the book or manual. *Finishing*

Spiral Binding - A method of bookbinding where a spiral wire is inserted into prepunched holes along one side of the book. This special type of binding, while expensive, is excellent for books that need to be used frequently and must lie flat while in use, like workbooks. See Wire-O-Binding. *Finishing*

Spirit Duplication - A form of printing where the image is transferred to the paper by moisture applied to the paper before it makes contact with the master (plate). Carbon from the master transfers to the wet paper, thus creating the impression. *Printing Processes*

Splitting - See Ink Splitting.

Spooling - Holding documents in memory until the printer can accept and process the files. See Print Spooler. *Software*

Spot Color - Extra colors that are used on specific elements in a page for highlighting. *Color Reproduction*

Spot Varnish - A specific area that is printed with a varnish for surface protection or for some type of special emphasis. *Printing Processes*

Spreads - This technique allows light color areas to spread into the black or darker areas to eliminate any possible gaps. *Image Assembly - Printing Processes*

Spreadsheet - A software application computer program that uses columns and rows of cells. The function of each cell can be programmed to produce specific results, i.e., budget forecasting, financial statement analysis, sales forecasting, and endless numbers of related possibilities. Spreadsheet programs have traditionally been one of the key driving forces in the growing use of microcomputers. *Software*

Square Dot - A halftone dot that is recommended for use in areas that require the greatest degree of definition. *Graphic Arts Photography*

Squeegee - A tool used to force ink through the screen in screen printing. *Printing Processes*

SRAM - See Static RAM.

Staging - A special coating that is used during the dot etching process to protect the non-image areas from the etching material. See Stopping Out. *Graphic Arts Photography - Image Carriers*

Static RAM - A faster RAM that can only store about 25 percent of the capacity of a Dynamic RAM. Ideal for cache memory. *Computer Hardware*

Stamping - The process of adhering foil to any material, i.e., cloth, paper, etc. *Finishing*

Standard Offset Color Bar - A device developed by GATF to control proofing. It contains slur, sharpness, trapping, density, and gray balance guides. See GATF. *Quality/Process Control*

Standard Viewing Conditions - A neutral gray area that uses a 5000K light source, where prints, transparencies, and printing is viewed and proofed. *Color Reproduction - Quality/Process Control - Standards*

Star Time For Windows - A presentation software package that allows users to integrate images from multiple applications, add speaker notes and exciting transition effects, and produce high resolution presentations. See General Parametrics. *Software*

Stat - A photographic process whereby a reproduction is created from another photostat, artwork, copy, or film. It is usually used to reduce or enlarge an image or text area. *Art and Copy Preparation - Graphic Arts Photography*

Static Neutralizer - A mechanism that removes static electricity from paper to avoid paper feeding and ink smudging problems. See Set-Off. *Printing Processes - Substrates*

Stem - The vertical portion of a type character. *Typography*

Stencil - The image is created in screen printing by a stencil. Stencils are produced by hand cutting or by a photographic process. *Printing Processes*

Step-And-Repeat - An image assembly or plate exposure process whereby one negative or positive is used to create duplicate and multiple images as required on film or on a plate. *Image Carriers - Image Assembly*

Step-And-Repeat Machine - A unit that is used to make multiple copies of the same image on film or on a plate. *Image Carriers*

Step Table - See Gray Scale.

Stereotype - A duplicate of a letterpress printing plate. *Image Carriers*

Stet - A proofreader's symbol which means that any marked corrections will remain unchanged, otherwise ignore the marked corrections. See Proofreaders Symbols. *Typesetting and Imagesetting*

Stick-Up Cap - Similar to a drop cap, except the enlarged letter is set on and above the top line of the text and is not embedded in the body of the paragraph. *Typography*

Still Video - Still Video allows one to capture digital images on electronic media via uniquely designed digital cameras. These images can then be stored and output as desired on various color and black and white laser proofers. *Digital Photography*

Still Video Camera - See Digitizer.

Stitch - The wire thread used in stitching. See Stitching *Finishing*

Stitching - A bookbinding technique that sews all the signatures together on any particular job. See Saddle-Stitched, Spiral Binding, Side Wire, and Wire-O-Binding. *Finishing*

Stochastic Screening - A screening technology that does not use fixed screen angles or frequencies. This method produces very small, identically sized dots with random appearing spaces between them and requires equipment that can repeatedly produce 14 to 20 micron dots (spots). Also known as FM (frequency modulated) Screening. *Color Reproduction - Graphics Arts Photography - Scanning*

Stock - This refers to the different types and grades of paper that are used in printing. *Substrates*

Stopping Out - See Staging.

Storage - See Store.

Store - To write data from main memory to secondary storage. *General Computer*

Storyboard - A series of small illustrations on a single board that portray the events or scenes that would be the basis for a TV commercial, multimedia project, movie, etc. These pictures are used as a guide for the producer and director in the project. *Multimedia*

Straight Matter - This refers to straight typeset text, all the same font and size, usually in galley form. *Typesetting and Imagesetting*

Strata, Inc. - A developer of computer-assisted visualization and illustration software programs. For Mac and PC. Contact numbers: 2 West St. George Blvd., Ancestor Square #2100, St. George, Utah 84770; (801)628-5218. *Software*

StrataClip 3d - 3-D clip art. See Strata, Inc. *Software*

Strata StudioPro - For professional Mac 3-D modeling, rendering, and animation and includes the features explode, shatter, atomize, and bounce. See Strata, Inc. *Software*

Strata Type - 3-D typography for the Mac. See Strata, Inc. *Software*

StrataVision 3d - 3-D modeling, rendering, and animation for the Mac. See Strata, Inc. *Software*

StrataVision 3d PC - Full-featured graphics package with 3-D modeling, rendering, morphing, and animation for the PC. See Strata, Inc. *Software*

Stream Feeder - The mechanism that keeps the paper sheets flowing to the press in an overlapping manner (no space between the sheets). *Printing Processes*

Streaking - On-press streaks caused by excess water or a dirty cylinder. *Printing Processes*

Streamline - Automated art production tool that converts bit-mapped images into compact PostScript language files. Allows for specification of levels of gray and standard or custom colors, and exporting of an image to a favorite page-layout program for scaling, skewing, rotating, editing, or shearing an image. For Mac and Windows. See Adobe Systems, Inc. *Software*

Strength - A substrate's on-press toughness. *Substrates* The percentage of pigment in an ink. *Ink*

Stress - The slant of a type character. *Typography*

Strike-On Composition - The creation of type by direct impression, as on a typewriter. This technique was used on some of the early composing machines, i.e., the IBM Composer. *Typesetting and Imagesetting*

Strike-On Type - See Strike-On Composition.

Strike-Through - See Show-Through.

Strip - See Stripping.

Stripper - A traditional term used in printing to describe the person who assembles the film into flats for final platemaking. Today's proper term is image assembler. See Stripping. *Image Assembly*

Stripping - The process of assembling film into flats or carriers in preparation for final platemaking and printing. *Image Assembly*

Stroke - The thickest portion of a type character. *Typography*

200

Stuffit - Data compression software for microcomputers. *Software*

Subcarrier - Any additional signals that have been added to a broadcasting basic signal to perform additional functions. *Telecommunications*

Substance Weight - The actual weight of a ream (500 sheets) of standard 17" X 22" paper, expressed in pounds. Same as basis weight for other paper. *Substrates*

Substrate - The surface that is used in printing for placement of the image, i.e., paper, plastic, cloth, etc. *Substrates*

Subtractive Color - The color system used in the printing process. Ink (which becomes an absorber of light) is printed on paper in order to create color. Light contacts the paper and ink, the ink absorbs the specific colors of red, green and blue (primary additive colors) in the light, then the ink reflects the colors that remain in the light. This reflected light is used to form the color in printing. Three types of ink are required to absorb all three of the primary colors. Cyan ink (C) absorbs the red light, yellow ink (Y) absorbs the blue light and magenta ink (M) absorbs the green light. When the density of any one of these three colors is modified, the degree of light reflection and absorption changes. This process allows the creation of a multitude of colors. Black is formed in the absence of light. Since the energy of light is absorbed and lost, this process of color creation is called subtractive. *Color Reproduction*

Subtractive Primaries - Yellow, magenta, and cyan. See Subtractive Color. *Color Reproduction*

Sulphate Pulp - A brown, inexpensive paper that is manufactured from wood fibers and is used for grocery bags, cardboard, etc. Is also known as kraft paper. *Substrates*

Sulphite Pulp - Another type of paper pulp that is manufactured from wood fibers. *Substrates*

Sunlight - The full spectrum of visible radiation. *Color Reproduction*

SuperATM - Enhanced version of Adobe Type Manager (ATM) software. Creates substitute fonts for viewing, editing, and printing files. As a result, line breaks, page breaks, spacing, and font styles stay put. For Mac. See Adobe Systems, Inc. *Software*

Supercell Screening - A sophisticated color separation technique developed for use on the more recent and more powerful desktop systems. *Color Reproduction*

Super VHS - A videocassette format upwardly compatible with standard VHS, but with two major advantages; it provides almost twice the resolution of standard VHS, and the chrominance and luminance signals are separated during recording and playback. *Digital Photography - Multimedia*

Supercalendering - The process of pressing paper between calender rolls with enough pressure to create smooth and shiny paper. A more intense process than calendering. See Calender Rolls and Calendering. *Substrates*

Superior - Characters that are dramatically smaller than the point size of the character that is next to them. They sit above the adjacent character. See Fig. 34. *Typography*

Surface Color - The way the color of an object that does not emit light is determined is by the light the object reflects and absorbs. *Color Reproduction*

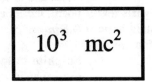

Fir. 34 - Superior

Surface Tension - Any on-press surface tension or resistance that could cause ink or other liquids to form into a droplet. *Printing Processes*

Surge Protector - A device that protects computers from damage due to electrical surges and spikes. *Computer Hardware*

Surprint - A final photographic print that is the result of superimposing one image over one other image. *Graphic Arts Photography*

S-VHS - A standard format for 1/2 inch video tape. See Super-VHS. *Multimedia*

Swatch - A small section of any material or color that is used as a reference sample. *Color Reproduction*

SWOP (Specifications for Web Offset Publications) - The recommended specifications of the quality standards for the printing of magazines on web presses. They are used as a standard for all printers in the magazine printing business. *Quality/Process Control - Standards*

Symmetric Multi-Processing - Ability to distribute tasks across multiple processors. *Software*

Synthesizer - A digital device that can simulate sounds and musical instruments. *Multimedia*

SyQuest - Removable magnetic hard disk. *Computer Hardware*

System Error - The computer's failure to complete a user command. *General Computer*

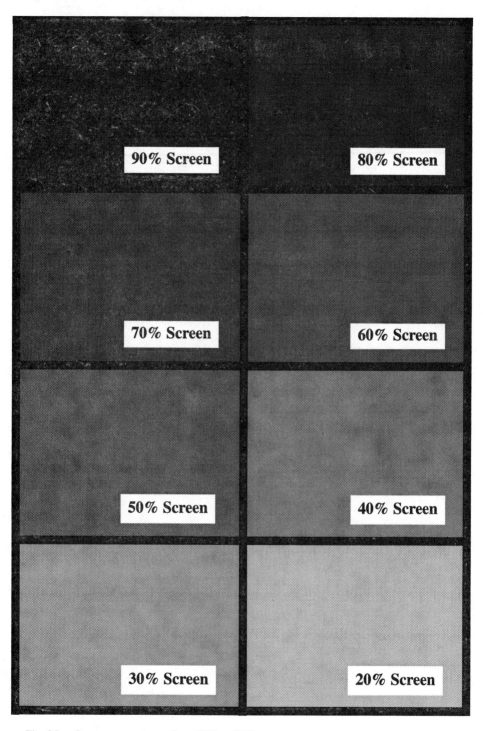

Fig. 35 - Screen percentages from 90% to 20%.

Tablet - A graphic digitizer. See Digitizer. *Desktop/Electronic Publishing*

Tabloid Page - 11" x 17" size sheet of paper. *Substrates*

Tack - The stickiness of an ink or the force required to split an ink film from a surface. The degree of tackiness can be measured with an inkometer or tackoscope. *Ink*

Tackoscope - See Inkometer.

Tagged Image File Format (TIFF) - A standardized format that is used to store and manipulate canned/bit-mapped files or images at varying resolutions. *Desktop/Electronic Publishing*

Tape - A magnetic tape that is used for storage of data. *Computer Hardware*

Tape Drive - A computer peripheral or device that stores data on magnetic tape. *Computer Hardware*

TCP/IP (Transport Control Protocol/-Interface Program) - Communication protocols that are used for sending data over networks. *Software*

Tear Sheets - Stories and other information that have been removed from a newspaper or magazine for reference purposes, i.e., copies of ads. These sheets can be used as a way of proving to a customer their ad or story was inserted in the newspaper. *Desktop/Electronic Publishing*

Technological Literacy - An individual's ability to understand and use technology. *General Computer*

Teleconferencing - An audio and visual link-up between different individuals at various locations. *Telecommunications*

Teletext - The all-text signals that are broadcast over the air or transmitted via cable to a television receiver. *Telecommunications*

Teminator - A network device that is used to absorb network signals that might be read as distinct signals. *Telecommunications*

Template - A pattern, usually made of plastic or metal, that is used as a guide when drawing circles (of various sizes), boxes, and numerous shapes with ink or pencil. *Art and Copy Preparation*

Text - The main body of words or copy in any type of document, i.e., book, advertisement, catalog, etc. *Art and Copy Preparation - Typesetting and Imagesetting*

Texture - The surface characteristics of a substrate. *Substrates*

Textured Mapping - The placement of a textured 2-D image on a 3-D image to create a textured 3-D image. *Multimedia*

Thermal Prints - An intermediate proofing system that gives a view of how the final printed piece will look before the final proof is created. *Proofing*

Thermo-Mechanical Pulp - A special type of steam treatment that is used on standard groundwood that will produce a higher grade (stronger) of groundwood pulp. *Substrates*

Text Box - An on-screen area where text can be entered and modified. *Software*

Textures Libraries - Collections of predefined real-world textures and details to be used with Studio Pro, Strata Vision 3d, and Strata Type 3d. See Strata, Inc. *Software*

Thermal Printer - A printer that forms characters by a heat process on treated paper. *Printing Processes*

Thick-Net - An Ethernet connection. See Ethernet. *Computer Hardware*

Thinner - A special type of liquid that is used to thin ink or glue, thus allowing them to flow more easily. *Finishing - Ink*

Thin-Net - An Ethernet connection. See Ethernet. *Computer Hardware*

Thin Space - A space that is equal in size to 1/4 the width of an em space and 1/2 the width of an en space. It is used when a very small amount of space between characters is needed. *Typography*

Three Color Black - A dark grayish color that occurs when equal amounts of cyan, magenta, and yellow are overprinted. *Color Reproduction*

Three Color Process - The printing of the three process colors (cyan, magenta, and yellow) without the black color. *Color Reproduction*

Three-Dimensional Graphics - Graphic objects that are viewed from many angles and tend to give the illusion they are 3-D. *Software*

Three Quarter Tone - Dot percentages in the 75 percent range. *Graphic Arts Photography - Printing Processes*

Threshold - That point where brightness can change from white to black or the reverse. *Digital Photography* A scanner technique that is used for the determination of gray levels. *Scanning*

Throughput - The measure of the total processing time for a computer system to handle specific data and program operations. *General Computer*

Thrust - See Creep.

Thumbnail Sketch - A layout in reduced size that roughly shows the basic form and content of a page or series of pages. *Art and Copy Preparation*

Thunder Cards - High-resolution graphics accelerators for the Mac and PC. *Computer Hardware*

TIFF - See Tagged Image File Format

Time-Based Data - Computer data samples that have been taken over a certain period of time and at specific intervals. *General Computer*

Time Code - The track that synchronizes all the other events of a multimedia project. *Multimedia*

Timeworks, Inc. - Publisher of computer software that features easy-to-use, and full-function productivity. Operates on five hardware platforms. Contact numbers: 625 Academy Dr., Northbrook, IL 60062; (708)559-1300. *Software*

Tinctorial Strength - A pigment's power to effect an ink's color. *Ink*

Tint - A printed area that is not a solid ink, but consists of dots of a particular color ink usually in increments of 10 percent. The higher the percentage the darker the tint. This allows the creation of many different color values and many different effects from just one color. See Fig. 35 - Screen Percentages on page 203. These are the same as tints. *Art and Copy Preparation* The appearance of ink in non-image areas. Also called tinting. *Printing Processes*

Tint Plate - A type of plate that allows the addition of a flat background color to a single color job. *Image Carriers*

Tip-In - See Tipping-In.

Tipping-In - The insertion of additional sheets of printed material between signatures, i.e., order forms. *Finishing*

Tissue - See Overlay Tissue.

Tissue Overlay - See Overlay Tissue.

T/Maker - Creator of a complete line of full-color and black and white clip art and cartoons. Contact numbers: 1390 Villa Street, Mountain View, CA 94041; (800)395-0195. *Software*

Token Ring - A LAN communication link or network that connects a series of computer workstations in a closed loop or ring. *Software*

Tone - Abbreviation for halftone. *Desktop/Electronic Publishing - Graphic Arts Photography* A specific color, color shade or color value. *Color Reproduction*

Tone-Line - A process that allows one to produce an outline reproduction (detailed

if required) of a continuous tone photograph. *Art and Copy Preparation*

Toner - A material that copiers and laser printers use to produce images onto paper. This term also refers to some of the dyes (most commonly black) used in ink. *Ink - Laser Applications*

Toner Cartridge - The actual container that holds a laser printer's toner. *Laser Applications*

Tone Scale - See Gray Scale.

Tongs - Instruments that are used to hold film and plates when placing them in various developing, etching, and washing solutions. *Graphic Arts Photography - Image Carriers*

Toning - The printing of ink in any non-image areas which result from ink-in-water emulsification. *Printing Processes*

Tooth - The rough texture of paper that will give it greater receptivity to ink. *Substrates*

Topology - The network hardware connections that exist between all the computers and their peripherals on a specific network. *Computer Hardware*

Touch Screen - A computer display that can respond to touch. *Computer Hardware*

Toxicity - A substance's ability to harm human tissue. *Environment*

Track - The circular storage area on a diskette or hard drive. Each diskette or hard drive is composed of many tracks for storage and retrieval of data, and each track is segmented into many sectors for faster retrieval and storage of data. *Computer Hardware*

Tractor Feed - A device that feeds computer paper through a printer by using pins that fit into the holes on the edges of the computer paper. As the pins revolve, the paper moves through the printer. *Computer Hardware*

Tracking - The overall character spacing between all characters, whereas kerning refers to spacing betweeen character pairs. *Typesetting and Imagesetting*

Trade Paperback - See Quality Paperback.

Transcoding - The conversion of a video image (still or a sequence) to another media type. *Multimedia*

Transfer Rate - The speed of data transfer. *General Computer*

Transfer Type - Sheets of various typefaces, symbols, graphics, tints, borders, etc., that are transferred to CRC or artwork. This transfer process usually involves burnishing. See CRC. *Art and Copy Preparation*

Transition - The movement from one scene into the next one. See Dissolve. *Multimedia*

Transmission - The sending or receiving of signals over communications lines. *Telecommunications*

Transmissive Media - Media that can only be viewed with backlighting. *Art and Copy Preparation - Desktop/Electronic Publishing - Multimedia*

Transmitted Color - This is where the light is transmitted through an object and that light which it absorbs determines the color. *Color Reproduction - Graphic Arts Photography*

Transmitter - The communication device for sending signals over the air or via cables. *Telecommunications*

Transparency - A full-color photographic output medium or film that must be viewed by transmitted light. *Art and Copy Preparation - Graphic Arts Photography*

Transparency Scanner - A particular type of scanner that was designed for scanning film transparencies. *Scanning*

Transparent - Paper, usually so thin, that it allows an image that is printed on one side to be seen through the paper on the other side. See Show-Through. *Substrates*

Transparent Copy - A type of material that requires the passage of light through the material to see or reproduce the image on the material. *Art and Copy Preparation - Graphic Arts Photography*

Transparent Ink - A type of printing ink that allows other ink colors that are layered under the transparent ink to be seen. The yellow, magenta, and cyan inks used in full-color printing are transparent inks. *Ink*

Transponder - A device that is housed on a satellite and is responsible for receiving signals from earth stations, then amplifies or changes them, and then resends them back to earth. *Telecommunications*

Transpose - The exchange of the position of one letter with another letter in a

208

word that creates a misspelling. Example: tranpsose. The"p" is transposed with the letter "s." *Desktop/Electronic Publishing*

Trapping - A printing and image assembly technique that uses two concepts - chokes and spreads - to eliminate any white gaps when printing a four-color job. See Chokes and Spreads. *Image Assembly* The ability of one ink film to adhere to another ink film in multi-color printing. *Printing Processes*

TrapWise - Creates electronic chokes and spreads that meet professional stripper standards and is able to trap spot and process colors, hairline rules, vignettes, thin text, images, and more. For Mac and PC. See Aldus Corporation. *Software*

Trim - The final bookbinding activity used in print production that removes all the excess edges from a book, catalog, or other printed piece that overlap the final and correct dimensions of the product. *Finishing*

Trim Size - A page, book, or other publication after it has been trimmed or cut to the desired size. See Trim. *Finishing*

Trimming - See Trim.

Trim Marks - See Crop Marks and Registration Marks.

Tritone - A three-color reproduction made from one-color copy. Typically, the original copy is a black and white photograph from which three halftones are made and overprinted on press. *Graphic Arts Photography - Printing Processes*

True Color - Color that is close to a natural-looking color, i.e., 24 bit color. *Color Reproduction*

True Rolling - The process of making adjustments to the plate, cylinder, and blanket packing to allow for rubber blanket distortion. *Printing Processes*

True Type - An Apple Computer font format. *Typography*

T-Square - A device that is used for a cutting and drawing edge where a line or cut is required that is straight. *Art and Copy Preparation - Image Assembly*

Turbo 040 Accelerator (Mac IIci, II, IIx, IIcx, IIsi, IIvi, IIvx, SE/30, Performa 600) - A 68040 accelerator that turbocharges all software up to 600 percent faster. Quadra-level compatibility with all standard software and hardware. See DayStar Digital. *Computer Hardware*

TurboRes - See Fine Print.

Turnaround Time - The time required to complete a job. *Desktop/Electronic Publishing - Printing Processes*

Tusche Stencil Screening - A special type of screen printing where the design to be printed is created directly on the screen in one step. This technique is best suited to fine artwork. See Screen Printing. *Printing Processes*

Twin-Wire Machine - A special papermaking machine that is frequently used to manufacture newsprint. *Substrates*

Twisted Pair - A special network cable (similar to a phone line) that contains two separate wires that have been twisted together for a low-cost, noise-free communications cable. It is commonly used with ethernet. See Ethernet. *Computer Hardware*

Two-Color Process - A printing technique that uses two ink colors in overprinting two halftones made from the same original photograph. See Duotone. *Printing Processes*

Two-Sheet Detector - A press device that monitors the flow of paper in the press to be sure that only one sheet of paper is being fed into the area of the press where the impression is produced. *Printing Processes*

Two-Sidedness - A paper with both a smooth and a rough side. *Substrates*

Two-Up Binding - The binding of two books at the same time and later cut apart. This reduces the per book cost of binding. *Finishing*

Type 1 - An Adobe Systems font format. *Typography*

TypeAlign - For creating logos, headlines, and type effects. Allows drawing a line, arc, or freehand curve and the text automatically follows, even around corners and inside shapes. Compatible with word processing, drawing, presentation and page-layout programs. For Mac and Windows. See Adobe Systems, Inc. *Software*

Typeface (or Font) - This refers to a specific set of characters and symbols having the same design. This dictionary uses the typeface Times. The definition terms are Times Bold and the cross references are Times Italic. *Typography*

Type Family - A specific style or design of type or font, i.e., Helvetica, that is available in various weights: light, condensed, medium, italic, bold, heavy, bold italic, etc. Not every family contains every weight. See Fig. 36. *Typography*

These are some sample typefaces from the Helvetica family of fonts. This is Helvetica Bold

Here is a sample of of straight Helvetica. This family is one of the most used typefaces in the world.

This is a sample of Helvetica Bold Italic, and is used were special emphasis is needed.

This is Helvetica Light. Another member of the family.

Fig. 36 - Type Family

Type Gauge - A graphic arts measurement tool that is based on picas and points, and is used in the measurement of type. *Art and Copy Preparation - Typography*

Type High - A letterpress standard, i.e., 0.918 of an inch. Refers to type slug height. *Typography*

Type On Call CD-ROM - Allows the purchase of Adobe type whenever needed by making a telephone call. One CD-ROM contains Adobe Type Library packages 1 through 265 - more than 1,300 encrypted Type 1 typefaces. For Mac and PC. See Adobe Systems, Inc. *Typography*

Type Reunion - Automatically sorts and displays all Type 1 typefaces alphabetically by family name, with a sub-menu that shows styles and weights. The program greatly reduces the length of a font menu and makes typefaces easily accessible. For Mac. See Adobe Systems, Inc and Type 1. *Software*

Typesetter - The person who operates the typesetting equipment. See Typesetting, Phototypesetting, and Phototypesetter. *Typesetting and Imagesetting*

Typeset - Handwritten or a monospaced typed manuscript that has been converted into composed type. *Typesetting and Imagesetting*

Typesetting - The process of converting a handwritten or monospaced typed manuscript into composed type. *Typesetting and Imagesetting*

Typesetting Commands - Commands in the form of alpha (A,B,C, etc.) or numer-ic (1,2,3, etc.) character combinations that control the position and characteristics of typeset characters. *Typesetting and Imagesetting*

Type Stress - The degree to which a character slants. See Stress. *Typography*

Typo - A word that has been misspelled. *Desktop/Electronic Publishing - Typesetting and Imagesetting*

Typographer - The person who chooses the specific typefaces for a job. *Typography*

Typography - The use of different styles of type to express ideas, concepts, and design. *Typography*

UCR - See Undercolor Removal.

Ultraviolet Light - Radiation that has shorter wavelengths than visible light and it quickens chemical reactions, i.e., platemaking, ink drying, etc. *Graphic Arts Photography - Image Carriers - Printing Processes*

Undeflected Ink-Jet - A type of ink-jet printing in which an array of closely spaced nozzles produce one line of dots in succession, without deflection, at rapid speeds. *Printing Processes*

Undercolor Removal (UCR) - In full-color printing, areas with equal amounts of cyan, magenta, and yellow (which produce gray) are replaced by carefully calculated amounts of black ink. This adds detail and sharpness by reducing the dull gray areas. This technique uses less ink overall and black ink is less expensive than colored inks. See Gray Component Replacement. *Color Reproduction*

Undercorrection - Inadequate color correction that allows unwanted colors to appear in a color and change its hue. *Color Reproduction*

Undercut - The space between the press cylinder bearers and cylinder body that provides room for the plate or the blanket and the packing. *Printing Processes*

Under-Exposure - Areas on film that have thickened and appear overpowering. *Graphic Arts Photography*

Under-Sampling - When video signals are sampled at rates less than the NyQuest Criterion. *Digital Photography*

Under-Trapping - The transfer of insufficient ink to printed areas than to unprinted areas. *Printing Processes*

Under-Run - The printing of a job in numbers smaller than originally ordered. *Printing Processes*

Unit - The combination of the plate, inking, and impression mechanisms that are used for each ink color on press, i.e., a four-color press would have four units. *Printing Processes* A character or space width in a font or typeface. *Typography*

Unit Cost - The individual cost of each printed item. *Printing Processes*

Unity - The combining of various elements on a page so they appear as one single, balanced, and harmonious unit. See Design Principles. *Art and Copy Preparation*

Universal Film Terms - Special film terms that were developed by Kodak for Photo CD which maintain the look of the original transparency or photograph. See Film Terms. *Digital Photography - Graphic Arts Photography*

Universal PowerCache Accelerator (Mac Classic, Color Classic, SE, SE/30, LC, LCII, LCIII, LC520, II, IIx, IIcx, IIsi, IIci, IIvi, Performa 400 series/600) - A 68030 CPU accelerator that offers speed increases from 200 percent for a IIci to 1,000 percent for a Mac Classic. See DayStar Digital. *Computer Hardware*

Universal Product Code (UPC) - See Bar Code.

UNIX - A multi-user operating system. *Software*

Unsharp Masking - A scanner technique that will sharpen or exaggerate image edges. *Scanning*

Unwanted Colors - The appearance of colors that are not wanted in specific areas. *Color Reproduction*

Uplink - The sending of signals to a satellite from an earth station. *Telecommunications*

Up - The printing of two or more pages or sides of a job on the same side of a sheet of paper at the same time. Often referred to as, printing 2-up, 3-up, etc. This technique will reduce the cost of printing each page, since multiples of one job are run simultaneously. *Printing Processes*

Uppercase - The larger version of a character. This dates back to the early days of type, when the larger version of each character was kept in the upper or top case and the smaller version of each character was kept in the bottom or lower case. See Fig. 37. *Typography*

User - Anyone who actually performs the computer functions. *General Computer*

User-Friendly - Computer or software that is easy-to-use. *General Computer*

User Group - A group of users that perform similar functions on the computer or have similar computer-related interests or needs. *General Computer*

User-Interface - That portion of the software or the computer that actually interfaces with the user, i.e., the pull down menu, mouse controlled commands, etc. *Software*

Utilities - Software that performs specific computer functions which enhance the use of the computer, but not essential to its operation. *Software*

UV Coating - A special coating that is applied to a book, booklet, or catalog which will protect it from damage due to handling. *Finishing - Printing Processes*

lower case
abcdefghijklmnopqrstuvwxyz
UPPER CASE
ABCDEFGHIJKLMNOPQRSTUVWXYZ

Fig. 37 - Lower and Uppercase

214

Vacuum Frame - A type of vacuum frame device designed to hold the reproduction medium, i.e., plate, and the information to be copied, i.e., film, in contact with each other during exposure. *Image Carriers*

Value 040 Accelerator (Mac LC, LC II, Performa 400/405/430) - Accelerators for the Mac LC, LCII, and Performa 400/405/430. Fully compatible with all Centris and Quadra software. Optional Ethernet Module allows full Ethernet support - Thick-Net, Thin-Net, or Twisted Pair (10 Base-T). See DayStar Digital. *Computer Hardware*

VAR (Value Added Reseller) - Companies that buy standard hardware and/or software, add some value (i.e., extra features, training, etc), and resell to another company. *General Computer*

Variable Speed Overdrive - CPU accelerator for Mac IIfx, Quadra 700, 900 and 950 that uses the existing CPU chip. Offers at least a 25 percent speed improvement. Control Panel document allows adjustment of the CPU speed on-the-fly in 1/10th MHz increments. See Newer Technology. *Computer Hardware*

Varnish - A coating that can be applied onto a printed piece for surface protection against wear and/or to highlight an area for special emphasis. See Varnish (Dull). *Printing Processes*

Varnish (Dull) - A dull coating that can be applied onto a printed piece for surface protection against wear and to de-emphasize a background area by making

that area more dull in appearance. See Varnish. *Printing Processes*

Vector Graphics - The representation of graphics by drawing lines between various points. *Desktop/Electronic Publishing*

Vehicle - A compound that is used in inks to be a carrier for any pigments in the ink. The vehicle used will aid in the determination of such properties of ink as tack, drying speed, wear resistance, etc. *Ink*

Vellum Finish - A type of paper with a slightly rough surface. This paper is very ink-absorbent and is excellent for high-speed print production. *Substrates*

Velox - A special photographic paper that is used for low-cost reproduction capabilities, i.e., the type of paper used in a graphic arts camera to prepare photostats and halftone screens. Also, refers to the actual print created on the velox paper, which is used on CRC. Another term for a stat. See CRC. *Art and Copy Preparation - Graphic Arts Photography*

Vertical Process Camera - A graphic arts camera that was designed with all the key components in a vertical position. See Graphic Arts Camera. *Graphic Arts Photography*

VGA (Video Gate Array) - A video circuit board that provides a high level of graphics on a PC microcomputer. *Computer Hardware*

VHS - See VHS Video Format.

VHS Video Format - An acronym for

Video Home System. It is the most popular of the half-inch video cassette formats. *Digital Photography*

Video - From the Latin term meaning "I See." Term for the technology dealing with the visual content of a television signal. *Digital Photography - Telecommunications*

Video Adapter - See Video Board.

Video Analyzer - A device that allows viewing of transparencies or color separations on a monitor. *Color Reproduction - Computer Hardware - Proofing*

Video Board - A circuit board that sends video signals to the computer monitor. This allows monitors to display text and graphics on-screen. *Computer Hardware*

Video Card - See Video Board.

Video Communication - Communication via television, i.e., video conferencing. *Multimedia - Telecommunications*

Videodisc - A record-like magnetic storage device that can hold video signals. *Computer Hardware*

Video Interface - A board that allows display (computer screen) data to be sent to a printer. *Computer Hardware*

Videophone - A telephone that allows those communicating to hear each other, speak to each other, and see each other. *Multimedia - Telecommunications*

Video RAM (VRAM) - 256K and 512K video memory for Mac Quadra 700, 800, 840AV, 900 and 950; LC, LC II, LCIII; Performa 400, 600, 600CD; Duo Docking Station; Mac IIvx; Centris 610, 650; and Color Classic. See Newer Technology. *Computer Hardware*

Videotex - Information that is collected and managed on a computer system and displayed on a computer monitor. Transmission occurs through telephone lines, i.e., Computer Bulletin Boards. *Telecommunications*

VIDIxpress - For use with Presenter Professional, this high-speed RISC-based 3-D imaging solution provides rendering speed and power that is, on average, nine times faster than a Mac IIfx. See Visual Information Development, Inc. *Software*

Vignette - A halftone or illustration where the background gradually fades away. The lightest portion being the closest to the unprinted or unphotographed area. *Art and Copy Preparation - Graphic Arts Photography*

Vignetting - The process of creating a vignette. *Art and Copy Preparation - Graphic Arts Photography*

Virtual - Real-time photorealism. Users move through a scene in a natural way using a mouse and the built-in "Virtual Navigator." See Strata, Inc. *Software*

Virtual Memory - A hardware/software technique that incorporates a portion of the hard drive into the RAM for faster processing. *Computer Hardware - Software*

Virtual Reality - Simulated images that react to the viewer's actions. *Multimedia*

Visual Information Development, Inc., (VIDI) - Developer of 3-D modeling, rendering, and animation software for the

216

Mac. Contact numbers:136 W. Olive Ave., Monrovia, CA 91016; (818)358-3936. *Software*

Viscometer - A device that measures viscosity. *Quality/Process Control*

Viscosity - The flow and tack properties of ink. *Ink - Quality/Process Control*

Visual Literacy - An understanding of the use of visual components to convey a message in the most meaningful way for a targeted audience. The components include text, pictures, color, white space, videos, and the aesthetic arrangement of these components in presenting a message effectively. *Desktop/Electronic Publishing - Marketing - Multimedia*

Voice Mail - A telephone system for the storage and retrieval of telephone messages. An advanced form of answering machine. *Multimedia - Telecommunications*

Voice Recognition - A computer's ability to accept spoken words as data input to the computer. *General Computer*

Volatile Organic Compounds (VOC's) Some specific hydrocarbon compounds that are considered harmful to health. *Environment*

Volatile Random Access Memory (VRAM) - See VRAM.

Volcano - A condition where an evaporating solvent will break through a heavy inked area and create a printing defect. *Printing Processes*

VRAM - RAM that supports monitors. *Computer Hardware*

Wafer Seal - Gummed labels that are attached to self-mailers and envelopes to keep them shut during mailing. These labels can have sales messages imprinted, such as "Special Offer Inside," on their surface to stimulate interest in the information inside. *Marketing*

Waist Line - An invisible line located above the top of the lower case characters. *Typography*

Walk-Off - A gradual deterioration of the plate's image area during the process of high-volume print production. *Printing Processes*

Wanted Colors - The appearance of the desired colors in the correct areas. *Color Reproduction*

WAN (Wide Area Network) - A computer network and its peripherals that are all connected and are able to share information over a wide geographic area. *General Computer*

Warm Color - The redddish and yellowish colors, such as pink and orange. *Color Reproduction*

Wash Marks - On-press streaks that are caused by too much water on lithographic presses. *Printing Processes*

Wash-Up - The general cleaning of a press during ink changing or at day's end. *Printing Processes*

Waterless Printing - Typically refers to lithography or offset printing that requires no fountain solution. *Printing Processes*

Watermark - A special or unique design pressed onto paper during manufacture. See Dandy Roll. *Substrates*

Wavelength - The basic characteristic of light that allows it to be measured by wave curves. The exact length of a wavelength is the exact distance between adjacent peaks in a wave curve. *Color Reproduction*

Wax - The material that is used to adhere graphic elements and copy to CRC. See CRC. *Art and Copy Preparation*

Web - The paper roll used in web printing. *Substrates*

Web Press - A printing press that uses one, long, continuous paper roll that is called a web. Images are printed on the web as the roll unwinds and passes through the press. The web press is best suited to high-speed and high-volume printing and is often used to print books, newspapers, magazines, and catalogs. Also, web paper is less expensive than cut paper of an equivalent quality. See Web. *Printing Processes*

Web Tension - The tension or pull needed to move a web through the web press. *Printing Processes*

Weight - The degree of thickness of a type character, i.e., bold, medium, light, etc. *Typography*

Wet Printing - Printing over already printed areas when the ink is still wet. Also referred to as wet trapping. *Printing Processes*

Wet Proofs - Proofs that are printed on a specific proofing press using plates that are created from the actual film. The ink and paper that are to be used on the final print run are used on the wet proofs to create a better likeness of the finished job. *Proofing*

Wet Strength - The strength of a substrate when it is wet. *Substrates*

Wetability - A surface's ability to accept a liquid. *Printing Processes*

Wet Trapping - In printing, the degree to which a wet ink film adheres to a previously printed wet ink film. See Wet Printing. *Ink - Printing Processes - Quality/Process Control*

Whirler - A device that was traditionally used to apply photo-sensitive coatings and materials to plates. *Image Carriers*

Whiskers - The hairy edges that are created by static electricity in the shadow areas of an image. *Printing Processes*

White Balance - A means of adjusting the color balance of a camera to reproduce white objects as white. With a Still Video Camera, white balance is achieved instantly as the subject is photographed. *Digital Photography*

White Light - The combination of all the colors in the visible spectrum. *Color Reproduction*

White-Out - An opaque material that will cover undesirable blemishes on the CRC when it is applied to the surface. See CRC. *Art and Copy Preparation*

White Point - The color temperature of a color monitor. The standard is 5000 K for most graphic arts applications. *Computer Hardware*

White Space - Areas on artwork or CRC that are free of type, graphics, and photos. *Art and Copy Preparation*

Wideband - A channel with a bandwidth greater than a purely voice channel. *Telecommunications*

Widow - A single word (usually the last word in a paragraph) that is left by itself at the top of a page or at the end of a paragraph. In fact, even two or three words is often unacceptable. It is considered unacceptable editorial practice and poor typography. *Desktop/Electronic Publishing - Typography*

Widths - See Set-Width.

Window - An on-screen area which can contain menu choices, icons, and other unique information, that is different from the information in other windows. *Software* The indicated locations on CRC where the photos and other graphics are to be positioned. See CRC. *Art and Copy Preparation*

Windows - See Microsoft Windows.

Wipe-On Plate - A plate that has had a light-sensitive material wiped onto the surface, either by hand or by machine. *Image Carriers*

Wire-O-Binding - See Spiral Binding.

Wire Side - This is the side of the paper that was created when in contact with the wire on the fourdrinier papermaking machine. *Substrates*

Wire Stitching - See Saddle Stitching.

With The Grain - Feeding a substrate into the press in the direction of the grain in the paper. It is easier to fold and tear paper with the grain. See Machine Direction. *Substrates*

Woodcut - A method of printing that uses a carved block of wood as the relief carrier for the image. *Image Carriers*

Word Perfect - A word-processing program. See Word Processing. *Software*

Word Processing - Computer software that is used to create letters, manuscripts, and other documents that are primarily text. *Software*

Word Star - Word processing software. See Word Processing. *Software*

WordScan 2.0 - Low-cost alternative for users who need to convert documents on an ad-hoc basis. It includes the same adaptive recognition engine and intuitive Windows interface as WordScan Plus 2.0. For PC and Windows. See Calera Recognition Systems. *Software*

WordScan Plus 2.0 - A Windows solution for time-critical or frequent use. Incorporates sophisticated document management tools, including page auto-orientation, de-skewing, and image/text proofing and editing. Works with third party scanners and fax hardware and software. See Calera Recognition Systems. *Software*

Word Space - See Letterspace.

WorkFlow Administrator - A client-server based publication management system that manages files from Mac applications. Provides unique file access throughout the work group, automatic archive and file backup, and advanced routing capabilities, including user notification. See North Atlantic Publishing Systems. *Software*

Work-And-Tumble - An imposition technique that prints the same image on either side of the paper with one plate. After printing the first side, the top that was on the gripper edge is tumbled and the bottom is now the gripper edge. However, the press guide is the same on this method. The disadvantage of this method is the need for two different gripper edges - this requires the printed sheets be trimmed and squared on all four sides. *Printing Processes*

Work-And-Turn - An imposition technique that prints the same image on either side of the paper with one plate. After printing the first side, the sheet is turned end to end to print the other side and the gripper edge is the same on both sides. The press guide is different each time. *Printing Processes*

Work-And-Twist - The technique of using two images on a plate that are in opposite directions. After one side of the sheet is printed it is turned over and printed so the different images overprint each other. *Printing Processes*

Work For Hire - Work that is performed for money without the right to ownership or copyright protection. *Desktop/Electronic Publishing*

Working Film - The film that is used to create the final plates. *Image Assembly - Image Carriers*

Work Order - See Job Ticket.

Workstation - A high-powered computer that is commonly part of a network. *Computer Hardware*

WORM (Write Once Read Many) - A disk drive that allows writing once to a file and then being able to read the file many times. *Computer Hardware*

Wove Paper - A type of paper with a uniform, smooth finish. *Substrates*

Wraparound Plate - A type of printing plate that wraps around the plate cylinder of a rotary press. *Image Carriers*

Wrapper - The jacket that is used on a hardcover or casebound book. It includes the front cover, the spine, and information about the author and the book content. *Finishing*

Wrinkles - Paper creases that are created during the printing process. *Printing Processes*

Write Once Read Many - See WORM.

Write-Protect - To set a magnetic storage device (diskette, disk drive, etc.) so a user cannot erase or write over any of the data on the magnetic storage. *General Computer*

Writer's Alterations - See Author's Alterations.

Wrong Font (WF) - The marking "WF" will indicate the wrong style of type or font. See Proofreaders' Symbols in Fig. 30 on page 176 and 177. *Typography*

Wrong-Reading Image - The reverse of an image, i.e., mirror image. *Graphic Arts Photography*

WYSIWYG (What You See Is What You Get) - Generally, this indicates the computer will output on paper a document that looks very similar to what is displayed on-screen. *General Computer*

X-Height - This is the height of a lower case character without considering the ascenders and descenders. The X is used to describe this aspect of type because it lacks ascenders and descenders and sits right on the baseline. See Fig. 38. *Typography*

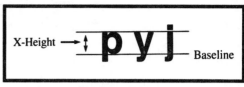

Fig. 38 - X-Height

Xerography - A dry photo electrostatic method of offset plate creation and copy reproduction. The plates may be metal or paper. *Image Carriers - Printing Processes*

XyWrite Filter - Allows XyWrite Plus III files to be imported and exported for QuarkXPress layouts. See North Atlantic Publishing Systems. *Software*

Yellow - One of the four-color process inks that are used in full-color printing. *Color Reproduction - Ink*

YCC - The color encoding system on a Kodak Photo CD. *Color Reproduction*

Zero Leading - A typesetting command that eliminates all leading from a section, word, or set of characters. *Typesetting and Imagesetting*

Zines - Small magazines that are focused on specific and very special interests. *Marketing*

Zip-A-Tone - A device that is used to apply shades or other special patterns to line artwork without a screening process. *Art and Copy Preparation*

Zoom - The enlargement or reduction of an on-screen document for a different or closer view of certain areas. *Art and Copy Preparation - Desktop/ Electronic Publishing*

Zooming - A special effect that will bring an image closer or move it further away in order to change the perspective. *Digital Photography - Graphic Arts Photography - Multimedia*

List of Figures

Art and Copy Preparation

Color Reproduction

Computer Hardware

Desktop/Electronic Publishing

Digital Photography

237

Environment

Finishing

General Computer

Graphic Arts Photography

243

Image Assembly

Image Carriers

Ink

Laser Applications

Marketing

Multimedia

Printing Processes

Proofing

Quality/Process Control

Scanning

Software

Standards

Substrates

Telecommunications

Typesetting and Imagesetting

Typography

American Business Press
675 Third Ave, Ste. 400
New York, NY 10017-5704
(212) 661-6360
FAX (212) 370-0736

Newspaper Association of America
The Newspaper Center
11600 Sunrise Valley Dr.
Reston, VA 22091
(703) 648-1000

American Paper Institute
260 Madison Ave.,
New York, NY 10016
(212) 340-0600

Binding Industries of America
Printing Industries of America Inc.
70 E. Lake St.,
Chicago, Il 60601
(312) 372-7606
FAX (312) 704-5025

Business Forms Management Association
519 S.W. Third Ave., Ste 712
Portland, OR 97204-2579
(503)227-3393
FAX (503) 274-7667

Direct Marketing Association
11 W. 42th St.
New York, NY 10036-8096
(212) 768-7277

Education Council of the Graphic Arts Industry
1899 Preston White Dr.
Reston, VA 22091
(703) 264-7200

Engraved Stationery Manufacturers Association, Inc
305 Plus Park Blvd.
Nashville, TN 37217
(615) 366-1798

Fibre Box Association
2850 Gold Rd.
Rolling Meadows, IL 60008
(708) 364-9600
FAX (708) 364-9639

Flexographic Technical Association, Inc
900 Marconi Ave.,
Ronkonkoma, NY 11779
(516) 737-6020

Graphic Arts Employers of America
Printing Industries of America, Inc
100 Daingerfield Rd.,
Alexandria, VA 22314
(703) 519-8150

Graphic Arts Literacy Alliance
P. O. Box 11712
Santa Ana, CA 92711
(714) 921-3120
FAX (714) 921-3126

Graphic Arts Marketing Information Service
Printing Industries of America, Inc
100 Daingerfield Rd.,
Alexandria, VA 22314
(703) 519-8179

Graphic Arts Sales Foundation
113 E. Evans St.,
West Chester, PA 19380
(215) 431-9780

Graphic Arts Show Company
1899 Preston White Dr.
Reston, VA 22091
(703) 264-7200

Graphic Arts Suppliers Association
1900 Arch St.,
Philadelphia, PA 19103
(215) 564-3484

Graphic Arts Technical Foundation
4615 Forbes Ave.,
Pittsburgh, PA 15213
(412) 621-6941

Graphic Communications Association
Printing Industries of America, Inc
100 Daingerfield Rd.,
Alexandria, VA 22314
(703) 519-8160
FAX (703) 548-2867

Gravure Association of America
1200 A Scottsville Rd.
Rochester, NY 14624
(716) 436-2150
FAX (716) 436-7689

Gutenberg Expositions
P. O. Box 11712
Santa Ana, CA 92711
(714) 921-3120
FAX (714) 921-3126

Hot Stamping Association
40 Melville Park Rd.,
Melville, NY 11747
(516) 694-7773

The International Association of Printing House Craftsmen
7599 Kenwood Rd.,
Cincinnati, OH 45236
(513) 891-0611

International Business Forms Industries
2111 Wilson Blvd., Ste. 350
Arlington, VA 22201
(703) 841-9191

International Graphic Arts Education Association
4615 Forbes Avenue
Pittsburgh, PA 15312
(412) 621-6941   FAX (412) 621-3069

International Printing Museum
8469 Kass Drive
Buena Park, CA 90621
(714) 523-4315

International Prepress Association
7200 France Ave S., Ste. 327
Edina, MN 55435
(612) 896-1908

International Thermographers Association
Printing Industries of America, Inc
100 Daingerfield Rd.,
Alexandria, VA 22314
(703) 579-8122

IPMA - In-Plant Management Association
The IPMA Building
1205 W. College Ave.
Liberty, MO 64068
(816) 781-1111

Italian Trade Commission
401 N. Michigan Ave., Ste. 3030
Chicago, IL 60611
(312) 670-4350

Label Printing Industries of America
Printing Industries of America, Inc
100 Daingerfield Rd.,
Alexandria, VA 22314
(703) 519-8122

Magazine Printers Section
Printing Industries of America, Inc
100 Daingerfield Rd.,
Alexandria, VA 22314
(703) 519-8100

Magazine Publishers of America
575 Lexington Ave.
New York, NY 10022
(212) 752-0055

Master Printers of America
Printing Industries of America, Inc
100 Daingerfield Rd.,
Alexandria, VA 22314
(703) 519-8130

National Association of Diemakers & Diecutters
P.O. Box 2; Mount Morris, IL 61054
(815) 734-4178

National Association of Litho Clubs
P.O. Box 1258
Clifton, NJ 07012
(201) 777-6727

National Association of Lithographic Plate Manufacturers
Printing Industries of America, Inc
100 Daingerfield Rd.,
Alexandria, VA 22314
(703) 519-8100

National Association of Printers and Lithographers
780 Palisade Ave.
Teaneck, NJ 07666
(201) 342--0700 (800) 642-NAPL

National Association of Printing Ink Manufacturers
47 Halstead Ave.
Harrison, NY 10528
(914) 835-5650

National Association of Quick Printers
401 N. Michigan Ave.
Chicago, Il 60611
(312) 644-6610

National Business Forms Association
433 E. Monroe Ave.
Alexandria, VA 22301
(703) 836-6232

National Composition & Prepress Association
Printing Industries of America, Inc
100 Daingerfield Rd.,
Alexandria, VA 22314
(703) 519-8165

National Computer Graphics Association
2722 Merrilee Dr., Ste. 200
Fairfax, VA 22031
(703) 698-9600

National Graphic Arts Dealers Association
116 W. Ottawa
Lansing, MI 48933

National Newspaper Association
1525 Wilson Blvd., Suite 550
Arlington, VA 22209
(703) 907-7900
FAX (703) 907-7901

National Paper Trade Association
111 Great Neck Rd.
Great Neck, NY 11021
(516) 829-3070

National Printing Equipment and Supply Association
1899 Preston White Dr.
Reston, VA 22091
(703) 264-7200

Non-Heatset Web Section
Printing Industries of America, Inc
100 Daingerfield Rd.,
Alexandria, VA 22314
(703) 519-8140

**Paper Industry Management
Association**
2400 E. Oakton St.
Arlington Heights, IL 60005
(708) 956-0250
FAX (708) 956-0520

Printing Industries of Wichita
P.O. Box 1377
Wichita, KS 67201
(316) 264-1363

Printing Industry of South Florida
6095 N.W. 167th St., Ste, D-7
Hialeah, FL 33015
(305) 558-4855

**Printing Industries
of the Gulf Coast**
1324 W. Clay St.
Houston, TX 77019
(713) 522-2046
FAX (713) 522-8342

Print/New Jersey
75 Keary Ave., P.O. Box 6
Keary, NJ 07032
(201) 99-PRINT

**Research and Engineering Council
of the Graphic Arts Industry**
P.O. Box 639
Chadds Ford, PA 19317
(215) 388-7394
FAX (215) 388-2708

**Screen Printing Association
International**
10015 Main St.
Fairfax, VA 22031
(703) 385-1335

**Screen Printing Technical
Foundation**
10015 Main St.
Fairfax, VA 22031
(703) 385-1417

Suburban Newspapers of America
401 N. Michigan Ave.
Chicago, IL 60611
(312) 644-5610

**Tag and Label Manufacturers
Institute, Inc.**
104 Wilmot Rd., Ste 201
Deerfield, IL 60015-5195
(708) 940-8800
FAX (708) 940-7218

**Technical Association
of the Graphic Arts**
P.O.Box 9887
Rochester, NY 14623
(716) 272-0557
FAX (716) 475-2250

**Typographers International
Association**
2233 Wisconsin Ave. N. W., Ste 235
Washington, DC 20007
(202) 965-3400

Web Offset Section
Printing Industries of America, Inc
100 Daingerfield Rd.,
Alexandria, VA 22314
(703) 519-8140

Printing Industries of America, Inc
Headquarters
100 Daingerfield Rd.,
Alexandria, VA 22314
(703) 519-8100
FAX (703) 548-3227

Printing Industries Association Inc. of So. California
P.O.Box 91-1151
Los Angeles, CA 90091
(213) 728-9500

Printing Industries Association of San Diego, Inc
3914 Murphy Canyon Rd., Ste, A-107
San Diego, CA 92123
(619) 571-6555
FAX (619) 571-7935

Printing Industries of Northern California
(Also incl. part of Nevada)
665 Third St., Ste. 500
San Francisco, CA 94107
(415) 495-8242

Printing Industries Association - Mountain States
(Also incl. New Mexico & part of Wyoming)
900 E. Louisiana Ave.
Denver, CO 80210
(303) 744-6007

Printing Industry Association of Connecticut & Western Massachusetts
1 Regency Dr., P.O.Box 30
Bloomfield, CT 06002
(203) 242-8991

The Printing Industry of Connecticut
P.O.Box 144
Milford, CT 06460
(203) 874-6793

Printing Industry of Metropolitan Washington
700 Landmark Bldg.
1333 H St. N.W.
Washington, DC 20005
(202) 682-3001

Printing Industries of Florida
4205 Edgewater Dr.
Orlando, FL 32804
(407) 290-5801 (800) 331-0461

Printing Industry Association of Georgia
5020 Highlands Pkwy.
Smyra, GA 30082
(404) 433-3050

The Printing Industry of Illinois/Indiana Association
70 E. Lake St.
Chicago, IL 60601
(312) 704-5000

Printing Industry Association of Kansas City
702 Midland Bldg
1221 Baltimore St.
Kansas City, MO 64105
(816) 421-7678

Printing Industry of St Louis
321 N. Spring Ave.
St. Louis, MO 63108
(314) 531-1610

Printing Industries of Maryland
2423 Maryland Ave.
Baltimore, MD 21218
(301) 366-0900

**Printing Industries
of Michigan**
23815 Northwestern Hwy. #2700
Southfield, MI 48075-3366
(313) 354-9200

**Printing Industries
of New England**
(Incl. Maine, Mass, New Hamphire,
Rhode Island and Vermont)
10 Tech Cir., P. O.Box 2009
Natick, MA 01760-0015
(508) 655-8700

**Printing Industries
of the Midlands**
(Incl. Iowa, Nebraska and South Dakota)
11009 Aurora Ave.
Urbandale, IA 50322
(515) 270-1009

Printing Industry of Minnesota
450 N. Syndicate, Ste. 200
St. Paul, MN 55104
(612) 646-4826

Association of the Graphic Arts
(Also incl. part of New Jersey)
330 7th Avenue
New York, NY 10001
(212) 279-2100
FAX (212) 279-5381

**Printing Industries Association
of New York**
455 Commerce Dr.
Amherst, NY 14228
(716)691-3211

**The Printing Industry
of the Carolinas**
P. O. Box 19889
Charlotte, NC 28219
(704) 357-1150

**Printing Industries
Association of No. Ohio**
30400 Detroit Rd.
Cleveland, OH 44145
(216) 835-6900

**Printing Industries
Association of So. Ohio**
1371 Glendale-Milford Rd.
Cincinnati, OH 45215
(513) 771-5422

**Printing Industry
of Central Ohio**
88 Dorchester Sq.
P. O. Box 819
Westerville, OH 43081
(614) 794-2300

**Printing Industries
of Oklahoma/S.W. Missouri**
5200 S. Yale, Ste. 101
Tulsa, OK 74135
(918) 496-1122

**Pacific Printing and
Imaging Association**
(Incl. Alaska, Hawaii, Idaho, Montana,
and Oregon)
180 Nickerson, Ste. 102
Seattle, WA 98109
(206) 285-8361   FAX (206) 282-0447
5319 S. W. Westgate Dr. Ste. 117
Portland, OR 97221
(503) 297-3328   FAX (503) 297-3320

Graphic Arts Association
1900 Cherry St.
Philadelphia, PA 19103
(215) 299-3300

**Printing Industry Association
of Western Pennsylvania**
925 Penn Ave., Ste. 401
Pittsburgh, PA 15222
(412) 281-0400

**Printing Industry Association
of the South**
(Incl. Alabama, Arkansas, Kentucky,
Louisiana, Miss. and West Virginia)
305 Plus Park Blvd.
Nashville, TN 37217
(615) 366-1799

**Printing Industries
of Utah**
445 E. Second St., Ste. 16
Salt Lake City, UT 84111
(801) 521-2623

**Printing Industries
of Virginia**
1108 E. Main St.
Richmond, VA 23219
(804) 643-1800

**Printing Industries
of Wisconsin**
P. O. Box 126
Elm Grove, WI 53122
(414) 785-9090

**Canadian Printing Industries
Association**
75 Albert St.,
Fuller Bldg. Ste. 906
Ottawa, Ontario K1P5E7
Canada
(613) 236-7208

Bibliography

Anon., "Print 2000," (Printing Industries of America, Inc., Arlington, Virginia, 1990), pp. x-1 - x-5.

Anon., "HiFi Color: Nonsense or Niche?" American Printer, 5/94, pp. 52-54.

Anon., Printing Ink Handbook, (National Association of Printing Ink Manufacturers, New York, NY, 1967), 94pp.

Anon., Satellite TV & You, (Triple D Publishing, Inc., Shelby, NC, 1988), 29pp.

Anon., "Standards Shape Print's Future," Graphic Arts Monthly, 10/93, pp. 70, 72, 74, 76, 81.

Anon., The Apple Guide to CD-ROM' Titles, (Apple Computer Co., Cupertino, CA, 1993), 147 pp.

Anon., The Printing Service Specialist's Handbook and Reference Guide, (Society for Service Professionals in Printing, Alexandria, VA, 1994), pp. G1 - G.37.

Bann, David and John Gargan, How To Check and Correct Color Proofs, (F & W Publications, Inc., Cincinnati, OH, 1990), 144pp.

Beach, Mark, Getting It Printed, (North Light Books, Cincinnati, OH, 1986), 199 pp.

Beale Stephen and James Cavuoto, The Scanner Book, (Micro Publishing Press, Torrance, CA, 1989), pp. 185-192.

Blair, Raymond and Charles Shapiro, (eds), The Lithographers Manual, (Graphic Arts Technical Foundation, Pittsburgh, PA, 1980), 20 chapters.

Bove, Tony, Cheryl Rhodes, Wes Thomas, Art of Desktop Publishing, (Bantam Books, New York, NY, 1986), 296 pp.

Broekhuizen, Richard J., Graphic Communications, (McKnight Career Publicaiton, 1973) 380 pp.

Bruno, Michael, Pocket Pal: A Graphic Arts Production Handbook, (International Paper Company, Memphis, TN, 1992), 233 pp.

Bruno, Michael, (ed.), Principles of Color Proofing, GAMA Communications, Salem, NH, 1986), 395 pp.

Cavuoto, James and Stephen Beale, Linotronic Imaging Handbook, (Micro Publishing Press, Torrance, CA 1990), 218 pp.

Compton, John, "Quality Concepts: Answers To Your Questions About ISO 9000 (Part 1)," RIT T&E News, (Rochester Institute of Technology, Rochester, NY, 1/94), pp. 5-7.

Conover, Theodore E., Graphic Communications Today, (West Publishing Co., St Paul, MN, 1985), 473 pp.

Crow, Wendell C., Communciation Graphics, (Prentice-Hall, Englewood Cliffs, NJ, 1986), 322 pp.

Curtiss, Wendall C., Introduction to Visual Literacy, (Prentice-Hall, Englewood Cliffs, NJ, 1987), 260 pp.

Dankert, Fred, "A Durable Waterless Planographic Plate," TAGA Conference paper, 5/1 - 5/4 1994, (to be printed in the 1994 TAGA Proceedings, Technical Association of the Graphic Arts, Rochester, NY).

Denton, Graig, Graphic For Visual Communications, (Wm. C. Brown Publishers, Dubuque, IA), 381 pp.

Eldred, Nelson, Package Printing, (Jelmar Publishing Co., Inc., Plainview, NY, 1993), 508 pp.

Field, Gary G., Tone and Color Correction, (Graphic Arts Technical Foundation, Pittsburgh, PA, 1991), 168 pp.

Haykin, Randy, (Ed.), Demystifying Multimedia, (Apple Computer, Inc., Cupertino, CA, 1993), pp. 272-283.

Hird, Kenneth, Offset Lithographic Technology, (The Goodheart-Willcox Co., Inc., 1991), 720 pp.

Hudson, Heather E., Communicaiton Satellites: Their Development and Impact, (The Free Press, New York, NY, 1990), 338 pp.

Larish, John, Digital Photography, (Micro Publishing Press, Torrance, CA, 1992), 208 pp.

Levenson, Harvey R., "Electronic Digital Photography," 1994 Technology Forecast, (Graphic Arts Technical Foundation, Pittsburgh, PA, 1994), pp, 10-12.

Levenson, Harvey R., "Multimedia," 1994 Technology Forecast, (Graphic Arts Technical Foundation, Pittsburgh, PA, 1994), pp, 14-16.

Levy, Uri and Gilles Biscos, Nonimpact Electronic Printing, (InterQuest, Ltd., Charlottesville, VA, 1993), 314 pp.

Lyman, Ralph, "Binding and Finishing," (Graphic Arts Technical Foundation, Pittsburgh, Pennsylvania, 1993), pp. 156-176.

McDowell, David Q., "Standards and Specifications: Standards for the Graphic Arts," 1993 Technology Forecast, (Graphic Arts Technical Foundation, Pittsburgh, PA, 1993), pp. 21-24.

McDowell, David Q., "Standards and Specifications: Standards for the Graphic Arts," 1994 Technology Forecast, (Graphic Arts Technical Foundation, Pittsburgh, PA, 1994), pp. 26-27.

McDowell, David Q., "Standards Update," TAGA Newsletter (Technical Association of the Graphic Arts, Rochester, NY, Fall, 1993), p. 7.

Molla, R. K., Electronic Color Separation, (R. K. Printing & Publishing Co., Montgomery, WV, 1988), 288 pp.

Mort, Richard A., How to Save a Bundle on Printing, (Richard A. Mort, Portland, OR, 1989), 149 pp.

Nothmann, Gerhard A., Nonimpact Printing, (Graphic Arts Technical Foundation, Pittsburgh, PA, 1989), 110 pp.

Prust, Dr, Zeke, A., Graphic Communications, The Printed Image, (Goodheart-Willcox Co., Inc.,, South Holland, IL, 1989), 544 pp.

Rea, Douglas Ford, "Electronic Still Photography," ESP '93 Teleconference Program Notes, (Rochester Institute of Technology, Rochester, NY, April-May, 1993), pp. 30-37.

Romano, Frank J. and Eileen McManus, Automated Typesetting: The Basic Course, (GAMA Commnications, Salem, NH, 1974), 220 pp.

Scarlett, Terry and Nelson Eldred, What the Printer Should Know About Ink, (Graphic Arts Technical Foundation, Pittsburgh, PA, 1984), 234 pp.

Seybold, John and Fritz Dressler, Publishing from the Desktop, (Bantam Books, New York, NY, 1987), 299 pp.

Wendal, Fred, Graphic Arts Photography: Color, (Graphic Arts Technical Foundation, Pittsburgh, PA, 1987), 151 pp.